This Far by Faith

This Far by Faith

An African American Resource for Worship

Augsburg Fortress
Minneapolis

THIS FAR BY FAITH
An African American Resource for Worship

This resource has been developed by a cooperative inter-church process involving the Evangelical Lutheran Church in America and the Lutheran Church—Missouri Synod. Each church body has been responsible for its own review process.

This resource is recommended for use in the Evangelical Lutheran Church in America.

The paper used in this publication meets the minimum requirements of American National Standard for Information Sciences—Permanence of Paper for Printed Materials, ANSI Z329.48-1984.
Printed in the USA.

Manufactured in the U.S.A.   ISBN 0-8066-3335-2   3-520

First Printing, April 1999

CONTENTS

PREFACE

Jesus whom we worship was born into a specific culture of the world. In the mystery of his incarnation are the model and mandate for the contextualization of Christian worship. God can be and is encountered in the local cultures of our world. A given culture's values and patterns, insofar as they are consonant with the values of the Gospel, can be used to express the meaning and purpose of Christian worship. Contextualization is a necessary task for the Church's mission in the world, so that the Gospel can be ever more deeply rooted in diverse local cultures.

From *The Nairobi Statement on Worship and Culture,* Lutheran World Federation, 1996.

> We've come this far by faith, leaning on the Lord,
> trusting in his holy word; he's never failed us yet.
> Oh, we can't turn back, *we've come this far by faith.*

These words describe the patient hope and prayerful expectation that have sustained the quest to turn *This Far by Faith,* an African American worship resource, from a dream into a reality.

Originally conceived as a concept paper by African American Lutherans within The Lutheran Church—Missouri Synod in 1990, the dream for the project took shape in 1993 when a small exploratory committee was formed of representatives from both the LCMS (Ulmer Marshall, Bryant Clancy, and Robert Malone) and the Evangelical Lutheran Church in America (Craig Lewis).

The dream for an African American worship resource that would supplement the principal worship books of the churches continued to develop. Aided by surveys conducted among African American pastors and congregations that showed great support for the idea, the project moved forward. The ELCA Division for Congregational Ministries and Commission for Multicultural Ministries, and the Commission for Black Ministries of the LCMS agreed to fund the project, but additional funds were still needed.

Walking by faith and not by sight, a steering committee and two subcommittees were formed and began working on the book in February 1995. In September 1995 the Lutheran Brotherhood Foundation approved a grant to assist the church bodies with funding, and work on the project accelerated. Development of the resource continued through the final steering committee meeting in January 1998, on the weekend commemorating the birth of Martin Luther King Jr.

A debt of gratitude is owed to the Lutheran Brotherhood Foundation for its assistance in funding the project and to all members of the steering, liturgy, music, and editorial committees, named below, without whose tireless efforts this book could not have been developed. We are thankful to Mary Ann Moller Gunderson (former director, ELCA Division for Congregational Ministries), Wyvetta Bullock (director, ELCA Division for Congregational Ministries), and Fred Rajan (director, ELCA Commission for Multicultural Ministries), who lent their leadership and support to the project.

Finally, we thank the African American Lutheran congregations of the LCMS and the ELCA for whom this project was conceived and without whose prayerful support the long struggle to produce this book of worship could not have been achieved.

Bryant Clancy
Project Manager
LCMS Commission
for Black Ministries

Karen M. Ward
Project Manager
ELCA Division for
Congregational Ministries

JOINT STEERING COMMITTEE

ELCA
Deborah Bagby, co-chair
Eric Campbell
Mark Coates
Fred Rajan
Frank Stoldt
Karen M. Ward

LCMS
Ulmer Marshall, co-chair
Minnie Brooks
Bryant Clancy
Stephen Everette
Robert Malone
Ida Odom

SUBCOMMITTEES

LITURGY
Donald Anthony
Barry Bobb
Joseph A. Donnella II
Emmanuel F. Y. Grantson
Robert Malone
Ulmer Marshall
John Nunes
Frank Stoldt
Karen M. Ward
Maxine Washington
Gregory Wismar

MUSIC
Deborah Bagby
Minnie Brooks
James Capers
Bryant Clancy
Mark Coates
Richard C. Dickinson
Wayne Dixon
Stephen Everette
Romenita Henderson
Sondra Nelson
Ida Odom
Martin A. Seltz
Lorraine Turner
Scott Weidler

EDITORIAL
Barry Bobb
Bryant Clancy
M. Alexandra George
Paul Grime
John Nunes
Martin A. Seltz
Frank Stoldt
Karen M. Ward
Scott Weidler

WORSHIP AND CULTURE

AN AFRICAN AMERICAN LUTHERAN PERSPECTIVE

The dialog between culture and the Christian faith expressed in worship is as old as the faith itself. The church's basic pattern of liturgy itself has antecedents both in the synagogue service and the festive meal practices of the Jewish people. The service of word and eucharistic meal was further shaped by the cultures in which the first Christians lived.

A recent Lutheran study presents helpful categories for framing and understanding this dialog:

> The reality that Christian worship is always celebrated in a given local cultural setting draws our attention to the dynamics between worship and the world's many local cultures.Christian worship relates dynamically to culture in four ways. First, it is *transcultural*, the same substance for everyone everywhere, beyond culture. Second, it is *contextual*, varying according to the local situation (both nature and culture). Third it is *counter-cultural*, challenging what is contrary to the gospel in a given culture. Fourth, it is *cross-cultural*, making possible sharing between different local cultures . . . (*Nairobi Statement on Worship and Culture,* Lutheran World Federation, 1996).

A Common Heritage
"They devoted themselves to the apostles' teaching and fellowship, to the breaking of bread and the prayers" (Acts 2:42). This is the *transcultural* pattern of weekly Christian worship that is the heritage of all Christians, regardless of culture. Word and sacraments are means of grace through which the gospel of Jesus Christ is communicated to all.

The baptized do not just "get together": they are called and gathered by the Spirit into the very presence of God. God's people do not hear just any word, but the Word of eternal life, Jesus Christ, who changes the heart and enlightens the mind. They do not share just any food, but the very body and blood of Christ. Those who have been gathered, enlightened, and fed do not just "leave," but as disciples of Christ, they are sent forth in mission to speak the word of God and do the work of God in the world. These things are the evangelical content of worship, a common "culture of the gospel" that unites and grounds the whole Christian community.

Worship in the Vernacular
This common heritage of Christian worship inevitably takes on a *contextual* dimension as it makes a home within a wide variety of situations. It reflects the astonishing particularity of

the incarnation: the eternal Word, through whom all things came into being (John 1:3), becomes contextual in a human body, a Jewish home, a first century Greco-Roman culture.

Scripture and the Lutheran confessions contain no specific word for culture. However, the Bible does refer to those elements that are understood today as components of culture: world, nation, generation, tribe, people, religion, form, language, custom. The teachings of Jesus in the gospels and the sermons of Paul in the Acts of the Apostles offer many examples of making connections to the cultural context of the hearers.

The confessional writings contain discussions on matters such as ceremonies and adiaphora (matters neither forbidden nor commanded). Furthermore, Martin Luther and other reformers were strong advocates for worship in the vernacular, worship that engaged the people in their own language and made connections to their daily lives. This emphasis on the vernacular is parallel to the contemporary attention given to the cultural contexts in which the people of God worship.

Components of Culture
Additional insight in understanding culture comes from 20th century liturgical scholar Anscar Chupungco, who proposes that culture includes three components: *values, patterns,* and *institutions. Values* are principles that shape the life and activities of a community and its members. Examples of values shared widely among cultures are hospitality, leadership and community. *Patterns* include a group's thought, spoken language, body language, concept of personal space, concepts of time, modes of dress, literature, music, architecture, and all forms of the fine arts. *Institutions* include the rites by which cultural groups celebrate or mark the cycles of life from birth to death.

African Americans within North American Lutheranism
North American Lutherans in the first centuries of immigration were people of Northern European ancestry, focused on nurturing and transmitting the faith primarily among their immigrant groups. It is true that Africans became Lutheran in the Americas beginning in the 1600s (records document that an African man named Emmanuel was baptized in a New York Lutheran congregation in 1669), and that especially in the last century, Lutheran domestic missions both in urban areas and the rural South have carried out ministries among African Americans.

Yet the challenge of transmitting the gospel to people of African descent in the Americas has been exacerbated by the "peculiar institution" of slavery and the seemingly intractable legacy of racism. In succeeding decades, as they continued to be baptized and catechized under Lutheran auspices, African Americans frequently found that their vernacular expressions of worship and song were not recognized by the wider Lutheran community.

A Common Contextual Heritage
While the African American community is not monolithic or uniform, there are many cultural commonalities among African Americans representing a rich cultural vernacular. Some of these similarities have been carried from the African continent, especially West Africa. These are shared with many who live in the "African diaspora" from Canada to the Caribbean. Most of the shared cultural features probably derive from a common experience of slavery (or cultural subjugation experienced by some Africans who were not

enslaved), racism, and the ongoing struggle for full recognition in the Americas. The following are examples of frequently-shared cultural features present in African American worship.

LANGUAGE AND IMAGERY

Not only were slaves discouraged from reading the Bible, it was actually illegal for slaves to read. This enforced a-literacy compelled many slaves and their progeny to rely on memory for biblical stories. Spirituals and hymns were an important aid to memory, and they often conflated or blended biblical narratives. The value of oral tradition among the people, however, helped to carry on the living voice of the gospel.

In the midst of struggle, Africans in the Americas developed rich and highly textured images to speak of God and of the relationship between God and humankind. This use of symbolic language is far more than a literary technique. The faith of an oppressed people served as a source of empowerment towards physical in addition to spiritual freedom Many spirituals deliberately used coded language, language useful both in worship and in communicating signals to enable the flight to freedom. At times this language contrasts with more verbally precise hymnological and theological traditions. One is more poetic and expressive, the other more concrete and propositional.

THE FUTURE PRESENT

Born out of the legacy of slavery, segregation, and social ostracism, African American prayer and song often speak of God's comfort in time of struggle, God's deliverance from oppression. Another common feature is a proleptic outlook towards heaven. God's future (heaven, kingdom, just reign) is anticipated, not as a means of escape from life, but as a source of sustenance for communal life which has often been difficult.

WORSHIP AS A VERB

Worship among African Americans is more verb than noun, a holistic engagement of head, heart and body touched by the sacred. Telling the story, testifying, preaching, and prayer are communal acts, set in the context of music, movement, and dance. All are infused with a deep awareness of the activity of the Holy Spirit within worship and a readiness for spontaneous response. Liturgy among African Americans often bears a similarity to jazz: improvisation and variation built upon the fundamental shape of the rite.

THE COMMUNAL "I"

The songs and prayers of African Americans often use first person language: "I want Jesus to walk with me" or "I've just come from the fountain." Observing this practice from outside the culture, some may conclude that this emphasis is individualistic. From within the culture, the opposite is true. There is a profound communal or tribal dimension among Africans and African Americans. In most African cultures, the base unit is the tribe or clan, rather than the individual or the nuclear family. Combine this African tribal antecedent with the African American history of group identity as slaves and the continuing reality of racial oppression, and one discovers a potent cultural undercurrent of collectivism.

In the popular aphorism of West Africa, "I am because we are, and because we are, I am." The use of the first person in worship is a communal "I," understood as "we" by worshipers who share a common history of struggle and striving for justice. Biblical precedents abound, especially in the psalms and in the letters of Paul.

An additional dimension of this communal sensibility is a profound awareness of the ties that bind living saints to the saints who dwell in light eternal. The African heritage of connectedness to one's ancestors is transformed in the context of Christian faith into a vivid appreciation for the communion of saints, the cloud of witnesses that accompany God's people on the journey of faith. Prayers that call upon the "God of our ancestors" have their lineage in the Old Testament invocation of the God of Abraham, Isaac, and Jacob, and in the frequent uses of this term in the letter to the Hebrews.

This Far by Faith

The interplay between worship and culture is often a messy enterprise. Practices that seem right and salutary in one era or within one culture may be judged odd or quaint in another. Fortunately, the Lutheran heritage welcomes this dialog, calling for unity in the common, evangelical core of worship and at the same time allowing for flexibility and freedom in the ways this essential core is communicated and celebrated.

As the first African American worship supplement prepared for use among Lutherans, *This Far by Faith* joyfully joins this conversation in progress. It is a proposal for addressing issues of worship from a perspective of particular culture and at the same time being faithful to the worship patterns of the church through the ages. To that end, this volume provides an important contribution to the global discussion on worship and culture by making available to African American Lutherans and to the wider church some of the riches of African American liturgy and song.

On these pages, witness a living chronicle of a faith journey begun on African soil. This is the pilgrimage of a people leaning on the Lord and trusting in God's holy word. Empowered by the Holy Spirit not to lay their religion down, African American Christians by the grace of God have overcome. They have overcome cultural marginality by finding family in the church. They have overcome dehumanization and oppression by knowing themselves to be God's children. They have overcome trials and tribulations, storms and tempests, to find joy and peace in believing. Hear them as they worship and sing the triumph of trust in God, having come *This Far by Faith*.

CONTEXTUAL WORSHIP PRACTICES

Symbolic actions and gestures used in worship are drawn from a variety of religious origins and the traditions of particular peoples. Christians have incorporated such cultural expressions within worship by interpreting the gesture in the light of Christian faith, in connection with biblical images, and in association with existing traditions of worship. Some examples include the use of the Advent wreath, candles, processions, and incense; the giving of rings in the marriage rite; or the pouring of earth in the funeral service.

The following practices and expressions, while not universal or exclusive, have been associated with the worship of Africans and African Americans at various times and places.

Space for worship

Some African traditions value the symbol of the circle or semi-circle. Moveable chairs or pews in the place of worship may be rearranged into such configurations.

Processional music and dance

Processions at the gathering or sending of the assembly may be accompanied by African drums and dance. Traditional African music forms such as the *lamba* and dances such as the *domba* may be used, and are especially fitting at the celebration of marriage.

Call to worship

This term is in widespread usage among African American churches, referring to the musical or spoken materials that gather the community for worship, or to a specific dialog, frequently scriptural, that articulates this invitation. Although not African in origin, the call to worship reflects the spirit of the African call-and-response pattern.

Acclamation

In many contexts joyous, vigorous, and physical response from worshipers is naturally expressed. Such acclamation can include handclapping and shouts of thanksgiving and jubilation. Ululation is one form of elevated vocal expression of African origin used to sound praise. At other times, the moan or lament is heard. Spontaneous dancing is a form of acclamation appropriate for certain festive contexts.

Posture and gesture for prayer

A bowed head, kneeling, and the folding of hands are common prayer postures. In addition, some may use the more ancient practice of extending open arms in prayer and praise, recalling the psalm, "Let my prayer rise before you as incense, and the lifting up of my hands as an evening sacrifice" *(Psalm 141:2)*.

Libation

Libation is a practice primarily used to accompany a call to worship or gathering prayer. The gesture of libation involves the pouring of a liquid such as water or a fermented drink into the earth or a container of soil. The leader pours from a pitcher or glass during a brief silence that follows each petition or response.

The Bible makes use of the image of pouring or libation in a number of places. These references help to supply meaning to the Christian use of this symbolic act. St. Paul says to the Philippians, "But even if I am being poured out as a libation over the sacrifice and the offering of your faith, I am glad and rejoice with all of you" *(Phil. 2:17)* and again in the letter to Timothy, " I am already being poured out as a libation. . . . I have finished the race, I have kept the faith" *(2 Tim. 4:6-7)*. Thus, the image of libation is a metaphor for the dedication of one's self in service for God's sake. The image of pouring is also used as an image for the outpouring of the gifts of the Spirit *(Acts 2:33, 10:45)*.

Communities of faith might consider the use of the libation gesture as a symbolic action of thanksgiving for the creation of humankind from the dust of this earthly home, and thanksgiving for those who have gone before, the mothers and fathers in faith whose mortal remains rest in the earth until the day of resurrection. The gesture may also be a sign of dedication to be poured out for the sake of the world in the same way Christ "poured out himself to death" *(Isa. 53:12)*, even as the church is empowered by the Holy Spirit who has been "poured out on us richly" *(Titus 3:6)*.

LEADING AFRICAN AMERICAN SONG

The variety of song that finds a home in African American worship presents a similar variety of challenges to those who lead the song of God's people. While many music leaders in communities that use this music have long-standing familiarity with these musical forms, others are seeking help in meeting these challenges, or desire to learn more about a specific genre. What follows is an introduction to the task of inspiring and enabling communities of faith to sing the liturgies and hymns in *This Far by Faith*. It may be a helpful summary and review for the experienced leader, or an overview for the novice with the goal of encouragement to pursue further study and practice.

Knowing and understanding the principles that undergird the performance of African American religious music is one thing, an important first step. Putting these principles into practice is quite another. Performances that look easy when executed by an experienced practitioner of spirituals and gospel music can be quite deceptive. The seemingly effortless melismatic passage or the brilliant display of polyrhythmic clapping comes not from mere spontaneous inspiration, but from years of persistent honing of skills through careful listening, observation, and practice.

For many church musicians, especially those with predominantly classical training, developing proficiency in African American music may pose a great challenge; after all, many of the principles of African American music performance are polar opposites of standard European American musical practices. The first and perhaps biggest challenge is coming to terms with the role of the musical score in African American music. In western music, the score reigns supreme; for the most part, performers are expected to adhere to tempo and dynamic markings. Beyond that, tampering with the melodic line, the rhythm, or the meter is often considered questionable. In contrast, the significance of the score in African American music is determined by the genre or type of music that it represents.

An example from the choral gospel music tradition may be illustrative. As a music whose foundation rests in the oral rather than the written tradition, African American gospel choirs typically learn new repertoire by rote, having heard the chosen selection sung by another group, or having heard the recording on CD, radio, or television. Frequently, no transcription of the selection exists or at least the choir does not have scores. It is the choir director's responsibility to know and demonstrate every vocal line and ensure that the parts blend harmonically.

Even though gospel music is often referred to as a "composed" music (distinguishing it from the spiritual created during slavery whose specific composers are unknown), writers of gospel songs both expect and accept deviation from the score. This improvisational dimension of gospel music performance does not mean that "anything goes." On the contrary, there are boundaries and principles and broadly accepted musical values to guide performers in deciding when, what, and how to do what they do. Only through the discipline of constant practice, generated by a sincere willingness and desire to learn, will the expression of African American music grow to assume personal and collective meaning in worship.

Performance Practice

Three primary areas of significance are identifiable in the performance of African American worship music regardless of genre: quality of sound (timbre); mechanics of delivery (manipulation of musical variables); and style of delivery (physical and visual dimensions of performance). Principles that govern this worship music leadership must not be viewed as inflexible rules that must be applied in the same way in every situation, for the underlying premise of this music is fluidity, constant change. The intent of sharing these fundamental, practical applications is to spark interest and confidence in creating a wider and stronger embrace of African American music, African American culture, and, with God's help, African American people.

Quality of Sound

Singing in traditional African American worship is an expression of jubilation, power, and praise. Even when the text of a spiritual communicates lament, the vocal quality of the singer remains strong. Vocalists are expected to convey their total sincerity and complete absorption in communicating both outward, to others present at the event, and upward to God. The vocal timbre in gospel solos may vary constantly, alternately utilizing moans, groans, shouts, wails, and growls. Similarly, in congregational singing the concluding verse or refrain may be hummed, allowing the assembly to experience the song's meaning through another timbral dimension. Whereas in the singing of spirituals the vocal timbre is more closely aligned with that of western music, maximizing the use of the head voice, in gospel music the commanding power of the chest voice is highly valued in women's singing, and male soloists frequently utilize falsetto.

Much congregational song takes the African-influenced form of call/response. The soloist, a strong and experienced singer, will issue the "call" in a firm manner that elicits an equally bold, full-voiced response from the congregation. It may take time and consistent use to develop the trust necessary for this assured back-and-forth song, but it is integral to African American worship.

A highly valued dimension of timbre, representing a continuing African tradition, is percussive delivery both in vocal and instrumental performance. Particularly in highly syncopated songs with faster tempos, short phrases are strongly punctuated to accent the rhythm. For example, in the opening line of "What a fellowship," breaks will commonly occur after "what" and "a." The line is not sung as a single continuing legato melodic phrase, but is instead chopped up into short, percussive fragments. The phrase is deliberately broken after the first word, adding rhythmic and timbral (percussive) interest.

Mechanics of Delivery

This broad category of performance describes the way time (rhythm, meter, tempo, duration), text, pitch, and harmony are conceived in African American sacred music expression, as well as the role of accompaniment and improvisation.

RHYTHM

More than by any other factor, African American music is driven by its rhythm. Rhythm is preeminent in both vocal lines and instrumental accompaniment; rhythm establishes the character of the piece. Each beat must be clearly sensed and heard. The principal pulse, of course, is given a strong accent. However, frequently the weak beats (such as 2 and 4 in 4/4) are given an even stronger accent than the primary and secondary ones. To illustrate, look at the spiritual "I'm so glad Jesus lifted me" (#191). It has four quarter note beats per measure and it is played with the accents not only on beats 2 and 4, but on the eighth note offbeats (1 and 2 and 3 and 4 and).

This sort of syncopation pervades all forms of African American worship music. It should never be rushed, always a temptation when you are anticipating the accent. Keep a firm sense of the tactus so that the syncopation can play off of it. As singers become more experienced in this style of music, they will often add layers of symmetrical and asymmetrical beat divisions over the basic pulse, contributing to the characteristic rhythmic complexity. Those less accustomed to the style, however, will be better off maintaining the basic rhythm. Above all, avoid smoothing out the rhythms; to do so will rob the music of its vitality and energy.

While rhythmic precision is critical to the performance of spirituals and gospel music, at the same time, rhythm must never be mechanical. Precision is one thing; rigidity is another. Notes may be held longer or shorter than written, and notes may even be anticipated—coming slightly earlier than indicated in the score. Even in congregational singing, each member of the congregation is free to personalize the singing experience—to make it one's own.

METER

Meter is another area in which oral tradition frequently takes precedence over what is written. Especially in the case of material borrowed from the classic or revival hymn traditions, a piece written in 4/4 routinely will be sung in 12/8, with a swing. So, for instance, "What a fellowship" (#220) is often written in 4/4, but played in 12/8. Even songs that keep their 4/4 feel will often have a flexibility in the meter that shows a triple-meter influence.

TEMPO

Tradition has come to dictate the tempos at which most African American songs are sung. Spirituals fall, for the most part, into either of two tempos. The sorrow song—such as "Go down, Moses" (#87)—is sung at a slow tempo, while the jubilee song—such as "Great day" (#164)—is taken at a brisk walking tempo. Within the arena of the gospel song, the gospel waltz is often employed for slower songs like "What a fellowship" while shout songs like "I'm so glad Jesus lifted me" would be sung at a quick tempo.

DURATION

In traditional African American worship neither the length of service in general nor the length of the songs in particular is dictated by the clock. Depending upon the quality of the interaction between the performer (preacher or singer) and the working of the Holy Spirit, extemporaneous elements of the worship may be extended or shortened. In congregational singing it is common for the final chorus of such well-loved hymns as "What a fellowship" to be repeated as directed by the song leader. Similarly, soloists frequently interject such textual phrases as "I believe I'll say that one more time" to signal repetition of a particular phrase or stanza. In neither of these instances is repetition viewed as boring or grandstanding; instead, repetition serves as an essential tool for generating and sustaining the spiritual fervor that has historically distinguished the worship of African Americans in the United States.

TEXT

Most spirituals and many gospel songs have very short texts, a feature which was helpful in committing them to memory. These brief texts are, however, repeated many times with improvised variations, the repetition helping to convey their message. Another way in which these texts are extended is through the interjection of "wandering," independent couplets and quatrains such as

> *If you cannot sing like angels, if you cannot preach like Paul,*
> *you can tell the love of Jesus and say he died for all.*

Sometimes these insertions are closely related to the text of the song, sometimes not. They are selected according to the spirit of the moment.

Although rhythm is unquestionably preeminent in African American religious music performance, text—the message—must not be minimized. Spirituals and gospel songs are filled with rich biblical imagery and intense devotion. The text, regardless of its relative simplicity or profundity, must be given its due.

PITCH

The concepts of pitch that characterize African American religious music are distinguished in some rather marked ways. First of all, melodic lines in both spirituals and gospel music include a preponderance of blue notes—lowered third, sixth, and seventh degrees in the major scale. Just as rhythms should not be smoothed out, neither should pitches. Even if a flatted seventh in the melody conflicts with a diatonic seventh in the accompaniment, this is considered an acceptable dissonance. Slides, scoops, and bends are all so fundamental to gospel music performance that soloists and congregations alike employ these vocal techniques intuitively. They have learned to value how pitch is conceived in their tradition through the process of years of exposure and practice.

HARMONY

Two styles of harmonization coexist with standard western harmony in unaccompanied singing. The first uses parallel thirds or sixths throughout the song, a constant parallel motion. In the second style, used especially with very slow-moving pieces, a parallel interval of a fourth or fifth predominates, creating an effect similar to organum.

ACCOMPANIMENT

When not sung unaccompanied, spirituals are often accompanied by acoustic piano alone. In gospel music, as well as gospel interpretations of hymns, piano is still the basis, but instrumentation is unlimited. African American churches often use some combination of piano, electric organ, drums, tambourine, and bass guitar. Accompaniment may also include instruments such as synthesizer, vibraphone, trumpet, saxophone, or flute. In virtually all forms of African American music, instrumental accompaniment functions to complement the voice; its role is not a secondary one, but rather one of equal importance to the voice. At the same time, instruments playing riffs or obbligatos should be careful to play on the "response" sections and not on the "calls" that are reserved for the leader.

IMPROVISATION

In orally based music like African American sacred song, improvisation plays an important role. At least some basic filling in beyond the written notation is essential to accompanying or leading this music. In singing the solo part, the leader will freely add runs, riffs, or motives to make the line more expressive. The melody line itself may be altered; rubato or rhythmic alteration may be employed.

A basic principle for accompanists is that open spaces in the gospel style are almost always filled in by the keyboard. At the very least this would require repeating chords during longer, held notes. Even more effective would be adding an arpeggiated figure; for instance, leading from one phrase to the next. It requires listening and practice, but such fills can add immeasurably to the song. A next step could be to add a moving bass line.

Few "upper limits" exist for the amount of improvising open to the keyboard player. Once the assembly is familiar with the hymn, even the melody is optional for the pianist. Arpeggios, scale passages, passing tones, upper and lower neighbor tones, even the occasional glissando are all possibilities within the style. Harmonic alterations that support the singing are also welcome. The player must sense when to "let loose" and when, especially as the vocalists become more active, to back off.

Style of Delivery

The style of delivery, or physical mode of presentation of much African American music includes variables which, in the European American tradition, may be considered extraneous. In the African American tradition, however, the visual and kinetic dimensions—the expressive behavior that characterizes performance—are of equal significance to the sonic dimension. In other words, it is not just what is sung, but how it is sung that counts.

The most striking aspect of delivery in African American music is the incorporation of dance. Although "flat-footed" singers have also been a part of African American song tradition, movement in synchrony to the rhythm of the song is very common in worship. However important these kinetic dimensions are to the African American worship experience, they never assume dominance over the singing itself.

Conclusion

These principles of African American musical performance are intended to serve as general guides toward developing musical facility and growth in these styles. Commitment and determination are necessary to internalize these principles, but the end result can be a richly rewarding experience.

A MUSICAL TIMELINE

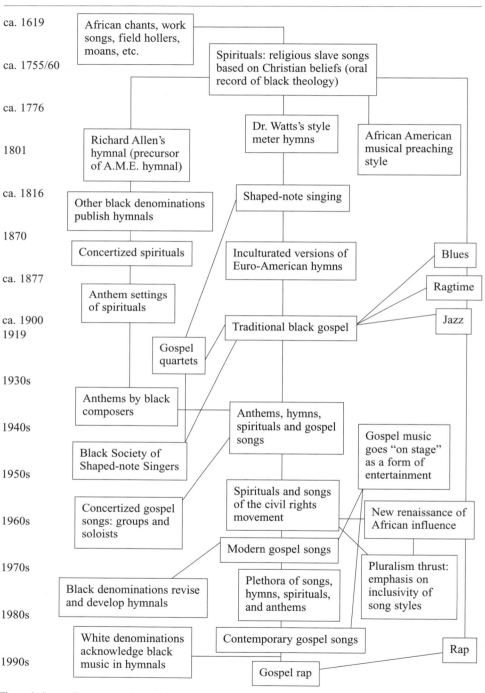

ca. 1619 — African chants, work songs, field hollers, moans, etc.

ca. 1755/60 — Spirituals: religious slave songs based on Christian beliefs (oral record of black theology)

ca. 1776

1801 — Richard Allen's hymnal (precursor of A.M.E. hymnal) — Dr. Watts's style meter hymns — African American musical preaching style

ca. 1816 — Other black denominations publish hymnals — Shaped-note singing

1870 — Concertized spirituals — Inculturated versions of Euro-American hymns — Blues

ca. 1877 — Anthem settings of spirituals — Ragtime

ca. 1900
1919 — Gospel quartets — Traditional black gospel — Jazz

1930s

1940s — Anthems by black composers — Anthems, hymns, spirituals and gospel songs — Gospel music goes "on stage" as a form of entertainment

1950s — Black Society of Shaped-note Singers

1960s — Concertized gospel songs: groups and soloists — Spirituals and songs of the civil rights movement — New renaissance of African influence

Modern gospel songs

1970s — Pluralism thrust: emphasis on inclusivity of song styles

1980s — Black denominations revise and develop hymnals — Plethora of songs, hymns, spirituals, and anthems

1990s — White denominations acknowledge black music in hymnals — Contemporary gospel songs — Rap

Gospel rap

The vertical center line represents the use of music for worship.
All musical styles overlap, continually influencing and nurturing each other.

© Melva Wilson Costen

THE LITURGY IS BIBLICAL

Sing to the Lord a new song, his praise in the assembly of the faithful. *(Psalm 149:1)*

Blow the trumpet in Zion; sanctify a fast; call a solemn assembly; gather the people. *(Joel 2:15-17)*

Assemble, all of you, and hear. *(Isaiah 48:14)*

For where two or three are gathered in my name, I am there among them. *(Matthew 18:20)*

When the day of Pentecost had come, they were all together in one place. *(Acts 2:1-13)*

CONFESSION AND FORGIVENESS
If we say that we have no sin, we deceive ourselves, and the truth is not in us. If we confess our sins, God who is faithful and just will forgive us our sins and cleanse us from all unrighteousness. *(1 John 1:8-9)*

GREETING
The grace of the Lord Jesus Christ, the love of God, and the communion of the Holy Spirit be with all of you. *(2 Corinthians 13:13)*

KYRIE
They called out, saying, "Jesus, Master, have mercy on us!" *(Luke 17:13)*

Pray for the peace of Jerusalem. Peace be within your walls. *(Psalm 122:6-7)*

HYMN OF PRAISE: GLORY TO GOD
Glory to God in the highest heaven, and on earth peace among those whom he favors! *(Luke 2:14)*

HYMN OF PRAISE: THIS IS THE FEAST
To the one seated on the throne and to the Lamb be blessing and honor and glory and might forever and ever! *(Revelation 5:13)*

SALUTATION
[Boaz] said to the reapers, "The Lord be with you." They answered, "The Lord bless you." *(Ruth 2:4)*

[The angel] came to her and said, "Greetings, favored one! The Lord is with you." *(Luke 1:28)*

So shall my word be that goes out from my mouth; it shall not return to me empty. *(Isaiah 55:10-11)*

One does not live by bread alone. *(Matthew 4:4)*

In the beginning was the Word. *(John 1:1-5)*

Let the word of Christ dwell in you richly. *(Colossians 3:16)*

Give attention to the public reading of scripture, to exhorting, to teaching. *(1 Timothy 4:13)*

I solemnly urge you: proclaim the message. *(2 Timothy 4:1-5)*

No prophecy of scripture is a matter of one's own interpretation. *(2 Peter 1:20-21)*

GOSPEL ACCLAMATION: GENERAL
Simon Peter answered him, "Lord, to whom can we go? You have the words of eternal life." *(John 6:68)*

GOSPEL ACCLAMATION: LENT
Return to the Lord, your God, for he is gracious and merciful, slow to anger, and abounding in steadfast love. *(Joel 2:13)*

THE PRAYERS
Hear my prayer, O Lord. *(Psalm 143:1)*

First of all, then, I urge that supplications, prayers, intercessions, and thanksgivings be made for everyone, for kings and all who are in high positions, so that we may lead a quiet and peaceable life in all godliness and dignity. *(1 Timothy 2:1-2)*

Then Jesus, crying with a loud voice, said, "Father, into your hands I commend my spirit." *(Luke 23:46)*

MEAL

For I received from the Lord what I also handed on to you. *(1 Corinthians 11:23-25)*

I am the bread of life. *(John 6:48-50)*

They devoted themselves to the apostles' teaching and fellowship, to the breaking of bread and the prayers. *(Acts 2:42)*

PEACE
So when you are offering your gift at the altar, if you remember that your brother or sister has something against you, leave your gift there before the altar and go; first be reconciled to your brother or sister, and then come and offer your gift. *(Matthew 5:23-24)*

Peace I leave with you; my peace I give to you. I do not give to you as the world gives. Do not let your hearts be troubled, and do not let them be afraid. *(John 14:27)*

Greet one another with a holy kiss. All the churches of Christ greet you. *(Romans 16:16)*

I am the vine, you are the branches. Those who abide in me and I in them bear much fruit. *(John 15:5)*

Create in me a clean heart, O God. *(Psalm 51:10-12)*

THANKSGIVING AND WORDS OF INSTITUTION

[The angels] called to another and said: "Holy, holy, holy is the Lord of hosts; the whole earth is full of his glory." *(Isaiah 6:3)*

The crowds that went ahead of him and that followed were shouting, "Hosanna to the Son of David! Blessed is the one who comes in the name of the Lord! Hosanna in the highest heaven!" *(Matthew 21:9)*

For I received from the Lord what I also handed on to you, that the Lord Jesus on the night when he was betrayed took a loaf of bread, and when he had given thanks, he broke it and said, "This is my body that is for you. Do this in remembrance of me." In the same way he took the cup also, after supper, saying, "This cup is the new covenant in my blood. Do this, as often as you drink it, in remembrance of me." For as often as you eat this bread and drink the cup, you proclaim the Lord's death until he comes. *(1 Corinthians 11:23-26)*

LORD'S PRAYER

Pray then in this way: Our Father in heaven. *(Matthew 6:9-13)*

BREAKING OF BREAD

The next day John saw Jesus coming toward him and declared, "Here is the Lamb of God who takes away the sin of the world!" *(John 1:29)*

SENDING

Go therefore and make disciples of all nations. *(Matthew 28:19)*

As the Father has sent me, so I send you. *(John 20:21)*

So if I, your Lord and Teacher, have washed your feet, you also ought to wash one another's feet. *(John 13:1-16)*

CANTICLE

Simeon took him in his arms and praised God, saying, "Master, now you are dismissing your servant in peace." *(Luke 2:28-32)*

Oh, give thanks to the Lord. Let the hearts of those who seek the Lord rejoice. *(Psalm 105:1-3, 42-45)*

BENEDICTION

You shall say to them, the Lord bless you and keep you; the Lord make his face to shine upon you, and be gracious to you; the Lord lift up his countenance upon you, and give you peace. *(Numbers 6:23-26)*

DISMISSAL

And [Jesus] said to the woman, "Your faith has saved you; go in peace." *(Luke 7:50)*

HOLY COMMUNION

SHAPE OF THE RITE

Sunday is the primary day on which the church assembles: the first day of creation when God transformed darkness into light and the day on which Christ rose from death and revealed himself to the disciples in the scriptures and the breaking of the bread. The baptized gather to hear the word of God, to pray for those in need, to offer thanks to God for the gift of salvation, to receive the bread of life and the cup of blessing, and to be renewed for the daily witness of faith, hope, and love. To guests, strangers, and all in need, the church proclaims the love of God in Christ Jesus.

GATHERING

Entrance Hymn
GREETING
Kyrie
Hymn of Praise
PRAYER OF THE DAY

God calls and gathers believers through the Holy Spirit, and in response the community acclaims this gracious God in song and prayer. The gathering of the congregation may begin with a brief order for confession and forgiveness and/or an entrance hymn. God's welcome is extended to the congregation by the presider. When appropriate, a litany or hymn of praise may be sung immediately before the prayer of the day. Through these actions, the congregation prepares to hear the word of God.

WORD

FIRST READING
Psalm
Second Reading
Gospel Acclamation
GOSPEL
SERMON
HYMN OF THE DAY
Creed
THE PRAYERS

In the rich treasure of scripture proclaimed by readers and preachers, the church hears the good news of God acting in this and every time and place. A three-year cycle of readings provides portions of the Old Testament narratives and prophetic writings, the New Testament letters, and the gospel books for each week. During Advent/Christmas, the lectionary reveals the mystery of the Word made flesh. In Lent/Easter, the paschal mystery of the Lord's death and resurrection is proclaimed. Throughout the season after Pentecost, the New Testament texts are read in a continuous order. During the last Sundays of the year, the readings present the final vision of a new heaven and a new earth.

This encounter with the living Word, Jesus Christ, is marked by proclamation and silence, psalm and hymn, singing and speaking, movement and gesture. Silence after the readings allows time for the word to be pondered. The sermon announces the good news of life in Christ to the community and the world; the hymn of the day both proclaims and responds to the word; the creed is a further response to it. God's word, read and preached and acclaimed, leads the community to pray for the church, the people of the world, and those who suffer or are in need.

MEAL

GREETING OF PEACE
PRESENTATION OF THE GIFTS
THANKSGIVING AND WORDS OF INSTITUTION
LORD'S PRAYER
COMMUNION
Canticle
Prayer

In word and gesture, prayer and song, the people lift up their hearts in praise and thanksgiving for the gifts of forgiveness, life, and salvation. To the table of the Lord are brought bread and wine, simple signs of God's love, humble signs of human labor. Over them are spoken Jesus' words by which he instituted this holy supper: "This is my body; this is my blood." The Holy Spirit is invoked with the prayer that all who eat and drink the body and blood of the Lord may do so with a living faith. With Jesus serving as host, all join in the prayer which he gave. Welcomed to the table, the communicants are united with God in Christ, with each other, and with the church's mission in the world. In their eating and drinking they remember the Lord's death and resurrection and proclaim his life-giving work until he comes. During the communion, hymns, songs, and psalms may be sung. As the table is cleared, the congregation may sing a canticle. A brief prayer concludes the liturgy of the meal.

SENDING

BLESSING
Dismissal

Worship on the Lord's day ends with simplicity. The community receives the blessing of God. All are invited to leave in peace, sent out to serve in word and deed: to speak the words of good news they have heard, to care for those in need, and to share what they have received with the poor and the hungry.

Central elements of the Holy Communion liturgy are noted in uppercase letters; other elements support and reveal the essential shape of Christian worship.

CONFESSION AND FORGIVENESS

ORDER A

℗ In the name of the Father, and of
the ✛ Son, and of the Holy Spirit.
🅲 **Amen**

℗ God of all mercy and consolation,
come to the aid of your people,
turning us from our sin
to live for you alone.
Give us the power of your Holy Spirit
that, attentive to your word,
we may confess our sins,
receive your forgiveness,
and grow into the fullness of your Son,
Jesus Christ our Lord.
🅲 **Amen**

℗ Let us confess our sin in the presence of
God and of one another.

Silence for reflection and self-examination.

℗ Gracious God,
🅲 **have mercy on us.
In your compassion forgive us
our sins, known and unknown,
things done and left undone.
Uphold us by your Spirit
so that we may live and serve you
in newness of life,
to the honor and glory
of your holy name;
through Jesus Christ our Lord. Amen**

℗ Almighty God have mercy on you,
forgive you all your sins
through our ✛ Lord Jesus Christ,
strengthen you in all goodness,
and by the power of the Holy Spirit
keep you in eternal life.
🅲 **Amen**

ORDER B

℗ In the name of the Father, and of
the ✛ Son, and of the Holy Spirit.
🅲 **Amen**

℗ Since we have such a great high priest
who has passed through the heavens,
Jesus Christ our Lord,
let us with confidence
draw near to God,
that we may receive mercy
and find grace in time of need.

Silence for reflection and self-examination.

🅲 **Have mercy on us, O God,
according to your lovingkindness.
In your great mercy,
wash away our iniquity
and cleanse us from our sin.**

**Create in us clean hearts, O God,
and renew a right spirit within us.
Do not remove us from your presence;
do not take your Spirit away.**

**Restore to us the joy of your salvation,
and sustain us with your Spirit. Amen**

℗ God is merciful and gracious,
granting forgiveness through Jesus
Christ to all who confess their sin.
As a called and ordained minister
of the church of Christ,
and by his authority,
I therefore declare to you
the entire forgiveness of all your sin,
in the name of the Father, and of
the ✛ Son, and of the Holy Spirit.
🅲 **Amen**

ORDER C

℗ In the name of the Father, and of
the ☩ Son, and of the Holy Spirit.
© **Amen**

℗ The Sun of righteousness shall rise
with shining beams of healing.
Let us gather under the wings
of God's mercy.

Silence for reflection and self-examination.

℗ Gracious God,
© **we acknowledge that we are sinners
and we confess our sins—those
known to us that burden our hearts,
and those unknown to us but seen by
you. We know that before you nothing
remains hidden, and in you everything is revealed. Free us from the
slavery of sin; liberate us from the
bondage of guilt; work in us that
which is pleasing in your sight; for
the sake of Jesus Christ our Lord.
Amen**

℗ From the house of David, God raised up
a mighty Savior.
© **Blessed be the Lord God of Israel,
who comes to set us free.**

℗ Remembering the covenant,
God delivered us from our enemies.
© **Blessed be the Lord God of Israel,
who comes to set us free.**

℗ Before God we are holy and righteous,
free to worship without fear.
© **Blessed be the Lord God of Israel,
who comes to set us free.**

℗ With a heart full of mercy and
compassion, God saves us and
forgives us all our sins. Christ, the
dawn from on high, shines upon us,
and by the light of the Holy Spirit
guides our feet into the way of peace.
© **Amen**

ORDER D

℗ In the name of the Father, and of
the ☩ Son, and of the Holy Spirit.
© **Amen**

℗ Beloved in the Lord: let us draw near
with a true heart, and confess our sins
to God our Father, imploring him in the
name of our Lord Jesus Christ to grant
us forgiveness.

Silence for reflection and self-examination.

℗ Our help is in the name of the Lord,
© **who made heaven and earth.**

℗ I said, I will confess my transgressions
to the Lord.
© **And you forgave the iniquity of my sin.**

℗ Almighty God, merciful Father:
© **I, a troubled and penitent sinner,
confess to you all my sins and
iniquities with which I have offended
you and for which I justly deserve
your punishment.
But I am sorry for them,
and repent of them,
and pray for your boundless mercy.**

**For the sake of the suffering and
death of your Son, Jesus Christ,
be gracious and merciful to me,
a poor sinful being; forgive my sins,
give me your Holy Spirit for the
amendment of my sinful life,
and bring me to life everlasting.
Amen**

℗ In the mercy of almighty God, Jesus
Christ was given to die for you, and for
his sake God forgives you all your sins.
To those who believe in Jesus Christ he
gives the power to become the children
of God and bestows on them the Holy
Spirit.
© **Amen**

HOLY COMMUNION

SETTING ONE
River of Life

An order for confession and forgiveness (pp. 24–25) may be used before this service.
The gathering rite may include a call to worship (pp. 72–76).
The minister may announce the day and its significance before the entrance hymn or the readings.

GATHERING

Stand

Entrance Hymn or Psalm

Greeting

> P̄ The grace of our Lord Jesus Christ, the love of God,
> and the communion of the Holy Spirit be with you all.
> C̄ **And also with you.**

Those assembled may be invited to welcome one another in the name of Christ.

Kyrie

The Kyrie may follow.

Ⓐ In peace, let us pray to the Lord.

C̄ Lord, have mer - cy.

A For the peace from a-bove, and for our sal-va-tion, let us pray to the Lord.

C Lord, have mer - cy.

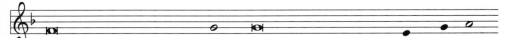

A For the peace of the whole world, for the well-being of the church of God,

and for the uni-ty of all, let us pray to the Lord.

C Lord, have mer - cy.

A For this ho-ly house, and for all who offer here their wor-ship and

praise, let us pray to the Lord.

C Lord, have mer - cy.

A Help, save, comfort, and de-fend us, gracious Lord.

C A - men

Hymn of Praise

The hymn of praise or another appropriate hymn may be sung.

C Glo-ry to God in the high-est, and peace to his peo-ple on earth.

I Lord God, heav-en-ly king, al-might-y God and Fa-ther, we wor-ship you, we give you thanks, we praise you for your glo-ry.

C Glo-ry to God in the high-est, and peace to his peo-ple on earth.

II Lord Je-sus Christ, on-ly Son of the Fa-ther, Lord God, Lamb of God, you take a-way the sin of the world: have mer-cy on us; you are seat-ed at the

right hand of the Fa - ther: re - ceive our prayer.

C Glo - ry to God in the high - est, and

peace to his peo - ple on earth.

For you a - lone are the Ho - ly One,

you a - lone are the Lord, you a - lone

are the Most High, Je - sus Christ, with the Ho - ly

Spir- it, in the glo - ry of God the Fa - ther.

C Glo - ry to God in the high - est, and

peace to his peo - ple on earth.

OR

C This is the feast of vic - to - ry for our God.

Al - le - lu - ia.

I Wor - thy is Christ, the Lamb who was slain, whose

blood set us free to be peo - ple of God.

Pow - er, rich - es, wis - dom, and strength, and

hon - or, bless - ing, and glo - ry are his.

C This is the feast of vic - to - ry for our God.

Al - le - lu - ia.

III Sing with all the peo - ple of God, and

join in the hymn of all cre - a - tion.

Blessing, honor, glory, and might be to God and the Lamb forever. A - men.

C This is the feast of victory for our God.

For the Lamb who was slain has begun his reign. Alleluia.

This is the feast of victory for our God.

Alleluia. This is the feast of victory for our God. Alleluia.

Prayer of the Day

The salutation may precede the prayer.

P The Lord be with you.

C And also with you.

P Let us pray. *(The prayer of the day is said, concluding:)*

C Amen

Sit

First Reading

Ⓐ A reading from _____.

After the reading, the reader may say: The word of the Lord.
All may respond: **Thanks be to God.**

Psalm

The psalm is sung or said.

Second Reading

Ⓐ A reading from _____.

After the reading, the reader may say: The word of the Lord.
All may respond: **Thanks be to God.**

Stand

Gospel Acclamation

The appointed verse may be sung by the choir, or the congregation may sing an acclamation or a hymn.

GENERAL

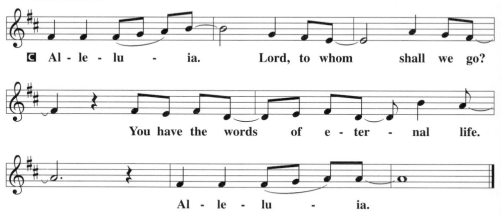

Ⓒ Al - le - lu - ia. Lord, to whom shall we go?

You have the words of e - ter - nal life.

Al - le - lu - ia.

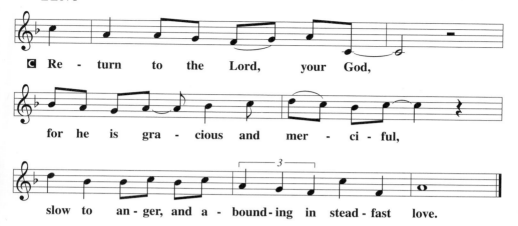

C Re - turn to the Lord, your God, for he is gra - cious and mer - ci - ful, slow to an - ger, and a - bound - ing in stead - fast love.

Gospel

P The Holy Gospel according to _____, the _____ chapter.
C Glory to you, O Lord.

After the reading:
P The Gospel of the Lord.
C Praise to you, O Christ.

The hymn of the day or another musical proclamation may precede the sermon.

Sit

Sermon

Silence for reflection may follow.

Stand

Hymn of the Day

Creed

The creed may be said: the Nicene Creed, on all festivals and on Sundays in the seasons of Advent/Christmas and Lent/Easter; the Apostles' Creed, at other times. When Holy Baptism or another rite with a creed is celebrated, this creed may be omitted.

NICENE CREED

C **We believe in one God,**
    the Father, the Almighty,
    maker of heaven and earth,
    of all that is, seen and unseen.

We believe in one Lord, Jesus Christ,
    the only Son of God,
    eternally begotten of the Father,
    God from God, Light from Light,
    true God from true God,
    begotten, not made,
    of one Being with the Father.
    Through him all things were made.
For us and for our salvation
    he came down from heaven;
    by the power of the Holy Spirit
        he became incarnate from the virgin Mary, and was made man.
For our sake he was crucified under Pontius Pilate;
    he suffered death and was buried.
    On the third day he rose again
        in accordance with the Scriptures;
    he ascended into heaven
        and is seated at the right hand of the Father.
He will come again in glory to judge the living and the dead,
    and his kingdom will have no end.

We believe in the Holy Spirit, the Lord, the giver of life,
    who proceeds from the Father and the Son.
    With the Father and the Son he is worshiped and glorified.
    He has spoken through the prophets.
    We believe in one holy catholic and apostolic Church.
    We acknowledge one Baptism for the forgiveness of sins.
    We look for the resurrection of the dead,
        and the life of the world to come. Amen

APOSTLES' CREED

C **I believe in God, the Father almighty,**
> **creator of heaven and earth.**

I believe in Jesus Christ, his only Son, our Lord.
> **He was conceived by the power of the Holy Spirit**
>> **and born of the virgin Mary.**
> **He suffered under Pontius Pilate,**
>> **was crucified, died, and was buried.**
> **He descended into hell.***
> **On the third day he rose again.**
> **He ascended into heaven,**
>> **and is seated at the right hand of the Father.**
> **He will come again to judge the living and the dead.**

I believe in the Holy Spirit,
> **the holy catholic Church,**
> **the communion of saints,**
> **the forgiveness of sins,**
> **the resurrection of the body,**
> **and the life everlasting. Amen**

*Or, He descended to the dead.

Stand/Kneel

The Prayers

The prayers begin with these or similar words:
A Let us pray for the whole people of God in Christ Jesus,
and for all people according to their needs.

Prayers are included for the whole church, the nations, those in need, the parish, and special concerns. The congregation may be invited to offer other petitions. Prayers of confession may be included if an order for confession and forgiveness has not been used earlier. The minister gives thanks for the faithful departed, especially for those who recently have died.

Each portion of the prayers concludes with these or similar words:

	OR
A Lord, in your mercy,	**A** Hear us, O God;
C **hear our prayer.**	**C** **your mercy is great.**

The prayers conclude with these or similar words:
P Into your hands, O Lord, we commend all for whom we pray,
trusting in your mercy; through your Son, Jesus Christ our Lord.
C **Amen**

Stand

Peace

> *The peace is shared at this time or prior to the distribution of communion.*
> P The peace of the Lord be with you always.
> C **And also with you.**
>
> *The ministers and congregation may greet one another with a gesture of peace, using these or similar words:* Peace be with you.

Sit

Offering and Preparation

> *The offering is received as the Lord's table is prepared.*
>
> *The appointed offertory may be sung by the choir as the gifts are presented, or the congregation may sing one of the following offertories, or an appropriate hymn or psalm may be sung.*

Stand

C Let the vine - yards be fruit - ful, Lord, and fill to the

brim our cup of bless - ing. Gath - er a

har - vest from the seeds that were sown, that we may be

fed with the bread of life.

Gath - er the hopes and dreams of all; u -

nite them with the prayers we of - fer.

Grace our ta - ble with your pres - ence, and
give us a fore - taste of the feast to come.

OR, especially in Lent:

C Cre - ate in me a clean heart, O God, and re -
new a right spir - it with - in me.
Cast me not a - way from your pres - ence, and take not your
Ho - ly Spir - it from me. Re -
store to me the joy of your sal - va - tion
and up - hold me with your free Spir - it.

This or another appropriate prayer (pp. 80–81) may be said.

A Let us pray.
Merciful God,

C we offer with joy and thanksgiving what you have first given us—
our selves, our time, and our possessions, signs of your gracious love.
Receive them for the sake of him who offered himself for us,
Jesus Christ our Lord. Amen

Thanksgiving

P The Lord be with you.

C And also with you.

P Lift up your hearts.

C We lift them to the Lord.

P Let us give thanks to the Lord our God.

C It is right to give our thanks and praise.

When a preface is prayed (pp. 82–83), the Sanctus follows:

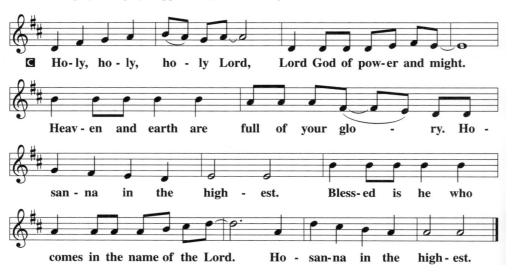

C Ho-ly, ho-ly, ho-ly Lord, Lord God of pow-er and might.
Heav-en and earth are full of your glo - ry. Ho-
san-na in the high - est. Bless-ed is he who
comes in the name of the Lord. Ho - san-na in the high-est.

The minister continues the thanksgiving, using one of the forms on pp. 84–88 or another appropriate form, in which the words of Christ's institution are proclaimed.

The thanksgiving may include this acclamation:

P . . . we proclaim the Lord's death until he comes.

C Christ has died. Christ is risen. Christ will come again.

When the thanksgiving includes a doxology, the following may be sung:

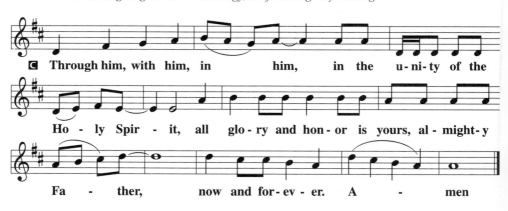

C Through him, with him, in him, in the u-ni-ty of the
Ho - ly Spir - it, all glo-ry and hon-or is yours, al-might-y
Fa - ther, now and for-ev - er. A - men

OR

C Our Father in heaven,
hallowed be your name,
your kingdom come,
your will be done,
on earth as in heaven.
Give us today our daily bread.
Forgive us our sins
as we forgive those
who sin against us.
Save us from the time of trial
and deliver us from evil.
For the kingdom, the power,
and the glory are yours,
now and forever. Amen

C Our Father, who art in heaven,
hallowed be thy name,
thy kingdom come,
thy will be done,
on earth as it is in heaven.
Give us this day our daily bread;
and forgive us our trespasses,
as we forgive those
who trespass against us;
and lead us not into temptation,
but deliver us from evil.
For thine is the kingdom,
and the power, and the glory,
forever and ever. Amen

If not included previously, the greeting of peace is now given and shared.

Sit

Communion

As the people commune, hymns and other music may be used.

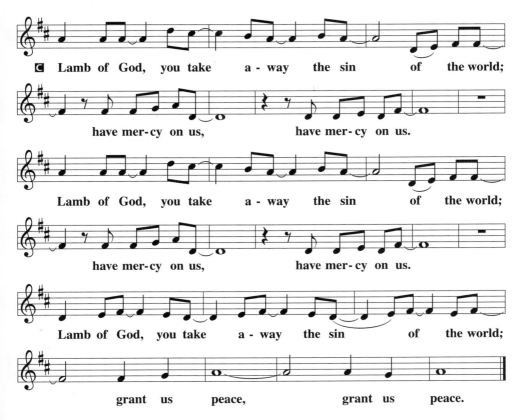

C Lamb of God, you take a - way the sin of the world;
have mer-cy on us, have mer-cy on us.

Lamb of God, you take a - way the sin of the world;
have mer-cy on us, have mer-cy on us.

Lamb of God, you take a - way the sin of the world;
grant us peace, grant us peace.

Canticle

After the people have communed, one of the following canticles or an appropriate hymn may be sung.

🅒 Lord, now you let your ser - vant go in peace; your word has been ful - filled. My own eyes have seen the sal - va - tion which you have pre - pared in the sight of all peo- ple: a light to re - veal you to the na - tions and the glo- ry of your peo- ple Is - ra - el. Glo - ry to the Fa - ther, and to the Son, and to the Ho - ly Spir - it: as it was in the be - gin - ning, is now, and will be for - ev - er. A - men

OR

C Thank-ful hearts and voic-es raise;

tell ev-'ry-one what God has done. Let all who seek the Lord re-

joice and bear Christ's ho-ly name.

Send us with your prom-is-es, O God, and

lead us forth in joy with shouts of thanks-giv-

repeat ad lib

ing, with shouts of thanks-giv-

ing. Al-le-lu-ia.

Prayer

The following or another post-communion prayer (p. 89) is prayed.

A Let us pray.

We give you thanks, almighty God, that you have refreshed us through the healing power of this gift of life; and we pray that in your mercy you would strengthen us, through this gift, in faith toward you and in fervent love toward one another; for the sake of Jesus Christ our Lord.

C **Amen**

Silence for reflection.

Benediction

The minister blesses the congregation. The benediction may be preceded by a charge to the people (pp. 90–93).

OR

P Almighty God,
Father, ✝ Son, and Holy Spirit,
bless you now and forever.

C **Amen**

P The Lord bless you and keep you.
The Lord make his face shine on you
and be gracious to you.
The Lord look upon you with favor and
✝ give you peace.

C **Amen**

When there is a procession from the church, a hymn, song, or canticle may be sung.

Dismissal

The minister may dismiss the congregation.
A Go in peace. Serve the Lord.
C **Thanks be to God.**

HOLY COMMUNION

SETTING TWO
Liturgy of Joy

An order for confession and forgiveness (see pp. 24–25) may be used before this service.
The gathering rite may include a call to worship (see pp. 72–76).
The minister may announce the day and its significance before the entrance hymn or the readings.

GATHERING

Stand

Entrance Hymn or Psalm

Greeting

> Ⓟ The grace of our Lord Jesus Christ, the love of God,
> and the communion of the Holy Spirit be with you all.
> Ⓒ **And also with you.**

Those assembled may be invited to welcome one another in the name of Christ.

Kyrie

The Kyrie may follow.

Ⓛ In peace, let us pray to the Lord.　　Ⓛ For the

Ⓒ Lord, have mer - cy.

peace from a-bove, and for our sal-va-tion, let us pray to the Lord.

L For the peace of the whole

C Lord, have mer - cy.

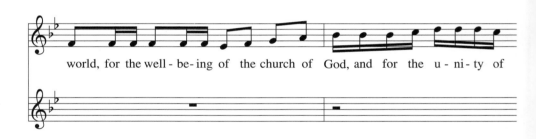

world, for the well-be-ing of the church of God, and for the u-ni-ty of

all, let us pray to the Lord.   L For this ho-ly

C Lord, have mer - cy.

house, and for all who of - fer here their wor - ship and praise, let us

pray to the Lord.

🅲 Lord, have mer - cy. A - men

🅻 Help, save, com - fort, and de - fend us, gra - cious Lord.

🅲 A - men

🅻 Help, save, com - fort, and de - fend us, gra - cious Lord.

🅲 A - men

Hymn of Praise

The hymn of praise or another appropriate hymn may be sung.

C Glo-ry to God in the high-est, and peace to his peo-ple on earth. Glo-ry to God in the high-est, and peace to his peo-ple on earth.

I Lord God, heav-en-ly king, al - might-y God and Fa-ther, we wor-ship you, we give you thanks, we praise you for your glo-ry.

C Glo-ry to God in the high-est, and peace to his peo-ple on earth. Glo-ry to God in the high-est, and peace to his peo-ple on earth.

II Lord Je-sus Christ, on-ly Son of the Fa-ther, Lord God, Lamb of God, you take a-way the sin of the world:

have mer-cy on us; you are seat-ed at the right
hand of the Fa-ther: re - ceive our prayer.

C Glo-ry to God in the high - est, and peace
to his peo-ple on earth. Glo-ry to God in the
high - est, and peace to his peo-ple on earth.

III For you a - lone are the Ho - ly One, you a - lone are the
Lord, you a - lone are the Most High, Je - sus Christ, with the
Ho - ly Spir-it, in the glo-ry of God the Fa - ther.

C Glo - ry to God in the high - est,
A - men, a - men.

OR

C This is the feast of vic-to-ry for our God. Al - le -
lu - ia, al - le - lu - ia.

I Wor - thy is Christ, the Lamb who was slain,
whose blood set us free to be peo - ple of God.
Pow - er, rich - es, wis - dom, and strength, and
hon - or, bless - ing, and glo - ry are his.

C This is the feast of vic-to-ry for our God. Al - le -
lu - ia, al - le - lu - ia.

II Sing with all the peo - ple of God, and
join in the hymn of all cre - a - tion:

Bless - ing, hon - or, glo - ry, and might be to God and the Lamb for - ev - er. A - men.

C This is the feast of vic-to-ry for our God. Al-le-lu - ia, al - le - lu - ia.

1 2 For the Lamb who was slain has be-gun his reign. Al - le - lu - ia.

C This is the feast of vic-to-ry for our God. Al-le-lu - ia, al - le - lu - ia. This is the feast of vic-to-ry for our God. Al-le-lu - ia, al-le-lu - ia.

Prayer of the Day

The salutation may precede the prayer.

P The Lord be with you.

C **And also with you.**

P Let us pray. *(The prayer of the day is said, concluding:)*

C **Amen**

Sit

First Reading

Ⓐ A reading from _____.

After the reading, the reader may say: The word of the Lord.
All may respond: **Thanks be to God.**

Psalm

The psalm is sung or said.

Second Reading

Ⓐ A reading from _____.

After the reading, the reader may say: The word of the Lord.
All may respond: **Thanks be to God.**

Stand

Gospel Acclamation

The appointed verse may be sung by the choir, or the congregation may sing an acclamation or a hymn.

GENERAL

Ⓒ Al - le - lu - ia.   Lord,   to whom shall we   go?

You have the words of e - ter - nal   life. Al - le - lu - ia.

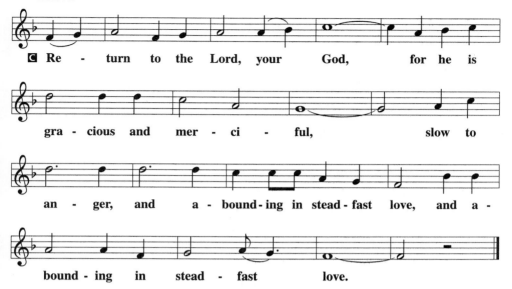

C Re - turn to the Lord, your God, for he is gra - cious and mer - ci - ful, slow to an - ger, and a - bound-ing in stead - fast love, and a - bound - ing in stead - fast love.

Gospel

P The Holy Gospel according to _____, the _____ chapter.

C Glory to you, O Lord.

After the reading:

P The Gospel of the Lord.

C Praise to you, O Christ.

The hymn of the day or another musical proclamation may precede the sermon.

Sit

Sermon

Silence for reflection may follow.

Stand

Hymn of the Day

Creed

The creed may be said: the Nicene Creed, on all festivals and on Sundays in the seasons of Advent/Christmas and Lent/Easter; the Apostles' Creed, at other times. When Holy Baptism or another rite with a creed is celebrated, this creed may be omitted.

NICENE CREED

C We believe in one God,
 the Father, the Almighty,
 maker of heaven and earth,
 of all that is, seen and unseen.

We believe in one Lord, Jesus Christ,
 the only Son of God,
 eternally begotten of the Father,
 God from God, Light from Light,
 true God from true God,
 begotten, not made,
 of one Being with the Father.
 Through him all things were made.
 For us and for our salvation
  he came down from heaven;
  by the power of the Holy Spirit
   he became incarnate from the virgin Mary, and was made man.
 For our sake he was crucified under Pontius Pilate;
  he suffered death and was buried.
  On the third day he rose again
   in accordance with the Scriptures;
  he ascended into heaven
   and is seated at the right hand of the Father.
 He will come again in glory to judge the living and the dead,
  and his kingdom will have no end.

We believe in the Holy Spirit, the Lord, the giver of life,
 who proceeds from the Father and the Son.
 With the Father and the Son he is worshiped and glorified.
 He has spoken through the prophets.
 We believe in one holy catholic and apostolic Church.
 We acknowledge one Baptism for the forgiveness of sins.
 We look for the resurrection of the dead,
  and the life of the world to come. Amen

APOSTLES' CREED

C **I believe in God, the Father almighty,**
creator of heaven and earth.

I believe in Jesus Christ, his only Son, our Lord.
He was conceived by the power of the Holy Spirit
and born of the virgin Mary.
He suffered under Pontius Pilate,
was crucified, died, and was buried.
He descended into hell.*
On the third day he rose again.
He ascended into heaven,
and is seated at the right hand of the Father.
He will come again to judge the living and the dead.

I believe in the Holy Spirit,
the holy catholic Church,
the communion of saints,
the forgiveness of sins,
the resurrection of the body,
and the life everlasting. Amen

*Or, He descended to the dead.

Stand/Kneel

The Prayers

The prayers begin with these or similar words:

A Let us pray for the whole people of God in Christ Jesus,
and for all people according to their needs.

Prayers are included for the whole church, the nations, those in need, the parish, and special concerns. The congregation may be invited to offer other petitions. Prayers of confession may be included if an order for confession and forgiveness has not been used earlier. The minister gives thanks for the faithful departed, especially for those who recently have died.

Each portion of the prayers concludes with these or similar words:

A Lord, in your mercy,	*OR*	**A** Hear us, O God;
C **hear our prayer.**		**C** **your mercy is great.**

The prayers conclude with these or similar words:

P Into your hands, O Lord, we commend all for whom we pray,
trusting in your mercy; through your Son, Jesus Christ our Lord.
C **Amen**

Stand

Peace

> *The peace is shared at this time or prior to the distribution of communion.*
>
> P The peace of the Lord be with you always.
>
> C **And also with you.**
>
> *The ministers and congregation may greet one another with a gesture of peace, using these or*
> *similar words:* Peace be with you.

Sit

Offering and Preparation

> *The offering is received as the Lord's table is prepared.*
>
> *The appointed offertory may be sung by the choir as the gifts are presented, or the congrega-*
> *tion may sing one of the following offertories, or an appropriate hymn or psalm may be sung.*

Stand

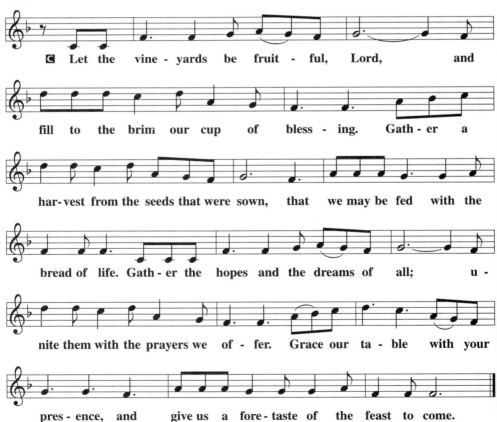

C Let the vine-yards be fruit-ful, Lord, and fill to the brim our cup of bless-ing. Gath-er a har-vest from the seeds that were sown, that we may be fed with the bread of life. Gath-er the hopes and the dreams of all; u-nite them with the prayers we of-fer. Grace our ta-ble with your pres-ence, and give us a fore-taste of the feast to come.

C Cre - ate in me a clean heart, O God, and re - new a right spir - it with - in me.

Cast me not a - way from your pres - ence, and take not your Ho - ly Spir - it from me. Re - store to me the joy of your sal - va - tion, and up - hold me with your free Spir - it. Cre - ate in me a clean heart, O God, and re - new a right spir - it with - in me.

This or another appropriate prayer (pp. 80–81) may be said.

A Let us pray.
Merciful God,

C we offer with joy and thanksgiving what you have first given us—
our selves, our time, and our possessions, signs of your gracious love.
Receive them for the sake of him who offered himself for us,
Jesus Christ our Lord. Amen

Thanksgiving

P The Lord be with you.

C And also with you.

P Lift up your hearts.

C We lift them to the Lord.

P Let us give thanks to the Lord our God.

C It is right to give our thanks and praise.

When a preface is prayed (pp. 82–83), the Sanctus follows:

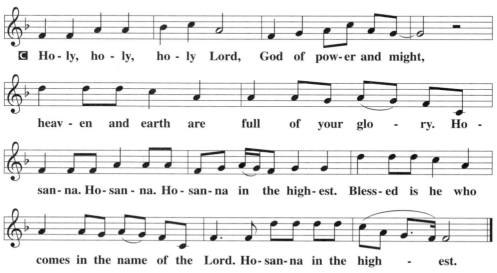

C Ho-ly, ho-ly, ho-ly Lord, God of pow-er and might,
heav-en and earth are full of your glo-ry. Ho-
san-na. Ho-san-na. Ho-san-na in the high-est. Bless-ed is he who
comes in the name of the Lord. Ho-san-na in the high - est.

The minister continues the thanksgiving, using one of the forms on pp. 84–88 or another appropriate form, in which the words of Christ's institution are proclaimed.

The thanksgiving may include this acclamation:

P . . . we proclaim the Lord's death until he comes.

C Christ has died. Christ is risen. Christ will come again.

When the thanksgiving includes a doxology, the following may be sung:

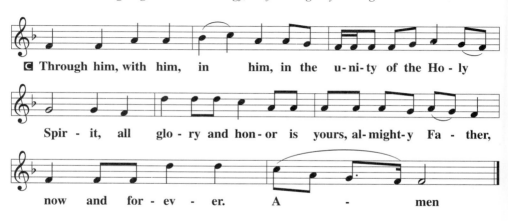

C Through him, with him, in him, in the u-ni-ty of the Ho-ly
Spir-it, all glo-ry and hon-or is yours, al-might-y Fa-ther,
now and for-ev-er. A - men

OR

C Our Father in heaven,
    hallowed be your name,
    your kingdom come,
    your will be done,
       on earth as in heaven.
Give us today our daily bread.
Forgive us our sins
    as we forgive those
       who sin against us.
Save us from the time of trial
    and deliver us from evil.
For the kingdom, the power,
    and the glory are yours,
    now and forever. Amen

C Our Father, who art in heaven,
    hallowed be thy name,
    thy kingdom come,
    thy will be done,
       on earth as it is in heaven.
Give us this day our daily bread;
and forgive us our trespasses,
    as we forgive those
       who trespass against us;
and lead us not into temptation,
    but deliver us from evil.
For thine is the kingdom,
    and the power, and the glory,
    forever and ever. Amen

If not included previously, the greeting of peace is now given and shared.

Sit

Communion

As the people commune, hymns and other music may be used.

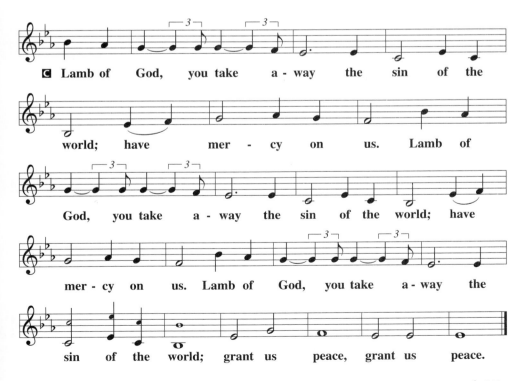

C Lamb of God, you take a - way the sin of the world; have mer - cy on us. Lamb of God, you take a - way the sin of the world; have mer - cy on us. Lamb of God, you take a - way the sin of the world; grant us peace, grant us peace.

Canticle

After the people have communed, the following canticle or an appropriate hymn may be sung.

C Thank-ful hearts and voic - es raise;

tell ev - 'ry-one what God has done. Let all who seek the

Lord re - joice and bear Christ's ho - ly name.

Send us with your prom-is - es, O God, and lead us forth in

joy with shouts of thanks-giv-ing. Al - le - lu - ia.

(Lent) **A - men, a - men.**

Prayer

The following or another post-communion prayer (p. 89) is prayed.

A Let us pray.

We give you thanks, almighty God, that you have refreshed us through the healing power of this gift of life; and we pray that in your mercy you would strengthen us, through this gift, in faith toward you and in fervent love toward one another; for the sake of Jesus Christ our Lord.

C **Amen**

Silence for reflection.

Benediction

The minister blesses the congregation. The benediction may be preceded by a charge to the people (pp. 90–93).

P Almighty God,
Father, + Son, and Holy Spirit,
bless you now and forever.
C **Amen**

OR

P The Lord bless you and keep you.
The Lord make his face shine on you
and be gracious to you.
The Lord look upon you with favor and
+ give you peace.
C **Amen**

When there is a procession from the church, a hymn, song, or canticle may be sung.

Dismissal

The minister may dismiss the congregation.
A Go in peace. Serve the Lord.
C **Thanks be to God.**

HOLY COMMUNION

SETTING THREE
A Pattern for the Service

This service follows the tradition of Luther's German Mass (1526), in which parts of the liturgy are replaced with appropriate hymns and songs.

GATHERING

An order for CONFESSION AND FORGIVENESS (pp. 24–25) may precede this service.

As a CALL TO WORSHIP, one or more of the following elements may be used: hymns, songs, psalms, song medleys, silence, spoken dialog (pp. 72–76).

<table>
<tr><td></td><td>OR</td></tr>
<tr><td>With a biblical GREETING, the minister declares God's welcome.</td><td>As the minister leads the INVOCATION, all may make the sign of the cross in remembrance of their baptism.</td></tr>
<tr><td>℗ The grace of our Lord Jesus Christ, the love of God, and the communion of the Holy Spirit be with you all.
𝗖 And also with you.</td><td>℗ In the name of the Father, and of the ✙ Son, and of the Holy Spirit.
𝗖 Amen</td></tr>
</table>

Those assembled may be invited to welcome one another in the name of Christ.

A KYRIE may be sung, using one of the following, or another litany or hymn focused on God's mercy.

    20 Kyrie
    21 Lord, have mercy
    22 Lord, have mercy / Nkosi, nkosi
    23 Lord, have mercy / Señor, ten piedad

A HYMN OF PRAISE may be sung, using "Glory to God" or an appropriate hymn, song, or canticle.

    24 Glory to God
  100 We praise thee, O God
  138 Come, all you people / Uyai mose

The PRAYER OF THE DAY is said, and the congregation responds, **Amen.**

The scripture READINGS for the day are proclaimed. Prior to the readings, the readers may receive a blessing (pp. 77–79). Silence for reflection may follow each reading.

After each reading, the reader may say: The word of the Lord.
The congregation responds: **Thanks be to God.**

The PSALM follows the first reading.

Before the Gospel, one of the following or another appropriate hymn or song may be sung as a GOSPEL ACCLAMATION.

	During LENT:
26 Alleluia	131 Lord, let my heart be good soil
25 Halle, halle, hallelujah	134 O Lord, open my eyes
27 Hallelujah	273 Bless the Lord

The GOSPEL is read.

At the announcement of the Gospel:
Ⓟ The Holy Gospel according to _____, the _____ chapter.
Ⓒ **Glory to you, O Lord.**

After the reading of the Gospel:
Ⓟ The Gospel of the Lord.
Ⓒ **Praise to you, O Christ.**

The acclamation may be repeated, or a hymn or other music sung in preparation for the sermon.

The SERMON follows. Silence for reflection may follow the sermon.

The HYMN OF THE DAY may be sung; or, an INVITATION TO CHRISTIAN DISCIPLESHIP may be extended, beginning with an appropriate hymn and continuing as the minister invites those who desire to come forward for prayer, creedal affirmation, or profession of faith. An invitation into catechumenal inquiry may occur at this time.

The CREED may be said: the Nicene Creed (p. 34 or p. 94) on all festivals and on Sundays in the seasons of Advent/Christmas and Lent/Easter; the Apostles' Creed (p. 35 or p. 95) at other times.

THE PRAYERS are said. Prayers are included for the whole church, the nations, those in need, the parish, the sick, special concerns, and in thanks for the faithful departed. The congregation may be invited to offer other petitions. Prayers of confession may be included if an order for confession and forgiveness has not been used earlier.

Each portion of the prayers may end with these or similar words:

	OR
Ⓐ Lord, in your mercy,	Ⓐ Hear us, O God;
Ⓒ **hear our prayer.**	Ⓒ **your mercy is great.**

The prayers conclude in these or similar words:
Ⓟ Into your hands, O Lord, we commend all for whom we pray, trusting in your mercy, through your Son, Jesus Christ our Lord.
Ⓒ **Amen**

The PEACE may be shared at this time or prior to the distribution of communion.

P The peace of the Lord be with you always.

C And also with you.

The ministers and congregation may greet one another with a gesture of peace, using these or similar words: Peace be with you.

The OFFERING is received as the Lord's table is prepared. The gifts may be presented at the altar.

As an OFFERTORY, one of the following, or another appropriate song or hymn may be sung.

28 Let the vineyards be fruitful

68 That priceless grace

129 Now we offer

216 Give me a clean heart

239 What shall I render

This or another appropriate prayer (pp. 80–81) may be said.

P Let us pray.

Merciful God,

**C we offer with joy and thanksgiving what you have first given us—
our selves, our time, and our possessions, signs of your gracious love.
Receive them for the sake of him who offered himself for us,
Jesus Christ our Lord. Amen**

The presiding minister begins the THANKSGIVING with this dialog.

P The Lord be with you.

C And also with you.

P Lift up your hearts.

C We lift them to the Lord.

P Let us give thanks to the Lord our God.

C It is right to give our thanks and praise.

When a preface is prayed (p. 82–83) one of the following or another version of the SANCTUS follows.

29 Holy, holy, holy Lord

32 Holy, holy, holy Lord

The minister continues the thanksgiving, using one of the forms on pp. 84–88 or another appropriate form, in which the words of Christ's institution are proclaimed. All join in saying or singing the Lord's Prayer (p. 39 or p. 57).

33 Our Father, who art in heaven

34 Let the words of my mouth

If not included previously, the greeting of peace is now given and shared.

The bread is broken, and the COMMUNION is shared.

Music during the communion may include one of the following as well as other appropriate hymns, psalms, songs, and anthems.

    35 Lamb of God
    36 O Lamb of God
  128 Now behold the Lamb

As a POST-COMMUNION song, one of the following or another appropriate hymn or song may be used.

  158 Hallelujah! We sing your praises
  292 Give thanks
  293 Thank you, Lord
  280 Thank you, Jesus

With the following or another appropriate prayer (pp. 89), the meal is concluded.

Ⓐ Let us pray.
We give you thanks, almighty God, that you have refreshed us through the healing power of this gift of life; and we pray that in your mercy you would strengthen us, through this gift, in faith toward you and in fervent love toward one another; for the sake of Jesus Christ our Lord.

Ⓒ **Amen**

SENDING

The minister blesses the congregation, using this or another appropriate BENEDICTION (pp. 93–95). The benediction may be preceded by a charge to the people (pp. 90).

Ⓟ The Lord bless you and keep you.
The Lord make his face shine on you and be gracious to you.
The Lord look upon you with favor and ☩ give you peace.

Ⓒ **Amen**

When there is a procession from the church, a hymn, song, or canticle may be sung.

With a DISMISSAL, the congregation is sent out in mission.

Ⓐ Go in peace. Serve the Lord.

Ⓒ **Thanks be to God.**

HOLY BAPTISM

This order normally follows the sermon in the liturgy. The hymn of the day or a baptismal hymn may be sung as candidates, sponsors, and family gather at the waters of baptism.

Introduction

P Hear the testimony of the Holy Scriptures concerning baptism:

Go and make disciples of all nations, baptizing them in the name of the Father and of the Son and of the Holy Spirit. *(Matt. 28:19)*

Repent, and be baptized every one of you in the name of Jesus Christ so that your sins may be forgiven; and you will receive the gift of the Holy Spirit. For the promise is for you, for your children, and for all who are far away. *(Acts 2:38-39)*

The Ethiopian said, "Look, here is water! What is to prevent me from being baptized?" . . . Philip and the Ethiopian went down into the water, and Philip baptized him. When they came up out of the water, the Spirit of the Lord snatched Philip away; the Ethiopian saw him no more, and went on his way rejoicing. *(Acts 8:36, 38-39)*

C **We obey our Lord's command and trust in his promise as we baptize into his name.** *(Acts 10:47-48; 19:5)*

P Very truly, I tell you, no one can enter the kingdom of God without being born of water and Spirit. *(John 3:5)*

C **What is born of the flesh is flesh, and what is born of the Spirit is spirit.** *(John 3:6)*

Presentation of Candidates

A sponsor for each candidate, in turn, presents the candidate with these or similar words:
Before the God of our ancestors and on behalf of this congregation, I present <u>name</u> to receive the sacrament of Holy Baptism.

The congregation may offer acclamation with applause after each candidate is presented, or after the welcome (p. 68).

Commitment and Promise

The minister addresses the sponsors, family, and congregation.

P In Holy Baptism God graciously delivers us from sin and death by joining us to the death and resurrection of our Lord Jesus Christ. Through water and the word the Holy Spirit calls us to walk a new life in God. In this new life we are joined across time and space to our ancestors who have lived and died trustingly and to the whole Christian community on earth. Their witness supports our Christian journey.

Nourished by the apostles' teaching and fellowship, the breaking of bread, and the prayers, *these* our *sisters/brothers* will be empowered to live in the fullness of their baptism and to join all of God's reborn people in serving the community with their gifts.

OR

When only young children are baptized:

P By presenting *these children* for Holy Baptism, you commit yourselves to providing for *their* growth in the knowledge and fear of the Lord. As Apollos was instructed in the way of the Lord, you join this community's teachers and elders in handing over the Holy Scriptures, the Lord's Prayer, the Creed and the Ten Commandments. Do you intend to act in this way for your *children* and for the sake of Jesus?

C **We do.**

When older children or adults are baptized also:

P In Christian love you have presented *these persons* for Holy Baptism. Do you intend faithfully to lift *them* up in prayer, nurture and help *them* grow in the Christian faith as you are empowered by God's Spirit? Do you promise to help *them* in *their* struggle to live in *their* baptismal covenant within the community of faith and in the world until Jesus comes again? Do you intend to act in this way for *their* sake and for the sake of Jesus?

C **We do.**

Thanksgiving

P The Lord be with you.
C **And also with you.**

P Let us give thanks to the Lord our God.
C **It is right to give our thanks and praise.**

P Blessed are you, O God, maker and ruler of all things. Your voice thundered over the waters at creation. You water the mountains and send springs into the valleys to refresh and satisfy us and all living things. Through the waters of the flood you carried those in the ark to safety. Through the sea you led your people Israel from slavery to freedom. In the wilderness you nourished them with water from the rock, and you brought them across the river Jordan to the promised land. By the baptism of his death and resurrection, your Son Jesus has carried us to safety and freedom. The floods shall not overwhelm us, the deep shall not swallow us up, for Christ has brought us over to the land of promise. He sends us to make disciples, baptizing in the name of the Father, and of the Son, and of the Holy Spirit.

Pour out your Holy Spirit; wash away sin in this cleansing water; clothe the baptized with Christ; and claim your daughters and sons, no longer Jew or Greek, no longer slave or free, no longer male or female, but one with all the baptized in Christ Jesus, who lives and reigns with you in the unity of the Holy Spirit, one God, now and forever.

C **Amen**

Profession of Faith

The minister addresses the baptismal group and the congregation.

P I ask you to profess your faith in Christ Jesus, reject sin, and confess the faith of the church, the faith in which we baptize.

Do you renounce all the forces of evil?

C **I renounce them.**

P Do you renounce the devil?

C **I renounce the devil.**

P Do you renounce all the devil's empty promises?

C **I renounce them.**

P Do you believe in God the Father?

C **I believe in God, the Father almighty,**
creator of heaven and earth.

P Do you believe in Jesus Christ, the Son of God?

C **I believe in Jesus Christ, his only Son, our Lord.**
He was conceived by the power of the Holy Spirit
and born of the virgin Mary.
He suffered under Pontius Pilate,
was crucified, died, and was buried.
He descended into hell.*
On the third day he rose again.
He ascended into heaven,
and is seated that the right hand of the Father.
He will come again to judge the living and the dead.

P Do you believe in God the Holy Spirit?

C **I believe in the Holy Spirit,**
the holy catholic Church,
the communion of saints,
the forgiveness of sins,
the resurrection of the body,
and the life everlasting. Amen

*Or, He descended to the dead.

Baptism

After each of the three phrases of the baptismal formula, the minister immerses the candidate in the baptismal water, or pours ample water over the candidate's head.

OR

P *Name*, I baptize you
 in the name of the Father,
 and of the Son,
 and of the Holy Spirit.
C **Amen**

P *Name* is baptized
 in the name of the Father,
 and of the Son,
 and of the Holy Spirit.
C **Amen**

A hymn, psalm, or other acclamation may follow.

Laying On of Hands

The minister lays both hands on the head of each of the baptized and prays for the Holy Spirit.
P God, the Father of our Lord Jesus Christ, we give you thanks for freeing your sons and daughters from the power of sin and for raising them up to a new life through this holy sacrament. Pour your Holy Spirit upon *name*: the spirit of wisdom and understanding, the spirit of counsel and might, the spirit of knowledge and the fear of the Lord, the spirit of joy in your presence.
C **Amen**

Sign of the Cross

The minister marks the sign of the cross on each of the baptized while saying the following or similar words. Oil prepared for this purpose may be used.
P *Name*, receive the sign of the holy cross upon your forehead ✝ [and upon your heart ✝] to mark you as one redeemed by Christ the crucified.

Images of Baptism

If desired, one or more of the following acts may be added, with care taken that they are supportive and do not overshadow the central sign of baptism: water with the word of God. These symbolic actions may be led by the minister or representative(s) of the congregation, accompanied with words such as those provided below.

Salt may be placed into the mouth of the baptized.
You are the salt of the earth. Receive the salt of wisdom, that you may conduct your life with the sound judgment of a child of God.

A garment of naturally colored fabric or a band of kente cloth may be placed upon the baptized.
You have been clothed in the righteousness of Christ to stand before the throne of the Lamb, joined with the great multitude of the communion of saints—our elders and ancestors, as well as generations yet to come.

A bangle (wristlet, bracelet) may be placed on the wrist of the baptized.
Receive this gift, in the shape of a circle with its unbroken oneness, as a sign of your belonging to a people chosen by God to be a blessing.

A baptismal candle may be lighted from the paschal or altar candle and given to each of the baptized (to the sponsor of a young child).

Receive this burning light. Let your light so shine before others that they may see your good works and give glory to God.

Certificates of baptism and of baptismal sponsorship may be given.

When infants or small children are baptized, this prayer may be said here or as a part of the prayers.

℗ O God, the giver of all life, look with kindness upon the *fathers* and *mothers* of *these children*. Let them ever rejoice in the gift you have given them. Make them teachers and examples of righteousness for their *children*. Strengthen them in their own baptism so they may share eternally with their *children* the salvation you have given them, through Jesus Christ our Lord.

Ⓒ **Amen**

Commission and Welcome

The ministers and the baptismal group turn to face the congregation. An elder or other representative of the congregation addresses the newly baptized, sponsors, and family.

Through baptism God has added your name to the roll of all our ancestors in faith. You are a part of the priesthood we share in Christ Jesus. You have not been called in vain. Therefore, take up your cross and follow Jesus through the prairies and grasslands, in the desert wilderness, along the freeways and back alleys of suburb and city. You belong now to God, sent to witness for Christ before all the world.

Ⓒ **We welcome you into the Lord's family. We receive you with great joy to live with us in the body of Christ, to share with us in God's new creation, to work with us by the power of the Holy Spirit.**

The congregation may express its welcome with singing, applause, or other signs of acclamation. Within the liturgy of Holy Communion, the prayers of the church follow. The greeting of peace may then be given and shared among the newly baptized, their sponsors and family, and all those assembled.

SERVICE OF THE WORD

This pattern for a Service of the Word may be used on an occasion when Holy Communion is not celebrated. When used on Sunday, prayers, psalms, and readings appointed for the day are appropriate.

GATHERING

As the congregation assembles, one or more of the following may occur: singing; individual prayer; meditation; sharing of announcements and community concerns; testimonies.

A CALL TO WORSHIP may include one or more of the following: scripture sentences; spoken or sung dialog; exhortations; musical solos; instrumental calls; dance. The invocation of God's name or an apostolic greeting are also included.

An order for CONFESSION AND FORGIVENESS may be used; the GREETING OF PEACE may be given and shared by all.

A HYMN, ANTHEM, or SCRIPTURE SONG may be sung.

The appointed prayer of the day or another GATHERING PRAYER is prayed.

WORD

The SCRIPTURE READINGS for the day are read, including a reading from the gospels. Psalms, hymns, songs, or anthems may be sung in response.

The SERMON follows. Response to the proclamation of God's word may include a hymn, song, or anthem, and the confession of the Apostles' or Nicene Creed.

THE PRAYERS include intercession for various needs and concerns.

The OFFERING may be followed by a concluding prayer.

SENDING

With a BENEDICTION, the minister blesses the congregation. The blessing may be preceded by a CHARGE TO THE PEOPLE.

A concluding hymn, song, or anthem may be sung. With a DISMISSAL, the congregation may be sent out in mission.

SERVICE OF PRAYER AND PREACHING

REVIVAL

Although the Lord's day, Sunday, is the primary time for Christians to assemble for worship, there are other occasions when sisters and brothers in Christ gather for corporate spiritual renewal. In many African American communities, these take the shape of revival services. Spanning a predetermined period of time (from two nights to two months, though ordinarily Monday through Friday evenings), these services focus on building up Christian discipleship and renewing the community of believers. In Lutheran settings, these services will focus on repentance, the celebration of salvation by grace, baptismal remembrance, and encouragement for those inquiring into the faith. The following may serve as a pattern for such a service.

GATHERING

Praise, prayer, and thanksgiving are joyously expressed. Flexibility is welcomed during this extended period of worship preparation. The gathering may conclude with a choir entrance.

Devotional Time
Choruses, songs, hymns
Testimony
Prayer

Call to Worship
Invocation
Welcome
Greeting of peace

Choir Entrance

WORD

Preaching, teaching, and public reading of God's word is central to these services. This speaking is God's action, revealed in the Old and New Testaments, and is reflected in preaching. The preacher is most often a guest missioner. Scriptures selected for revival services may be many, or may be more specific in scope, perhaps with one thematic reading for each service. The preaching event is the climax and focus of revival worship.

Choral Offering
Offering
Scripture Readings
Prayer
Congregational Song, Choral Music
Sermon

These services provide many opportunities to focus on God's gift of saving faith. The ongoing work of the Holy Spirit is to call, gather, enlighten, sanctify, and keep the church in the true faith. After the sermon, the worship leader may invite those who desire to come forward for prayer, creedal affirmation, or profession of faith. An invitation to catechumenal inquiry may occur at this time.

SENDING

The grace of God, proclaimed in this worship, moves the assembly to go forth boldly in faith. With the promise of salvation, the redeemed are charged to extend this saving message to everyone. Often, the guest missioner will capsulize the message and service theme with a concluding word of blessing and dismissal.

Blessing
Dismissal

VARIABLE WORSHIP TEXTS

CALLS TO WORSHIP

These calls to worship stand in the tradition of sounding the shofar in ancient Israel or intoning the introit in the historic Western rite. With words of scripture, hymns, or other exhortations, the leader invites the assembly into the worship of God.

In addition to spoken dialog, calls to worship based on hymns and songs (such as those suggested below) may be spoken or sung in call-and-response form by leader and congregation.

Advent

Ⓛ Church of God, are you ready?

Ⓒ **We're ready!**

Ⓛ Are you ready to meet the Lord?
Church of God, are you ready?

Ⓒ **We're ready!**

Ⓛ Are you ready to greet the Lord?
Church of God, get ready!

Ⓒ **We're ready!**

Ⓛ Get ready and wait for the Lord.
Those who wait for the Lord shall
renew their strength; they shall soar
with wings like eagles;
they shall run and not be weary,
they shall walk and not grow faint.

(Isaiah 40:31)

OR

Ⓛ The earth is the Lord's, and the fullness
thereof; the world, and they that dwell
therein.

Ⓒ **Lift up your heads, O gates;**
be lifted up, O everlasting doors,
and the King of glory shall come in.

Ⓛ Who is this King of glory?

Ⓒ **The Lord of hosts is the King of**
glory! The Lord of hosts is the King
of glory!

Ⓛ Who is this King of glory?

Ⓒ **The Lord of hosts is the King of**
glory!

(Psalm 24:1, 7, 10)

Hᴍɴ ᴀɴᴅ Sᴏɴɢꜱ

38 Soon and very soon

44 Somebody's knockin' at your door

Christmas

[L] Oh, sing to the Lord a new song!
Sing to the Lord, all the earth.

[C] **Declare his glory among the nations, his wonders among all the peoples.**

[L] Give to the Lord the glory due his name; bring an offering, and come into his courts.

[C] **Worship the Lord in the beauty of holiness; tremble before him, all the earth.**

[L] Let the heavens rejoice,
let the earth be glad,
let the sea roar,
let the field be joyful!

[C] **All the trees of the forest, shout for joy before the Lord, who comes to judge the earth with righteousness and the peoples with truth.**

(Psalm 96:1-2, 8-9, 11-13)

OR

[L] Joy to the world.

[C] **Joy, joy, joy!**

[L] Joy to the world.

[C] **Joy, joy, joy!**

[L] Joy to the world.

[C] **Joy, joy, joy!
Joy! For the Lord is come!**

[L] Let every heart prepare him room.

[C] **Let heaven and nature sing!**

[L] Let every heart prepare him room.

[C] **Let heaven and nature sing!**

[L] Let every heart prepare him room.

[C] **Let heaven and nature sing!
Let heaven and nature sing!
Let heaven, let heaven and nature sing!**

HYMNS AND SONGS
52 Go tell it on the mountain
55 Mary had a baby

Epiphany

[L] Arise, shine, for your light has come!

[C] **The glory of the Lord has risen upon us.**

[L] Lift up your eyes and look around:

[C] **all gather together to proclaim the praise of the Lord.**

[L] Your sun will never set again.

[C] **The Lord is our light and our salvation!**

[L] Your moon will wane no more.

[C] **The Lord is our light and our salvation!**

[L] Your days of sorrow will end.

[C] **The Lord is our light and our salvation!**

[L] Whom shall we fear?

[C] **Whom shall we fear?
The Lord is the strength of our life; whom shall we fear?**

(Isaiah 60:1, 4, 20; Psalm 27:1)

OR

[L] This little light of mine,

[C] **I'm goin'-a let it shine!**

[L] This little light of mine,

[C] **I'm goin'-a let it shine!**

[L] This little light of mine,

[C] **I'm goin'-a let it shine,
let it shine, let it shine,
let it shine.**

[L] Everywhere I go

[C] **I'm goin'-a let it shine!**

[L] Everywhere I go

[C] **I'm goin'-a let it shine!**

[L] Everywhere I go

[C] **I'm goin'-a let it shine,
let it shine, let it shine,
let it shine.**

HYMNS AND SONGS
59 Jesus, the light of the world
165 In the morning when I rise

Lent

    Ⓛ Seek the Lord while he may be
    found.

    Ⓒ Call upon God while he is near.

    Ⓛ Wicked, forsake your ways!

    **Ⓒ Unrighteous, forsake your
    thoughts!**

    Ⓛ Come back to God.

    Ⓒ Return to the Lord!

    Ⓛ Come back to God.

    Ⓒ Return to the Lord!

    Ⓛ The Lord is gracious and merciful,
    slow to anger and abounding in
    steadfast love.

    (Isaiah 55:6-7; Joel 2:13)

OR

    Ⓛ Great is the Lord and greatly to be
    praised;

    Ⓒ God's greatness is unsearchable.

    Ⓛ O Lord, you are just in all your ways,
    faithful in all your works.

    **Ⓒ You are near to all who call upon you,
    to all who call upon you in truth.**

    Ⓛ Great is the Lord and greatly to be
    praised;

    Ⓒ God's greatness is unsearchable.

    (Psalm 145:3, 17-18)

Hymns and Songs

    69 What can wash away my sin?
   153 Guide my feet

Easter

    Ⓛ This is the day that the Lord has
    made;

    Ⓒ we will rejoice and be glad in it!

    Ⓛ The Lord is my strength and my
    song.

    Ⓒ The Lord has become my salvation.

    Ⓛ Open to me the gates of
    righteousness;

    **Ⓒ I will go through them and praise
    the Lord.**

    Ⓛ I shall not die, but live,

    Ⓒ and declare the works of the Lord.

    Ⓛ This is the day that the Lord has
    made;

    Ⓒ we will rejoice and be glad in it!

    (Psalm 118:14, 17, 19, 24)

OR

    Ⓛ Christ the Lord is risen.

    Ⓒ The stone is rolled away!

    Ⓛ Death has now been vanquished.

    Ⓒ The stone is rolled away!

    Ⓛ Come, bow down and worship.

    Ⓒ The stone is rolled away!

    Ⓛ Come, let us adore him.

    Ⓒ The stone is rolled away!

    Ⓛ Give God all the glory.

    Ⓒ The stone is rolled away!

    Ⓛ Alleluia! Christ is risen!

    Ⓒ Christ is risen indeed. Alleluia!

Hymns and Songs

   191 I'm so glad Jesus lifted me
   262 This is the day

Pentecost

L Gracious Spirit, heed our pleading.
C Come, Holy Spirit, come.
L It's your leading that we're needing.
C Come, Holy Spirit, come.
L Guide our thinking and our speaking.
C Come, Holy Spirit, come.
L Motivate all in their seeking.
C Come, Holy Spirit, come.
L Keep us fervent in our witness.
C Come, Holy Spirit, come.
L Keep us fervent in our witness.
C Come, Holy Spirit, come.
L Ever grant us zealous fitness.
C Come, Holy Spirit, come!

HYMNS AND SONGS
101 Spirit of the living God
106 Come, O Holy Spirit, come

Season after Pentecost, General

A

L I was glad when they said unto me,
C let us go to the house of the Lord!
L I was glad when they said unto me,
C let us go to the house of the Lord!

L Unless the Lord builds the house,
C in vain do the builders labor.
L Unless the Lord builds the house,
C in vain do the builders labor.

L Surely the Lord is in this place.
**C This is the house of God,
this is the gate of heaven!**
L Surely the Lord is in this place.
**C This is the house of God,
this is the gate of heaven!**
L Oh, come let us worship!
**C Oh, come let us worship!
Oh, come let us worship!
Oh, come let us worship!**

(Ps. 122:1; Ps. 127:1; Gen. 28:16-17)

B

L Come unto me, all who labor and are heavy laden, and I will give you rest.
C Take my yoke upon you, and learn of me; for I am meek and lowly in heart; and you shall find rest for your souls.
L For my yoke is easy, and my burden is light.
**C Come unto me, all who labor and are heavy laden, and I will give you rest.
I will give you rest,
I will give you rest,
I will give you rest.**

(Matthew 11:28-30)

C

L Make a joyful noise unto the Lord, all you lands.

C **Serve the Lord with gladness; come before his presence with singing.**

L Enter into his gates with thanksgiving, and into his courts with praise.
Be thankful to him and bless his name.

C **For the Lord is good; his mercy is everlasting, and his truth endures to all generations.**

(Psalm 100:1-2, 4-5)

D

L Rejoice in the Lord always. Say it again: Rejoice! Let gentleness be evident to all, for the Lord is near.

C **Let us not be anxious about anything, but in everything by prayer and petition with thanksgiving, present our requests to God.**

L Rejoice in the Lord always. Say it again: Rejoice!

C **Let gentleness be evident to all, for the Lord is near.**

(Philippians 4:4-6)

E

L Praise the Lord! Praise God in his sanctuary; praise God in the firmament of his power!

C **Praise God for his mighty acts; praise God according to his excellent greatness!**

L Let everything that has breath praise the Lord!

C **Praise the Lord!**

(Psalm 150:1-2, 6)

F

L Give thanks unto the Lord, for he is good; for his mercy endures forever.

C **Let the redeemed of the Lord say so, whom he has redeemed from the hand of the enemy.**

L For God satisfies the longing soul, and fills the hungry soul with goodness.

C **Give thanks unto the Lord, for he is good; for his mercy endures forever.**

(Psalm 107:1-2, 9)

G

L Come, let us sing for joy to the Lord; let us shout aloud to the rock of our salvation!

C **Let us come before him with thanksgiving, and extol him with music and song!**

L For the Lord is a great God, and a great king above all gods.

C **In his hand are the depths of the earth; and the mountain peaks belong to him.**

L The sea is his, for he made it, and his hands formed the dry land.

C **Come, let us bow down in worship, let us kneel before the Lord our maker!**

L For he is our God, and we are the people of his pasture, and the flock under his care.

C **Come, let us sing for joy to the Lord; let us shout aloud to the rock of our salvation!**

(Psalm 95:1-7a)

HYMNS AND SONGS
   141 Come and go with me
   145 Jesus, we want to meet

These prayers for illumination may be used to bless those who serve as readers of scripture and to prepare the assembly for the hearing of God's word. This action underscores the importance of the ministry of lectors and of the public reading of the scriptures as an event that brings Christ, the Word, into the midst of his people. The blessings also echo African and African American tradition: in need of and out of respect, those seeking blessing come before the elder(s), in this case the pastor, to be prayed over.

After the prayer of the day and just before the readings, the lector(s) may come forward for the blessing and stand before the presider, who may be standing beside or seated in the presider's chair. This chair may be adorned with ethnic cloth coordinated with the liturgical season or with some other appointments (candles, for example), in accordance with liturgical tradition and with the African practice of designating seating for tribal leaders and elders.

These prayers can be used as printed or as models for presiders who choose to pray freely over the readers. They may be adapted for use with more than one reader.

Advent

P The Spirit and the church cry out,
   come, Lord Jesus.
Everyone who awaits his
appearance cries out,
   come, Lord Jesus.
The whole creation cries,
   come, Lord Jesus.

Let us pray.
Come to us, Lord Jesus, as *name*
reads for us your holy word.
Keep us attentive to the truth of
the scriptures; turn us away from
myths; and turn us in faith to you,
our strength and our redeemer.
C **Amen**

OR

P Oh, come, oh, come, Emmanuel,
   and ransom captive Israel,
   that mourns in lonely exile here
   until the Son of God appear.
   Rejoice! Rejoice! Emmanuel
   shall come to you, O Israel.

Let us pray.
Be with us, O God, as *name*
opens for us the scriptures, and open
our ears to hear the good Word,
Jesus Christ our Lord.
C **Amen**

Christmas

P Joy to the world, the Lord has come! Let earth receive her King.
Let every heart prepare him room, and heaven and nature sing.

Let us pray.
Bless *name*, O God, as *he/she* proclaims to us the scriptures,
and open the mangers of our hearts to welcome the King,
Jesus Christ the Lord.
C **Amen**

Epiphany

P Let us pray.
Gracious God, your word is a lamp
to our feet and a light to our path.
Send your Holy Spirit upon _name_ as
he/she proclaims the word,
so that all who receive it will no
longer dwell in the shadows,
but will have the light of life.

C **Amen**

OR

P _Name_, may God bless you as you read
for us the scriptures.
May the word of God dwell in us richly
so that everything we do in word or
deed will be done in the name of the
Lord Jesus, giving thanks to God the
Father through him.

C **Amen**

Lent

P Even now, says the Lord, return
to me with all your heart.
Return to the Lord, your God,
who is gracious and merciful,
slow to anger, and abounding in
steadfast love.

Let us pray.
Bless _name_, O God of mercy, and
bless us as we listen to the words of
the scriptures. May they touch our
hearts and lead us to return to you,
through Jesus Christ our Lord.

C **Amen**

OR

P Let us pray.
Oh, that today we would hear God's
voice. May we hear your voice today,
Lord, as _name_ reads to us the scriptures.
Let not our hearts be hardened, but
open to the word of life.

C **Amen**

Easter

P Christ is risen!
The word of God is living and
active, sharper than a two-edged
sword. _Name_, as you read to us the
scriptures, may they pierce our
souls and judge the thoughts and
the intentions of our hearts.

C **Amen**

OR

P Let us pray.
Bless, O Lord, your servant _name_ as
he/she reads to us the holy word. May
our hearts burn within us as you open to
us the scriptures; through Jesus Christ
our Lord.

C **Amen**

Pentecost

P Let us pray.
Spirit of the living God,
fall fresh on us;
Spirit of the living God,
fall fresh on us.

Holy God, send your Spirit to fall
fresh upon us and upon _name_ as
he/she proclaims to us the scriptures. Mold our minds and melt our
hearts to receive what the Spirit is
saying to the churches; through
Jesus Christ our Lord.
C **Amen**

Season after Pentecost

P Let us pray.
Gracious God, we do not live by
bread alone, but by every word that
comes from you. Bless _name,_ who
will read to us the scriptures.
Make us hunger for the Word of
life, Jesus Christ our Lord.
C **Amen**

_OR_
P Let us pray.
Bless _name_, O Lord, as _he/she_ reads
to us the scriptures.
As rain and snow come down from
heaven and do not return until the
earth is watered, let your word not
return empty, but accomplish your
purpose and succeed in that for
which it was sent;
through Jesus Christ our Lord.
C **Amen**

_OR_
P Let us pray.
O God, source of our salvation:
Open our ears to hear what the Spirit is
saying to the churches.

The Word is among us.
The Spirit is present.
May the Lord add a blessing to this
reading.
C **Amen**

_OR_
P Let us pray.
God Almighty, we ask your blessing
upon _name_ as _he/she_ reads to us the
scriptures. May the words of _his/her_
mouth and the meditations of our hearts
be acceptable in your sight, O Lord,
our rock and our redeemer.
C **Amen**

One of the following, or another appropriate sentence of scripture, may precede the offering.

A

I appeal to you, brothers and sisters, by the mercies of God, to present yourselves as a living sacrifice, holy and acceptable to God, which is your spiritual worship. *(Rom. 12:1)*

B

If you are offering your gift at the altar, and there remember that your brother or sister has something against you, leave your gift there before the altar and go; first be reconciled to your brother or sister, and then come and offer your gift. *(Matt. 5:23, 24)*

C

Offer to God a sacrifice of thanksgiving, and make good your vows to the Most High. *(Ps. 50:14)*

D

Walk in love, as Christ loved us and gave himself for us, an offering and sacrifice to God. *(Eph. 5:2)*

E

Let us with gladness present our lives and the fruits of our labor to the Lord.

OFFERTORY PRAYERS

Advent

A O Mighty One,

C **you have done great things for us,
and holy is your name.
Bless all we offer you—
our selves, our time, and our
possessions—that through us
your grace and favor may be
made known to all the world;
for the sake of Jesus Christ,
our Redeemer. Amen**

Christmas

A God of wonder,

C **we offer you these humble gifts,
signs of your goodness and
mercy. Receive them with our
gratitude, that through us,
all people may know the riches
of your love in the Word-made-
flesh. Amen**

Epiphany

A God of all creation,

C **all you have made is good
and your love endures forever.
You bring forth bread from the
earth and fruit from the vine.
Nourish us with these gifts,
that we might be for the world
signs of your gracious presence
in Jesus Christ our Lord. Amen**

Lent

A Compassionate God,

C **we offer you these gifts
as signs of our time and labor.
Receive the offering of our lives,
and feed us with your grace,
that, in the midst of death,
all creation might feast on
your unending life
in Jesus Christ our Lord. Amen**

Holy Week, The Three Days

Ⓐ God of glory,

Ⓒ receive these gifts and the
offering of our lives.
As Jesus was lifted up from
earth, draw us to your heart
in the midst of this world,
that all creation may be brought
from bondage to freedom,
from darkness to light,
and from death to life;
through Jesus Christ our Lord.
Amen

Easter

Ⓐ Good Shepherd,

Ⓒ you spread a table before us.
We offer you the gifts of this
money, bread, and wine,
signs of your gracious love,
and tokens of our grateful hearts.
Nourish us at the feast of the
Lamb, that we may proclaim to
all the world your triumphant
love in Jesus Christ our Lord.
Amen

Season after Pentecost A

Ⓐ Wise and gracious God,

Ⓒ receive the labor of our hands—
these gifts of money, bread, and
wine—along with the offering of
our lives. Nourish us with the life
of your Son, that we might be his
body in the world, making known
your abundant mercy
in Jesus Christ our Lord. Amen

Season after Pentecost B

Ⓐ Generous God,

Ⓒ all good gifts come from your
gracious hand. We offer you this
bread, wine, and money, the har-
vest of our time and labor.
Make us wise stewards of all your
gifts, that your name may be
exalted in all the world, through
Jesus Christ our Lord. Amen

Season after Pentecost C

Ⓐ God of the harvest,

Ⓒ receive these gifts of the earth
and human labor with the offering of our hearts.
Feed us with your bread and cup,
that we may be signs of your
gracious life made known
in Jesus Christ, our Lord. Amen

General

Ⓐ Blessed are you, O Lord our God,
creator of all things:
through your goodness you have
given us this bread, fruit of the
earth and of human labor.

Ⓒ **Blessed be God forever!**

Ⓐ Blessed are you, O Lord our God,
creator of all things:
through your goodness you have
given us this wine, fruit of the vine
and the work of human hands.

Ⓒ **Blessed be God forever!**

Ⓐ Merciful God,
as the grains once scattered in the
fields and the grapes once
dispersed on the hillside are now
united on this table in bread and
wine, may we who celebrate this
Holy Communion be gathered into
one in you.

Ⓒ **Amen**

General

℗ It is right and good that we should offer you thanks and praise, O God, for with great love you have led us out of slavery into the freedom of the promised land. You guided us along the way, giving us power to rejoice in the face of evil and death, and, fulfilling your ancient promise, you continue to lift up the broken-hearted even in our own day. And so, with the multitude from east and west, from north and south, with angels and archangels and all the company of heaven, we lift our voices in the unending hymn:

OR

℗ It is indeed right and salutary that we should at all times and in all places offer thanks and praise to you, O Lord, holy Father, through Jesus Christ our Lord. Although our road has been stony going, you have given us the power to stand firm in the face of wickedness and to rejoice in triumph over death and the grave. And so, with the multitude from east and west, from north and south, with angels and archangels and all the company of heaven, we lift our voices in the unending hymn:

Advent

℗ It is indeed right and salutary that we should at all times and in all places offer thanks and praise to you, O Lord, holy Father, almighty and everliving God. You comforted your people with the promise of the Redeemer, through whom you will also make all things new in the day when he comes again to judge the world in righteousness. And so, with the church on earth and the hosts of heaven, we praise your name and join their unending hymn:

Christmas

℗ It is indeed right and salutary that we should at all times and in all places offer thanks and praise to you, O Lord, holy Father, through Christ our Lord. In the wonder and mystery of the Word made flesh you have opened the eyes of faith to a new and radiant vision of your glory; that, beholding the God made visible, we may be drawn to love the God whom we cannot see. And so, with the church on earth and the hosts of heaven, we praise your name and join their unending hymn:

Epiphany

℗ It is indeed right and salutary that we should at all times and in all places offer thanks and praise to you, O Lord, holy Father, through Christ our Lord. haring our life, he lived among us to reveal your glory and love, that our darkness should give way to his own brilliant light. And so, with the church on earth and the hosts of heaven, we praise your name and join their unending hymn:

Lent

℗ It is indeed right and salutary that we should at all times and in all places offer thanks and praise to you, O Lord, holy Father, through Christ our Lord. You bid your people cleanse their hearts and prepare with joy for the paschal feast. Renew our zeal in faith and life, and bring us to the fullness of grace that belongs to the children of God. And so, with the church on earth and the hosts of heaven, we praise your name and join their unending hymn:

Passion

P It is indeed right and salutary that we should at all times and in all places offer thanks and praise to you, O Lord, holy Father, through Christ our Lord; who on the tree of the cross gave salvation to all, that, where death began, there life might be restored, and that he, who by a tree once overcame, might by a tree be overcome. And so, with the church on earth and the hosts of heaven, we praise your name and join their unending hymn:

Easter

P It is indeed right and salutary that we should at all times and in all places offer thanks and praise to you, O Lord, holy Father, almighty and everliving God. But chiefly we are bound to praise you for the glorious resurrection of our Lord; for he is the true Passover Lamb who gave himself to take away our sin, who by his death has destroyed death, and by his rising has brought us to eternal life. And so, with Mary Magdalene and Peter and all the witnesses of the resurrection, with earth and sea and all their creatures, and with angels and archangels, cherubim and seraphim, we praise your name and join their unending hymn:

Ascension

P It is indeed right and salutary that we should at all times and in all places offer thanks and praise to you, O Lord, holy Father, through Christ our Lord; who, after his resurrection, appeared openly to his disciples and, in their sight, was taken up into heaven, that he might make us partakers of his divine nature. And so, with the church on earth and the hosts of heaven, we praise your name and join their unending hymn:

Pentecost

P It is indeed right and salutary that we should at all times and in all places offer thanks and praise to you, O Lord, holy Father, through Christ our Lord; who rose beyond the bounds of death, and, [on this day,] as he had promised, poured out your Spirit of life and power upon the chosen disciples. At this the whole earth exults in boundless joy. And so, with the church on earth and the hosts of heaven, we praise your name and join their unending hymn:

Holy Trinity

P It is indeed right and salutary that we should at all times and in all places offer thanks and praise to you, O Lord, holy Father, almighty and everliving God. You have revealed your glory as the glory also of your Son and of the Holy Spirit: three persons, equal in majesty, undivided in splendor, yet one Lord, one God, ever to be adored in your everlasting glory. And so, with the church on earth and the hosts of heaven, we praise your name and join their unending hymn:

Sundays after Pentecost

P It is indeed right and salutary that we should at all times and in all places offer thanks and praise to you, O Lord, holy Father, through Christ our Lord; who on this day overcame death and the grave, and by his glorious resurrection opened to us the way of everlasting life. And so, with the church on earth and the hosts of heaven, we praise your name and join their unending hymn:

A   🄿 God of our weary years, God of our silent tears,
        you have brought us this far along the way.
    In times of bitterness you did not abandon us,
        but guided us into the path of love and light.
    In every age you sent prophets
        to make known your loving will for all humanity.
    The cry of the poor has become your own cry;
        our hunger and thirst for justice is your own desire.
    In the fullness of time, you sent your chosen servant
        to preach good news to the afflicted,
        to break bread with the outcast and despised,
        and to ransom those in bondage to prejudice and sin.

    In the night in which he was betrayed,
        our Lord Jesus took bread, and gave thanks;
        broke it, and gave it to his disciples, saying:
        Take and eat; this is my body given for you.
        Do this for the remembrance of me.
    Again, after supper, he took the cup, gave thanks,
        and gave it for all to drink, saying:
        This cup is the new covenant in my blood,
        shed for you and for all people for the forgiveness of sin.
        Do this for the remembrance of me.

    For as often as we eat of this bread and drink from this cup
        we proclaim the Lord's death until he comes.
🄈 **Christ has died. Christ is risen. Christ will come again.**

🄿 Remembering, therefore, his death and resurrection,
        we await the day when Jesus shall return to free all the earth
        from the bonds of slavery and death.
    Come, Lord Jesus! And let the church say "Amen"!
🄈 **Amen**

🄿 Send your Holy Spirit, our advocate,
        to fill the hearts of all who share this bread and cup
        with courage and wisdom to pursue love and justice in all the world.
    Come, Spirit of freedom! And let the church say "Amen"!
🄈 **Amen**

🄿 Join our prayers and praise with your prophets and martyrs of every age,
        that, rejoicing in the hope of the resurrection,
        we might live in the freedom and hope of your Son.
🄈 **Through him, with him, in him,**
    in the unity of the Holy Spirit,
    all glory and honor is yours, almighty Father,
    now and forever. Amen

B   P Holy God, holy and mighty, holy and immortal,
in the beginning you formed the heavens and earth
and created us in your likeness.
You made us guardians of your good creation and left the earth in our care.
All through our weary years and our silent tears,
you did not abandon us to ourselves,
but sought us out in love.
When we were captives in Egypt, you did not abandon us.
When we wandered in the wilderness, you did not abandon us.
When we turned to false gods, you did not abandon us.
Through your holy prophets you called us to return
to your graciousness, to your mercy, and to your steadfast love.

In the crowning act of love you gave your only Son,
that whoever believes in him will have eternal life.
For you sent Jesus not to condemn the world,
but to save the world from sin.
Through his death on the cross, we who were once far off
have been brought near by the blood of Christ.

In the night in which he was betrayed,
our Lord Jesus took bread, and gave thanks;
broke it, and gave it to his disciples, saying:
Take and eat; this is my body given for you.
Do this for the remembrance of me.
Again, after supper, he took the cup, gave thanks,
and gave it for all to drink, saying:
This cup is the new covenant in my blood,
shed for you and for all people for the forgiveness of sin.
Do this for the remembrance of me.

For as often as we eat of this bread and drink from this cup,
we proclaim the Lord's death until he comes.

C Christ has died. Christ is risen. Christ will come again.

P With this bread and cup, we remember Christ's life among us;
his association with outcasts, his eating with sinners,
his healing of the sick, his care for the poor.

Send, we pray, your Holy Spirit
upon us and upon this bread and wine,
that we who share this meal
may become a holy communion,
the body of Christ in the world.

C Through him, with him, in him,
in the unity of the Holy Spirit,
all glory and honor is yours, almighty Father,
now and forever. Amen

C   *When this prayer is used, it follows immediately the third sentence of the preface dialog, "Let us give thanks to the Lord our God . . ." The preface itself and Sanctus are omitted.*

P God of our ancestors, friend in our midst, your children come before you.
Here is food! Here is drink!
These things are yours before they are ours.

Now we are making a feast, but it is a thanksgiving:
God, we are thanking you.
With our ancestors in faith and all the hosts of heaven,
    O God, we thank you and rejoice.
This food—we shall eat it in your honor!
This drink—we shall drink it in your honor!

P We thank you for giving us life.

C **We thank you!**

P We thank you for giving us freedom.

C **We thank you!**

P We thank you for bringing us peace.

C **We thank you!**

P We thank you for the one who bore our sins upon the cross.

C **We thank you!**

P We thank you for the one who brought us over from death to life.

C **We thank you!**

P Father, send the Spirit of life,
    the Spirit of power and fruitfulness.
With the Spirit's breath, speak your Word into these things.
Give us who eat and drink the living body and the lifeblood of Jesus, our brother,
    life and power and fruitfulness of heart and body.
Give us true communion with your Son.

On the night of his suffering,
    he gave thanks for the bread that he held in his hands.
This bread he shared among his followers, saying:
    All of you, take this, eat this;
    it is my body, handed over for you.
    Do this and remember me.

C **The body of Christ! Amen**

P Then he shared drink with them, saying:
    All of you, take this, drink this;
    it is my blood, the blood of the new covenant
    that begins now and lasts forever.
This blood is poured out for you and for all people
    so that sins may be taken away.
    Do this and remember me.

C **The blood of Christ! Amen**

P Let us proclaim the mystery of faith.

C Hail, hail, hail
   Jesus Christ our Lord,
   death, resurrection, and return!
   May happiness come!

P Lord, you are resurrection and life.
   You, Crucifixion, are here!
   You, Resurrection, are here!
   You, Ascension, are here!
   You, Spirit—Medicine of Life—are here!

   Father, bring us life;
       give us kinship and fellowship
       with Mary, the mother of our Lord,
       with all the elders and ancestors of your people,
       and with all your children.

C **And you, our prayer—**
   Prayer of the long-distant past;
   you, ancient Word, spoken by the Father;
   you, Breath of the Spirit—
   Prayer of the ancestors,
   you are spoken now! Amen

PRAYERS OF THANKSGIVING

These prayers may be used within the context of praying at the table that always includes the proclamation of the words of institution of the holy supper and the praying of the Lord's Prayer.

General

℗ Blessed are you, Lord of heaven and earth, for you have had mercy on us and given your only-begotten Son that whoever believes in him should not perish but have eternal life. We give you thanks for the redemption you have prepared for us through Jesus Christ. Send your Holy Spirit into our hearts to establish in us a living faith and prepare us joyfully to receive our Redeemer who comes to us in his body and blood.

Advent, Christmas, Epiphany

℗ Blessed are you, Lord of heaven and earth, for you have had mercy on us and given your only-begotten Son that whoever believes in him should not perish but have eternal life. We give you thanks for the salvation you have granted to us through Jesus, the Word made flesh, the child of Mary; the Light of the world, our Immanuel. Send the Spirit of your Son into our hearts, that as your beloved children we may welcome our Savior who comes to us in his body and blood.

Lent, Easter, Pentecost

℗ Blessed are you, Lord of heaven and earth, for you have had mercy on us and given your only-begotten Son that whoever believes in him should not perish but have eternal life. We give you thanks for the priceless grace you have bestowed upon us through Jesus Christ, who died upon the tree of Calvary and rose again to make us living branches, drawing our life from him and bearing fruit in all the world. Send your Holy Spirit, the Spirit of truth and power, to renew our faith as we receive our crucified and risen Lord who comes to us in his body and blood.

WORDS OF INSTITUTION

℗ In the night in which he was betrayed,
    our Lord Jesus took bread,
    and gave thanks; broke it,
    and gave it to his disciples, saying:
    Take and eat;
    this is my body, given for you.
Do this for the remembrance of me.

Again, after supper,
    he took the cup, gave thanks,
    and gave it for all to drink, saying:
    This cup is the new covenant
    in my blood,
    shed for you and for all people
    for the forgiveness of sin.
Do this for the remembrance of me.

OR

℗ Our Lord Jesus Christ, on the night
    when he was betrayed, took bread,
    and when he had given thanks,
    he broke it and gave it to the disciples
    and said: Take, eat;
    this is my body, which is given for you.
This do in remembrance of me.

In the same way also he took the cup after
    supper, and when he had given thanks,
    he gave it to them, saying: Drink of it,
    all of you; this is my blood of
    the new covenant, which is shed for you
    for the forgiveness of sins.
This do, as often as you drink it,
    in remembrance of me.

A   Ⓐ Let us pray.
     God of our ancestors,
     God of all people,
     before whose face the human generations pass away,
     we thank you that as the broken bread was gathered into one loaf,
     the broken fragments of our history are gathered up
     and healed by the redeeming act of Christ.
     Send us forth in peace,
     form us into what we celebrate,
     the body of Christ in the world.
     Nourished by this sacrament,
     give us strength and courage to serve you in daily life
     with joy and singleness of heart.
     In the name of Christ we pray.
     Ⓒ Amen

B   Ⓐ Let us pray.
     Almighty God,
     we thank you for feeding us with spiritual food,
     the body and blood of Christ.
     All who come to you will not hunger,
     all who believe in you will not thirst.
     Empowered by this sacrament,
     send us back into the world
     to do the work you have given us to do:
     to share the gospel and be faithful disciples
     of Jesus Christ our Lord.
     Ⓒ Amen

C   Ⓐ Almighty God,
     you provide the true bread from heaven,
     your Son, Jesus Christ our Lord.
     Grant that we who have received
     the sacrament of his body and blood
     may abide in him and he in us,
     that we may be filled
     with the power of his endless life,
     now and forever.
     Ⓒ Amen

CHARGES TO THE PEOPLE

A charge (an exhortation to mission) such as those that follow may be used before the benediction.
When a charge is given, the benediction that follows should be brief.

A   Ⓛ Go out into the world in peace;
have courage;
hold on to what is good;
return no one evil for evil;
strengthen the fainthearted;
support the weak, and help the suffering;
honor all people;
love and serve the Lord,
rejoicing in the power of the Holy Spirit.

B   Ⓛ Go out into the world in peace.
Love the Lord your God
with all your heart,
with all your soul,
with all your mind;
and love your neighbor as yourself.

C   Ⓛ Beloved in the Lord,
God has shown you what is good.
What does the Lord require of you
but to do justice,
and to love kindness,
and to walk humbly with your God?

D   Ⓛ People of God,
you have been called to be disciples of Christ.
Whatever you do, in word or deed,
do everything in the name of the Lord Jesus,
giving thanks to God through him.

P The peace of God,
which passes all understanding,
keep your hearts and minds
in the knowledge and love of God,
in Jesus Christ our Lord;
and the blessing of almighty God,
Father, + Son, and Holy Spirit,
be among you and remain with you
always.
C **Amen**

OR

P The God of peace, who brought
back from the dead our Lord Jesus,
make you complete in everything
good so that you may do God's
will, working among you that
which is pleasing in God's sight,
through Jesus Christ our Lord.
C **Amen**

THREEFOLD BENEDICTIONS

Advent

P You believe that God came to us in
Jesus Christ, and look for him to
come again. May the advent of his
coming bring you comfort and joy.
C **Amen**

P May God make you steady in faith,
full of hope, and abounding in
love.
C **Amen**

P Rejoice that Jesus is Emmanuel,
God with us. When he comes again
in glory, may he bring you to everlasting life.
C **Amen**

P Almighty God,
Father, + Son, and Holy Spirit,
bless you now and forever.
C **Amen**

Christmas

P Jesus is the Word made flesh
in our midst. May his incarnation
fill your hearts with joy and peace.
C **Amen**

P Jesus is the promised Savior,
born of Mary. May his birth among
us renew your hope.
C **Amen**

P Jesus is the King of kings and the
Lord of lords. May the gift of his
presence bring forth rejoicing.
C **Amen**

P Almighty God,
Father, + Son, and Holy Spirit,
bless you now and forever.
C **Amen**

New Year

℗ God is the Alpha and the Omega,
the beginning and the end. May
God grant you grace and peace at
the dawn of this new year.

℃ **Amen**

℗ All flesh is grass, but the word of
God remains forever. May God
who is eternal keep you in hope of
the resurrection.

℃ **Amen**

℗ The past, the present, and the future
rest in God's hands. May God
guard your coming in and your
going forth, this new year and
forevermore.

℃ **Amen**

℗ Almighty God,
Father, ✝ Son, and Holy Spirit,
bless you now and forever.

℃ **Amen**

Epiphany

℗ The magi found the infant Jesus by
following his star. May you seek
the Lord where he is found and call
upon him while he is near.

℃ **Amen**

℗ Christ Jesus is the sun of righteousness. May his radiance bring you
warmth and cheer.

℃ **Amen**

℗ Light and peace are yours through
Jesus Christ. May your light so
shine before others, that they see
your works and glorify your Father
in heaven.

℃ **Amen**

℗ Almighty God,
Father, ✝ Son, and Holy Spirit,
bless you now and forever.

℃ **Amen**

Passion

℗ Jesus took the form of a servant
and was obedient to death, even
death on a cross. May you follow
his example and share in the
resurrection.

℃ **Amen**

℗ In faithfulness to God, Jesus gave
his life as a ransom for many.
May you walk in love as Christ
loved us and gave himself for us,
an offering and sacrifice to God.

℃ **Amen**

℗ On the cross of Calvary Jesus bore
our grief and carried our sorrows.
May his Passion bring you healing
and peace.

℃ **Amen**

℗ Almighty God,
Father, ✝ Son, and Holy Spirit,
bless you now and forever.

℃ **Amen**

Easter

℗ "I am the resurrection and the life,"
says the Lord. May Christ's rising
lift your spirits and gladden your
hearts.

℃ **Amen**

℗ All those who believe in Christ will
never perish. May you pass with
Christ from death to life.

℃ **Amen**

℗ Christ has gone to prepare a place
for us. May his resurrection bring
you all joy and peace in believing,
so that you may abound in hope.

℃ **Amen**

℗ Almighty God,
Father, ✝ Son, and Holy Spirit,
bless you now and forever.

℃ **Amen**

Pentecost, Holy Spirit

P At Pentecost, the Spirit of God was poured out upon believers. May the Spirit's flame burn brightly in your hearts.

C **Amen**

P The wind of the Spirit blows where it wills. May the breath of the Spirit rouse you for life.

C **Amen**

P Christ said to the disciples, "Receive the Holy Spirit." May you be enlightened and sanctified in his name.

C **Amen**

P Almighty God, Father, ✝ Son, and Holy Spirit, bless you now and forever.

C **Amen**

Season after Pentecost A

P We do not live by bread alone, but by every word that comes from God. May the word of God be upon your lips and written on your hearts.

C **Amen**

P The word that goes out from God does not return empty. May the word bear fruit, accomplishing its purpose in you.

C **Amen**

P May your minds be set on things above, where Christ is seated, at God's right hand.

C **Amen**

P Almighty God, Father, ✝ Son, and Holy Spirit, bless you now and forever.

C **Amen**

Season after Pentecost B

P Jesus is the great shepherd of the sheep. May you hear his voice and obey his commands.

C **Amen**

P Jesus is the pathway that leads to life. May you follow in the narrow way.

C **Amen**

P Jesus is the vine and we are the branches. May you be rooted and grounded in his love.

C **Amen**

P Almighty God, Father, ✝ Son, and Holy Spirit, bless you now and forever.

C **Amen**

Season after Pentecost C

P The church is surrounded by a great cloud of witnesses. May you find strength and courage in their presence.

C **Amen**

P The devil prowls like a lion, seeking someone to devour. May you be freed from all sin and protected from all evil.

C **Amen**

P Christ has run the good race of faith and finished the course. May you run with perseverance the race set before you.

C **Amen**

P Almighty God, Father, ✝ Son, and Holy Spirit, bless you now and forever.

C **Amen**

The Lutheran Church—Missouri Synod has provided these versions of the creeds for the use of its congregations.

Nicene Creed

☐ I believe in one God,
    the Father Almighty,
    maker of heaven and earth,
        and of all things visible and invisible.

And in one Lord Jesus Christ,
    the only-begotten Son of God,
    begotten of his Father before all worlds,
    God of God, Light of Light,
    very God of very God,
    begotten, not made,
    being of one substance with the Father,
    by whom all things were made;
    who for us men and for our salvation
        came down from heaven,
        and was incarnate by the Holy Ghost of the virgin Mary,
        and was made man;
    and was crucified also for us under Pontius Pilate.
    He suffered and was buried;
    and the third day he rose again
        according to the Scriptures,
        and ascended into heaven,
        and sitteth on the right hand of the Father.
    And he shall come again with glory
        to judge both the quick and the dead;
    whose kingdom shall have no end.

And I believe in the Holy Ghost,
    the Lord and Giver of life,
    who proceedeth from the Father and the Son,
    who with the Father and the Son together
        is worshiped and glorified,
    who spake by the prophets.
    And I believe one holy Christian and apostolic Church.*
    I acknowledge one Baptism for the remission of sins.
    And I look for the resurrection of the dead,
    and the life of the world to come. Amen

*Or, one holy catholic and apostolic Church, *the original and generally accepted text.*

Apostles' Creed

C I believe in God, the Father Almighty,
    maker of heaven and earth;

And in Jesus Christ, his only Son, our Lord,
    who was conceived by the Holy Ghost,
    born of the virgin Mary,
    suffered under Pontius Pilate,
    was crucified, dead, and buried.
    He descended into hell;
    the third day he rose again from the dead;
        he ascended into heaven
        and sitteth on the right hand of God the Father Almighty;
    from thence he shall come to judge the quick and the dead.

I believe in the Holy Ghost;
    the holy Christian Church,*
    the communion of saints;
    the forgiveness of sins;
    the resurrection of the body,
    and the life everlasting. Amen

*Or, the holy catholic Church, *the original and generally accepted text.*

THE WAY OF THE CROSS

The Way of the Cross may be used for individual prayer or as a public liturgy, particularly on the Fridays in Lent. The congregation may assemble in the church, or at another appointed place (especially if outdoor stations are to be made).

L In the name of the Father, and of the ✝ Son, and of the Holy Spirit.
C Amen

L Lord, have mercy.
C Christ, have mercy.
L Lord, have mercy.

Lord's Prayer

OR

C Our Father in heaven,
    hallowed be your name,
    your kingdom come,
    your will be done,
        on earth as in heaven.
Give us today our daily bread.
Forgive us our sins
    as we forgive those
        who sin against us.
Save us from the time of trial
    and deliver us from evil.
For the kingdom, the power,
    and the glory are yours,
    now and forever. Amen

C Our Father, who art in heaven,
    hallowed be thy name,
    thy kingdom come,
    thy will be done,
        on earth as it is in heaven.
Give us this day our daily bread;
and forgive us our trespasses,
    as we forgive those
        who trespass against us;
and lead us not into temptation,
    but deliver us from evil.
For thine is the kingdom,
    and the power, and the glory,
    forever and ever. Amen

L We will glory in the cross of our Lord Jesus Christ,
C in whom is our salvation, our life, and resurrection.

L Let us pray.
    Mercifully assist us, O Lord God of our salvation, that we may remember with joy the mighty acts whereby you have given us life everlasting; through Jesus Christ our Lord.
C Amen

The procession moves to the first station.

First Station

JESUS IS CONDEMNED TO DEATH

[L] We adore you, O Christ, and we bless you.
[C] **By your holy cross you have redeemed the world.**

As soon as it was morning, the chief priests held a consultation with the elders and scribes and the whole council. They bound Jesus, led him away, and handed him over to Pilate. Pilate spoke to the crowd: "What do you wish me to do with the man you call the king of the Jews?" They shouted back, "Crucify him!" Pilate said to them, "Why, what evil has he done?" But they shouted all the more, "Crucify him!" So, after flogging Jesus, Pilate handed him over to be crucified.

[L] God did not spare his own Son,
[C] **but delivered him up for us all.**

HYMNS　　80　He never said a mumbalin' word
　　　　　193　Precious Lord, take my hand

[L] Let us pray.
Almighty God, your Son our Savior suffered at the hands of sinners and endured the shame of the cross. Grant that we may walk in the way of his cross and find it the way of life and peace; through your Son, Jesus Christ our Lord.
[C] **Amen**

[L] Holy God, holy and mighty, holy and immortal,
[C] **have mercy and hear us.**

The procession moves to the second station.

Second Station

JESUS TAKES UP HIS CROSS

[L] We adore you, O Christ, and we bless you.
[C] **By your holy cross you have redeemed the world.**

Carrying the cross by himself, Jesus went out to the place called The Place of the Skull, which in Hebrew is called Golgotha. Although he was a Son, he learned obedience through what he suffered. Like a lamb that is led to the slaughter and like a sheep that before its shearers is silent, so he did not open his mouth. Worthy is the Lamb who was slain to receive power and riches, and wisdom and strength, and honor and glory and blessing.

[L] The Lord has laid on him the iniquity of us all:
[C] **for the transgression of my people was he stricken.**

HYMNS　　73　Jesus, keep me near the cross
　　　　　282　Let all that is within me cry, "Holy!"

L Let us pray.
Almighty God, whose beloved Son willingly endured the agony and shame of the
cross for our redemption: Give us courage to take up our cross and follow him;
who lives and reigns forever and ever.

C **Amen**

L Holy God, holy and mighty, holy and immortal,

C **have mercy and hear us.**

The procession moves to the third station.

Third Station
THE CROSS IS LAID ON SIMON OF CYRENE

L We adore you, O Christ, and we bless you.

C **By your holy cross you have redeemed the world.**

As they led Jesus away, they seized a man, Simon of Cyrene, who was coming from
the country, and they laid the cross on him, and made him carry it behind Jesus. "If
any want to become my followers, let them deny themselves and take up their cross
and follow me. Take my yoke upon you, and learn from me; for my yoke is easy, and
my burden is light."

L Whoever does not carry the cross and follow me

C **cannot be my disciple.**

HYMNS   70 Lead me, guide me
        235 All to Jesus I surrender

L Let us pray.
Heavenly Father, whose blessed Son came not to be served but to serve:
Bless all who, following in his steps, give themselves to the service of others;
that with wisdom, patience, and courage, they may minister in his name to the
suffering, the friendless, and the needy; for the love of him who laid down his life
for us, your Son our Savior Jesus Christ.

C **Amen**

L Holy God, holy and mighty, holy and immortal,

C **have mercy and hear us.**

The procession moves to the fourth station.

Fourth Station
JESUS MEETS THE WOMEN OF JERUSALEM

L We adore you, O Christ, and we bless you,

C **By your holy cross you have redeemed the world.**

A great number of the people followed Jesus, and among them were women who were wailing for him. But Jesus turned to them and said, "Daughters of Jerusalem, do not weep for me, but weep for yourselves and for your children."

L Those who sowed with tears
C **will reap with songs of joy.**

HYMNS   66 I want Jesus to walk with me
            67 By the waters of Babylon

L Let us pray.
Teach your church, O Lord, to mourn the sins of which it is guilty, and to repent and forsake them; that, by your pardoning grace, the results of our iniquities may not be visited upon our children and our children's children; through Jesus Christ our Lord.
C **Amen**

L Holy God, holy and mighty, holy and immortal,
C **have mercy and hear us.**

The procession moves to the fifth station.

Fifth Station
JESUS IS STRIPPED OF HIS GARMENTS

L We adore you, O Christ, and we bless you,
C **By your holy cross you have redeemed the world.**

When they came to a place called Golgotha, they offered him wine to drink, mixed with gall; but when he tasted it, he would not drink it. The soldiers divided his garments among them by casting lots. This was to fulfill what the scripture says, "They divided my clothes among themselves, and for my clothing they cast lots."

L They gave me gall to eat,
C **and when I was thirsty they gave me vinegar to drink.**

HYMNS 198 When the storms of life are raging
           208 Oh, freedom

L Let us pray.
O God, your Son chose the path which led to pain before joy and the cross before glory. Plant his cross in our hearts, so that in its power and love we may come at last to joy and glory; through your Son, Jesus Christ our Lord.
C **Amen**

L Holy God, holy and mighty, holy and immortal,
C **have mercy and hear us.**

The procession moves to the sixth station.

Sixth Station
JESUS IS NAILED TO THE CROSS

L We adore you, O Christ, and we bless you.

C By your holy cross you have redeemed the world.

When they came to the place that is called The Skull, there they crucified Jesus; and with him they crucified two criminals, one on the right, and one on the left. He poured out himself to death, and yet he bore the sin of many.

L They pierce my hands and my feet;

C they stare and gloat over me.

HYMNS   77 On a hill far away
        81 Were you there (sts. 1–3)

L Let us pray.
Lord Jesus Christ, you stretched out your arms of love on the hard wood of the cross that everyone might come within the reach of your saving embrace. So clothe us in your Spirit that we, reaching forth our hands in love, may bring those who do not know you to the knowledge and love of you; for the honor of your name.

C Amen

L Holy God, holy and mighty, holy and immortal,

C have mercy and hear us.

The procession moves to the seventh station.

Seventh Station
JESUS DIES ON THE CROSS

L We adore you, O Christ, and we bless you.

C By your holy cross you have redeemed the world.

When Jesus saw his mother and the disciple whom he loved standing beside her, he said to his mother, "Woman, behold your son." Then he said to the disciple, "Behold your mother." And when Jesus had received the vinegar he said, "It is finished!" Then he bowed his head and gave up his spirit.

L Christ for us became obedient unto death,

C even death on a cross.

HYMNS   68 That priceless grace
        85 Calvary

L Let us pray.
O God, you gave your only Son to suffer death on the cross for our redemption, and by his glorious resurrection you delivered us from the power of death. Make us die every day to sin, so that we may live with him forever in the joy of the resurrection; who lives and reigns now and forever.

C Amen

L Holy God, holy and mighty, holy and immortal,
C have mercy and hear us.

The procession moves to the eighth station.

Eighth Station
JESUS IS LAID IN THE TOMB

L We adore you, O Christ, and we bless you.
C By your holy cross you have redeemed the world.

When it was evening, there came a rich man from Arimathea, named Joseph, who was also a disciple of Jesus. He went to Pilate and asked for the body of Jesus. Then Pilate ordered it to be given to him. So Joseph took the body and wrapped it in a clean linen cloth and laid it in his own new tomb, which he had hewn in the rock. He then rolled a great stone to the door of the tomb.

L You will not abandon me to the grave,
C nor let your holy one see corruption.

HYMNS   81 Were you there (sts. 4–5)
         86 King of my life

L Let us pray.
O God, your blessed Son was laid in a tomb in a garden, and rested on the Sabbath day. Grant that we who have been buried with him in the waters of baptism may find our perfect rest in his eternal and glorious kingdom;where he lives and reigns forever and ever.
C Amen

L Holy God, holy and mighty, holy and immortal,
C have mercy and hear us.

The procession may move to the chancel or the place of gathering.

Conclusion

L Savior of the world, by your cross and precious blood you have redeemed us.
C Save us and help us, we humbly beseech you, O Lord.

L Let us pray.
We thank you, heavenly Father, that you have delivered us from the dominion of sin and death and brought us into the kingdom of your Son; and we pray that, as by his death he has recalled us to life, so by his love he may raise us to eternal joys; who lives and reigns with you, in the unity of the Holy Spirit, one God, now and forever.
C Amen

L To Christ our Lord who loves us, washed us in his own blood, and made us a kingdom of priests to serve his God and Father, to him be glory and dominion forever and ever.
C Amen

NOTES

▶ The Way of the Cross is a devotion adapted from a custom observed by Christian pilgrims who said prayers in Jerusalem at a series of places in that city associated with the passion of Jesus.

▶ Traditionally, there have been as many as fourteen stations. Of these, eight are based directly on events of scripture and are included in this rite. Each station includes sentences and responses, scripture verses, a prayer, and a hymn.

▶ Although the rite is especially appropriate on the Fridays in Lent, it does not displace the proper liturgy for Good Friday.

▶ The Way of the Cross resonates with several aspects of African and African American Christian traditions: an association with struggle and suffering; the concepts of pilgrimage and marching for justice; and a hymnic tradition that proclaims the saving blood and cross of Christ.

▶ Traditionally, the procession moves to stations at a series of plain wooden crosses placed along the walls of the church. With each cross there may also be a pictorial representation of the event being remembered.

▶ Stations may also be made outside the church walls as a public witness. Outdoor stations may be made at significant locations in the immediate neighborhood where healing is needed and where associations between the contemporary struggles of life and the events of Christ's suffering can be made (for example, sites where crimes have occurred, abandoned buildings, or other places of human struggle).

▶ Visual depictions for the stations may include sculpture, paintings, murals, photographs, or modern images, possibly created by people from the community.

▶ The hymns listed are suggestions. Other appropriate hymns and songs may be sung, and individual stanzas may be selected as needed.

▶ The one who presides may lead sentences and prayers; the prayer provided for each station or an appropriate free prayer may be used. One or more readers may proclaim the scripture verses. An assisting minister may carry a large, rough-hewn wooden cross in procession.

THE JOURNEY OF FAITH

PRAYERS, SIGNS, AND BLESSINGS

In addition to the principal forms of worship for the assembly, the church celebrates occasions and transitions in the lives of individual Christians and their families. Sometimes these points of recognition occur within the principal gathering of the community; at other times they are celebrated independently in the church or the home. The church lifts up the lives of its people in these ways not merely as a matter of social congratulation. Intercessions and blessings, symbolic actions and gestures, songs and acclamations are ways in which the community supports and accompanies its members along the journey of faith. Through such rites people are helped through the passages of human experience with the word of God, with prayer, and with mutual love.

The church recognizes and supports its members at various times in childhood and adolescence, in the stages of adult life, and in the face of illness and death. These occasions, by their very combination of the personal and the communal, have often employed particular cultural expressions of various times and places to proclaim the church's universal witness to every time and place.

African and African American Christians are among the many peoples who have incorporated cultural expressions to support primary Christian words and actions in connection with these life passages. These practices often make use of the physical elements of the world as an affirmation of God's good gifts in creation.

Some of these cultural expressions have identifiable points of origin. However, one consequence of the many years of slave trading is that later generations are often not able to trace the source of their traditions to specific nations or tribes on the African continent. Thus, cultural expressions that may derive from a particular region are now available to the larger community to support Christian proclamation in a given context.

The following pages offer resources that Christian communities may use in their ministry with people on the journey of faith. This representative selection provides resources for use with young people coming into adulthood, those entering marriage, men and women in the life of the community, and elders with the gifts they bring.

YOUNG PEOPLE COMING TO ADULTHOOD

The life transition through adolescence into adulthood may be marked with prayers of support and encouragement. Congregations may select as desired from the following elements in order to offer public affirmation of growth into maturity and prayer for the future.

Following the hymn of the day in the liturgy the young people, accompanied by family members (including baptismal sponsors when possible), may gather at the front of the congregation or at the place of baptism.

Introduction

A representative of the congregation may present the young people:
These persons seek the prayers and support of the community as they grow into maturity by the grace and power of God.

P In response to Jesus' invitation, "Let the children come unto me and do not hinder them," these young persons have been baptized into Christ and clothed with Christ. As members with us in the baptismal priesthood of Christ, they have been called to be disciples of Christ and servants of God in the world. As these young people stand on the verge of adulthood, we ask God to guide them into maturity and to walk with them as they begin to discern where adulthood may lead.

Invitation to Vocation

Each young person may be invited to express hopes and intentions for the call of God in their adult lives; these may include a desired occupational direction.

P *Name,* what do you desire for your future?

R I desire _____, and I ask the God of our ancestors and the people of Christ to strengthen, lead, and guide me.

P St. Paul writes: "For as in one body we have many members, and not all the members have the same function, so we, who are many, are one body in Christ, and individually we are members one of another. We have gifts that differ according to the grace given to us." *(Rom. 12:4-6)*

In the use of these differing gifts within the family, the school, the church, the society, and the world of work, we recognize the gift of vocation, our calling to various places of responsibility. Know that each one affords an opportunity to serve. "Like good stewards of the manifold grace of God, serve one another with whatever gift each of you has received." *(1 Peter. 4:10)*

Feeding

From a dish containing bread or a traditional food, the mother or another family representative may offer the young person a small amount, saying in these or similar words:

Name, it is I, your *relationship*, feeding you today. I represent the generations of your family and of the extended human family. We are feeding you today. When you were a child, we fed you. We clothed you. We took care of you. We brought you to Jesus. Now you are a *woman/man*. You will feed yourself, clothe yourself, take care of yourself, and grow in your own relationship to Jesus. This does not mean that we have abandoned you. We will support and nourish you in time of need. But you will be responsible for yourself. We feed you today, remembering how you have been fed in body and spirit until now. We feed you today, entrusting you to the grace of God who will supply your every need. In the name of Jesus we feed you. In the power of the Holy Spirit of God we feed you.

G In the name of Jesus. Amen

Commitment and Communal Support

The young person may tie a knot in a length of cord, saying these or similar words:

I, *name*, tie this knot in the presence of God and of this community. This knot is a sign of my pledge to follow in the way of Jesus and climb the ladder of growth that is before me. I ask the God of our ancestors and the people of Christ to strengthen, lead, and guide me; in the name of Jesus.

G In the name of Jesus. Amen

The cord is passed on to family members, who tie another knot on the first one, saying these or similar words to the young person:

We, too, tie a knot on your knot, a sign of the promise we make to you today in the presence of God and of this community. We will support and help you in any way and by any means necessary. We will pray for you, advise you, and help you to discern and carry out your calling. We ask the God of our ancestors and the people of Christ to strengthen, lead, and guide us; in the name of Jesus.

G In the name of Jesus. Amen

Affirmation of Identity

The minister addresses each young person in turn.

P Who are you?

R My name is_____. I am a *woman/man*. A young *woman/man*, but still a *woman/man*. My roots are *name of heritage*. My people and my community need me. My church and my family need me. My friends and the whole of creation need me. I ask the Holy Spirit of God and the people of Christ to strengthen, lead, and guide me; in the name of Jesus.

G In the name of Jesus. Amen

Call to Maturity in Christ

The young people may face the congregation. A representative of the congregation says:

We are called to the unity of the faith and of the knowledge of the Son of God, to maturity, to the measure of the full stature of Christ. We must no longer be children, tossed to and fro and blown about by every wind of doctrine, by trickery and scheming. But speaking the truth in love, we must grow up in every way into him who is the head of the body, into Christ. *(based on Eph. 4:13-16)*

C **Sisters and brothers** **in Christ, today we have heard wonderful things from you. You have shared your hopes and dreams with this community. We invite you to a more mature and responsible participation in the world, to live in word and deed the faith that we confess. We receive you with open hearts and arms, in the name of Jesus.**

The congregation may offer its acclamation with applause and shouts of thanksgiving.

Prayer

The following prayer may be included in the prayers of the church or used independently.

A Lord God of our ancestors, we thank you for what you have done and will continue to do with our *daughters and sons.* Walk with them in life, and keep the evil one from obstructing their path. You see all; you know where the water is deep. Keep them from danger. Order their steps and guide their feet while they run the race of faith. May the good work that you have begun in them be brought to completion at the day of Jesus Christ.

C **Amen**

NOTES

▶ These resources acknowledge the movement away from childhood and dependence towards maturation and independence—a transition that often includes discernment and planning for adult responsibilities.

▶ The North American cultural setting offers no uniform norm as to when childhood/adolescence ends and adulthood begins. Some consider an age tied to physical maturation, such as age 13; others, age 15 or 16, such as "sweet sixteen," the first driver's license, and the Hispanic celebration of Quince Años; others, age 18, the age of eligibility for voting and for military conscription. Recognizing that coming to adulthood is a process spanning a number of years, particular communities of faith and their young people may discern appropriate times and adapt these resources accordingly.

▶ As a resource to help mark a life-cycle transition, this recognition is independent from and is not intended to replace the affirmation of baptism (confirmation) that occurs in the catechetical ministry of many congregations. It may, however, provide a more suitable setting for certain life passage dimensions that have become attached to the confirmation rite.

▶ It is suggested that this recognition be celebrated only once in the life of each young person. The recognition may be offered once or twice per year within the weekly assembly or at a special parish celebration. Sundays and seasons for which the color is green are recommended times.

MARRIAGE

At the heart of the rite of marriage is the promise of love and faithfulness by which two people bind themselves to one another in a lifelong commitment. The church celebrates and accompanies the couple through this life passage by witnessing their promises, proclaiming the word of God in connection with this transition, and praying for God's blessing on the couple and their household.

These universal features of marriage within the Christian tradition are supplemented here by particular expressions of African and African American cultures. Congregations may select as desired from the following prayers, ceremonies, and blessings.

A Form of the Vows

The bride and groom face each other and join hands. Each, in turn, promises faithfulness to the other in these or similar words.

I, *name*, give you my hand this day. I open my mouth to declare before God, our ancestors, and this congregation, that I take you, *name*, to be my *wife/husband*. I love you. In bitter days and in days of sweetness, in darkness and in light, in life and until death, I will walk in step with you. Your concerns will be my concerns. Your joys will be my joys. We will share our struggles, and we will share our triumphs. I will be with you all the days of my life. This is my vow. I have spoken.

Cord of Family Unity

The symbolic gesture of tying a cord of family unity may follow the exchange of vows and rings. The minister may take up a length of cord and present it to representatives of the bride's and groom's families with these or similar words:

Ⓟ This cord represents an unbroken chain of life: given by God to our first parents, sustained by God through the generations of our ancestors, flowing to our families today. I invite you to tie this cord in the presence of God and these witnesses as a sign that you are joining the life of your two families.

Then, addressing representatives of each family in turn:

Ⓟ Are you prepared to be joined to the family of *name of bride/groom*?

The family representatives respond:

Ⓡ Yes, we are.

The family representatives tie a knot into the cord.

The family representatives pass the cord to the bride and groom, who tie another knot, saying:

Ⓡ We have together tied a knot with this cord. Our families are joined into one family, our peoples are joined into one people.

Broom of New Beginning

The symbolic gesture of jumping over a broom may follow the exchange of vows and rings.
The minister may address the couple in these or similar words:

P The broom represents cleansing and the hearth at the center of the home. I invite you to jump over the broom as a sign of your passage out from the past and into a new day begun as you make a home together.

The broom is laid down and the bride and groom hop over it, with the right foot and then the left.

Blessing and Declaration of Marriage

A length of kente cloth may be unfolded and held around the couple and over their heads.
Other family members may gather under the cloth as well. The minister may say:

P As you are wrapped in this cloth, may it remind you of the energy, the beauty, and the sheltering warmth of God's gift of the family. As our merciful God first made garments for humankind, as our gracious God clothes all who are in Christ, so may God clothe you with compassion and love for one another, for your family and community, and for the whole of creation.

The couple may share a kiss, and as they kiss the cloth is lowered. Then the marriage may be announced:

P What God has joined together, let no one put asunder. Elders of the community, family and friends, behold *name* and *name;* they are now husband and wife.

C **Hail! Hail ! Hail! May happiness come!**

The congregation may offer its acclamation, which may include applause, shouts of thanksgiving, music, dance.

Prayers

A God of our ancestors, the one on whom we lean and do not fall: when you close, no one can open, and when you open, no one can close. Your children come before you. We call on you to bless *name* and *name,* married this day.

Our Savior Jesus Christ, who freely gives us life, who turned water into wine at the wedding at Cana, we call on you. Strengthen in love and faithfulness the hearts of *name* and *name*. Keep them forever in your path, we pray.

Spirit of God, great and old and wise, our companion and guide, we lift up your name. Pour out your gifts upon *name* and *name*, that they may be rich in peace and joy, gentleness and wisdom. Give them understanding toward one another and a generous heart toward others.

A Holy One, we pray to you for *name* and *name* in the name of Jesus.
C **In the name of Jesus.**
A Give them fruitfulness of mind and body.
C **In the name of Jesus.**
A Give them peace of mind.
C **In the name of Jesus.**

Ⓐ Give them happiness and prosperity.
Ⓒ In the name of Jesus.
Ⓐ Give them patience with one another.
Ⓒ In the name of Jesus.
Ⓐ Protect them from enemies and tricksters.
Ⓒ In the name of Jesus.
Ⓐ Wrap them in the strength of the community.
Ⓒ In the name of Jesus.
Ⓐ Use us to support one another.
Ⓒ In the name of Jesus.
Ⓐ Give us wisdom to raise our children.
Ⓒ In the name of Jesus.
Ⓐ Bless every human bond of love and commitment.
Ⓒ In the name of Jesus.
Ⓐ Bless all husbands and wives, parents, and children.
Ⓒ In the name of Jesus.

Other petitions may be added as desired.

Ⓐ In the name of Jesus we ask this.
Ⓒ In the name of Jesus. Amen

NOTES

▶ The above resources do not constitute a complete marriage rite. One or more of these elements may be added to or substituted within the marriage rite in use by the congregation.

▶ Various traditions have incorporated symbolic elements and gestures into the marriage rite to underscore the spoken vows of marriage. The exchange of rings is a long-standing practice. The additional options presented here are linked to several African and African American traditions. Other practices may also be found. For example, in some regions fruits of the earth are offered to the couple, such as an orange, signifying fruitfulness of mind and body; a cluster of bananas, signifying the potential gift of children; and a coconut, with its hidden milk signifying the mystery of love that God has placed in the hearts of the newly married.

▶ An entrance procession of the wedding party, family members, and ministers may include art forms appropriate to the context and cultural traditions represented, such as music, textile art, or dance. Symbolic elements to be used in the service may be carried in procession.

▶ For the cord of family unity, an alb cincture or similar length of cord may be used.

▶ The kente cloth used in the blessing and declaration of marriage should be of an appropriate size for the action (6 feet by 9 feet is a useful size). One common kente cloth pattern is named *ebusa ye dom,* "the family is a crowd," symbolizing the vibrancy of a strong community.

▶ The prayer gesture of libation may accompany the prayers at the conclusion of each petition.

BLESSING OF WOMEN AND MEN

Some congregations observe men's day or women's day at various times of the year to recognize the contributions of women and men to the whole community on its journey of faith. On such occasions the following prayers of blessing may be added to the prayers of the church or included in the sending rite prior to the benediction.

For Women's Day

℗ God, who knit us together in
    the womb,
God of Eve, made in your image,
God of Sarah, Hagar, and Keturah,
God of Ruth and Naomi,
God of Mary Magdalene,
God of Mary, mother of our Lord:
    we ask your blessing upon all
    the women of this congregation.
Help them to be
    good daughters and sisters,
    good friends and spouses,
    good mothers and grandmothers,
    good women of faith.
Stir up in them
    the power of your Spirit.
Kindle in them
    the fire of your love.
Call forth in them
    the strength to serve you.
Through word and sacrament
    in the community of faith,
    renew in them the blessed
    assurance of salvation
    and the promise of eternal glory
    in your presence,
through Jesus Christ our Lord.
☖ **Amen**

For Men's Day

℗ God, our everlasting Father,
    God of Adam, made in your image,
    God of Abraham and Isaac,
    God of Nimrod and Phinehas,
    God of Simon the Cyrenian,
    God of Joseph, guardian of Jesus:
    we ask your blessing upon all
    the men of this congregation.
Help them to be
    good sons and brothers,
    good friends and spouses,
    good fathers and grandfathers,
    good men of faith.
In the midst of struggles,
    give them patience and strength.
In the midst of persecution,
    keep them steadfast in your Word.
For freedom Christ has set them
    free.
Help them stand firm,
    and not submit to the yoke
    of any slavery.
Through word and sacrament
    in the community of faith,
    may they be renewed
    in body, mind, and spirit,
through Jesus Christ our Lord.
☖ **Amen**

OR

For Women's Day

P   Blessed are you, O Lord our God,
creator of heaven and earth.
We give thanks to you for all the
women of faith who have done
your will throughout the ages.
We thank you
for Rebekah, Leah, and Rachel,
for Deborah and Esther,
for Anna and Elizabeth,
for Joanna and Susanna,
for Lydia, Dorcas, and Phoebe,
for Mary Magdalene, first witness
of the resurrection,
and for Mary, the blessed mother
of our Lord.

God of our ancestors in faith,
we ask your blessing
upon the faithful women
of this congregation,
our sisters and friends,
our spouses and daughters,
our grandmothers and mothers.
Bless them and all women
who place their trust in you.
Keep them steadfast in your Word.
Look with favor upon their lives
in Christ.
May they wait upon the Lord
and renew their strength,
soaring up with wings
like eagles,
running and not growing weary,
walking and not becoming faint;
through Jesus Christ our Lord.

C   **Amen**

For Men's Day

P   Blessed are you, O Lord our God,
creator of heaven and earth.
We give thanks to you for all the
men of faith who have done
your will throughout the ages.
We thank you for Abraham,
the father of Israel,
Moses the deliverer,
Samuel the judge,
David the king,
Isaiah the prophet,
Simeon the Black and Lucius of
Cyrene, prophets in Antioch,
and for Joseph, husband of Mary
and guardian of our Lord.

God of our ancestors in faith,
we ask your blessing
upon the faithful men
of this congregation,
our brothers and friends,
our spouses and sons,
our grandfathers and fathers.
Bless them and all men
who place their trust in you.
Empower them to hold fast their
faith and reject all that is evil.
May they not be conformed to
this world, but be transformed
by the renewing of their minds,
so that they may discern
what is the will of God,
what is good and acceptable
and perfect;
through Jesus Christ our Lord.

C   **Amen**

BLESSING OF ELDERS

The elders of the community are acknowledged in many congregations to have an important place and vocation. Elders are recognized by those around them as people who, through years of human experience and faithful presence in the community, bring various gifts of wisdom, steadfastness, caring, and leadership. Congregations may have various ways of identifying the elders in their midst.

This prayer of blessing for elders may be added to the prayers of the church or included in the sending rite prior to the benediction.

P Blessed are you, O Lord our God,
    maker of heaven and earth.
From everlasting to everlasting you are God,
    our dwelling place in all generations.
You are the source of holy wisdom,
    and the fountain of all truth.

We give thanks to you for the elders among us.
We are graced by their wisdom and seasoning.
We are touched by their knowledge and faith.
Bless them, O God, as they are a blessing to us.
Pour out your Spirit,
    that our elders may continue to dream dreams
    and testify to the Light of their salvation, Jesus Christ.
May we find inspiration in their years of faithfulness.
May we follow their example
    by serving you with steadfastness and singleness of heart;
    through Jesus Christ our Lord.

C **Amen**

BURIAL OF THE DEAD

NOTES

▶ The Burial of the Dead expresses the church's confident faith and hope in the forgiveness of sins, the resurrection of the body, and the life everlasting. Christian funeral rites mark the final stage of the journey of faith, the passing over of the baptized from this world to God. They also provide an opportunity to give thanks for the life of the deceased and to provide solace to those bereaved through the word of God proclaimed and sung in the context of a supportive community of faith.

▶ Traditional Christian funeral practices have often followed a pattern that includes washing, anointing, and dressing the body (practices reminiscent of baptism); communal gathering of family and friends for support and prayer; a service of the word (and Holy Communion); and a final commendation and procession to the grave.

▶ Within African American communities, a variety of burial traditions build upon this foundation. Coming from the harsh circumstances of slavery and its legacy, African Americans have often viewed death as a release from this "vale of tears" and a home-going to a better hereafter. Thus, African American burial traditions are often emotive, dignified, and celebratory. They are emotive as they provide deep catharsis for mourners. They are dignified as they honor the dead and assert the dignity of the living. And as the deceased crosses over, there is joy-filled celebration for the unity of life, death, and the new life in Christ. These rituals of comfort are also helpful in many modern urban communities where there is often a tragically high rate of premature death, especially among young African American males.

▶ African American burial practices vary from region to region. In some places, for example, the procession to the grave has taken on major significance, accompanied with celebratory music and rhythmic step. Other practices take place informally, rather than as part of the communal rites. These include leaving cooked food at grave sites; scattering dirt into graves; decorating graves with pieces of glass, pottery, and personal belongings; and funeral parties. The custom—informally observed by some African Americans—of delaying burial after death may have roots in the Igbo tradition of the second funeral.

▶ Because of the great regional variety, no specific resources for funeral rites are included here. Congregations may evaluate the practices of their communities and determine those aspects that can be used to supplement the church's rites for the burial of the dead.

WITNESSES TO THE FAITH

The piety of many African and African American Christians includes a vivid appreciation for the ancestors in faith. Those who walk the way of faith by the grace of God are strengthened by the biblical assurance: "Since we are surrounded by so great a cloud of witnesses, let us also lay aside every weight and the sin that clings so closely, and let us run with perseverance the race that is set before us, looking to Jesus" (Heb. 12:1-2).

The Lutheran confessional writings (Apology to the Augsburg Confession, Article XXI) note several ways God's people may recognize such witnesses to the faith from previous generations: giving thanks for their lives, allowing their example to motivate us, and entrusting our own growth in faith and service to the abounding grace of God.

The following is a sampling of persons and groups of persons, witnesses to the faith through the centuries, who may have particular significance to African Americans. Some of these are persons, recognized ecumenically, who are linked to the African continent by ancestry or by area of service; others have become known through their witness among African Americans. Such a list can never be comprehensive; it serves to supplement other available lists of commemorations, and may be supplemented further by local practice.

Where available, a calendar date has been included (traditionally that of a person's death, the "heavenly birthday"). On or near the appropriate date, the prayers of the church may include thanksgiving by name for the faithful departed. The church's life and mission may be strengthened by additional uses of these and other stories of witnesses to the faith; for example, in various aspects of educational ministry, or in the celebration of Black History Month.

Adrian of Canterbury, teacher
African by birth, Adrian (or Hadrian, d. 709–10) worked with Theodore, archbishop of Canterbury, in developing the church in England, particularly through his direction of an influential school where many church leaders were instructed. *January 9*

The Alpha Synod
In 1868 Michael Cobble was licensed by the North Carolina Synod to begin an African American mission congregation. Years later, the synod ordained D. J. Koontz and licensed Nathan Clapp, but did not grant equal pastoral privileges, suggesting they support their own ministries through secular employment. Continued lack of support for these missions led Koontz, Clapp, Sam Holt, and W. Philo Phifer to petition the North Carolina Synod for the formation of a synod for African American Lutherans, called the Alpha Synod (1889–1891).

Koontz was the first African American to become a synod president. After the Alpha Synod dissolved due to financial difficulties, Koontz's work was taken up in 1891 by Phifer with the help of the synodical conference of The Lutheran Church—Missouri Synod.

Antony of Egypt, renewer of the church
Born in Qemen-al-Arous, Upper Egypt, Antony (c. 251–356) was one of the earliest Egyptian "desert fathers." He established monasteries for Christian learning and devotion, was active in refuting the Arian heresy, and exerted a strong influence upon Athanasius, who made a record of his life. *January 17*

Augustine, bishop of Hippo
Originally from Algeria, Augustine (354–430) was converted as an adult through the influence of Ambrose, bishop of Milan, and was baptized at the Easter Vigil in 387. His theological writings and gifts of organization helped to shape the church of the fourth century in both Africa and Europe. *August 28*

Benedict the African, confessor
Born a slave on the island of Sicily, Benedict (d. 1589) joined a community of hermits when he was freed, serving as superior but later returning to his former position of cook. His fame as a confessor brought many visitors to the humble and holy cook. A patron saint of blacks in the United States, Benedict is remembered for his patience and understanding when confronted with racial prejudice. *April 4*

Marmaduke N. Carter, pastor
In 1916 Marmaduke Carter became the principal of the Christian Day School (formerly called the Rosebud School) and the first pastor of Christ Church, Rosebud, Alabama, a pioneering congregation in African American ministry among Lutherans in the South.

Peter Claver, missionary
A Jesuit missionary, Peter Claver (d. 1654) served in Cartagena (in what is now Colombia) by teaching and caring for the black slaves. Meeting them as they arrived after experiencing horrible conditions on slave ships, Claver tended to their physical needs and baptized the newborn. Though committed to speaking more with his hands than with his lips, he also advocated for the improvement of the slaves' living conditions. *September 9*

Cyprian, bishop of Carthage, martyr
Cyprian (c. 200–258) worked for the unity of the church and cared for his flock in North Africa during a time of great persecution. For refusing to take part in official pagan worship under Valerian, Cyprian was exiled and later executed. *September 16*

Emma Francis, deaconess
Emma Francis opened the Ebenezer Home for Girls in Frederiksted, Virgin Islands. In 1922 she moved to the United States and helped found a Lutheran church in New York. As a parish worker at Transfiguration Lutheran Church in New York, she became the first African American deaconess in the Lutheran church.

Frederick Lutheran Church
Frederick Lutheran Church, located on the island of St. Thomas in the U.S. Virgin Islands, is the second-oldest congregation in the Evangelical Lutheran Church in America. It was founded by the Church of Denmark in 1666.

Jehu Jones, missionary

A native of Charleston, South Carolina, Jehu Jones (1786–1852) was ordained by the New York Ministerium in 1832, the Lutheran church's first African American pastor. Upon returning to South Carolina he was arrested under a law prohibiting free blacks from re-entering the state, and so was unable to join the group of Charlestonians he had been commissioned to accompany to Liberia. For nearly twenty years Jones carried out missionary work in Philadelphia in the face of many difficulties. Here he led in the formation of the first African American Lutheran congregation (St. Paul's) and the construction of its church building. *September 28*

Martin Luther King, Jr., renewer of society, martyr

Martin Luther King, Jr. (1929–1968) is remembered as an American prophet of justice among races and nations, a Christian whose faith undergirded his advocacy of vigorous yet nonviolent action for racial equality. Pastor of churches in Montgomery, Alabama, and Atlanta, Georgia, his witness was taken to the streets in such other places as Birmingham, Alabama, where he was arrested and jailed while protesting against segregation. Awarded the Nobel Peace Prize in 1964, he was killed by an assassin on April 4, 1968. *January 15 (to coincide with national holiday) or April 4*

Massie L. Kennard, renewer of the church

Massie L. Kennard (1918–1996), a native of Chicago, Illinois, was a major figure in championing ethnic and racial inclusiveness in the former Lutheran Church in America. Ordained in 1958, he served the church in various staff positions, including director for Minority Concerns of the Division for Mission in North America. *October 10*

Monica, mother of Augustine

Monica (c. 322–387) is remembered as the mother of Augustine, praying and working fervently for his conversion through many years of his waywardness. A disciple of Ambrose, Monica assisted in bringing her son under Ambrose's influence, and eventually Augustine was baptized. In his *Confessions,* Augustine speaks tenderly of his mother's "zeal in good works and faithfulness in worship." *May 4*

Moses the Black, monk

A man of great strength and rough character, Moses the Black (died c. 400) was converted to the Christian faith toward the close of the fourth century. The change in his heart and life had a profound impact on his native Ethiopia. *August 28*

Pachomius, renewer of the church

Pachomius (d. 346), born in Upper Egypt and later conscripted into the army, is recognized as the founder of Christian community monasticism. He translated the administrative skills learned in the military into a highly organized system for communal life. Communities for women as well as men were established, emphasizing work according to one's craft, a pattern for life in community, and common prayer. *May 14*

Daniel Payne, teacher

Educator Daniel Payne organized a school for African Americans in Charleston, South Carolina, that eventually became the largest school in Charleston. In 1835 the school was closed when the General Assembly of South Carolina passed a law preventing free African Americans and slaves from operating schools. Payne eventually enrolled in

Gettysburg Seminary and was ordained by the Franckean Synod of Upper New York. No call was available to him in the Lutheran church, so he served a Presbyterian congregation in East Troy, New York. He went on to found Wilberforce College in Ohio.

Perpetua and Felicity and companions, martyrs
Among the earliest martyrs remembered by the church are Perpetua, a noblewoman from North Africa, and Felicity, a slave, together with several others who were arrested for their enrollment and participation in the catechumenate. The early account of their martyrdom in 202 records that Perpetua and Felicity survived the wild beasts in the arena at Carthage and were killed by the sword, having first exchanged the kiss of peace. *March 7*

Martin de Porres, renewer of society
Born in Peru to Don Juan de Porres and Ana Velázquez, a freed black slave from Panama, Martin (1575–1639) learned the healing arts from his mother's knowledge of herbal medicine and his own apprenticeship to a barber–surgeon in Lima. A lay brother in the Dominican order, Martin engaged in many charitable works, including the founding of an orphanage and hospital as well as the administration of the convent's food program. He is recognized as an advocate for Christian charity and interracial justice. *November 3*

Tertullian, theologian
Born in Carthage, North Africa, Tertullian (c. 160–c. 225) wrote forcefully in defense of the Christian faith and in opposition to various heresies, and is credited with such memorable words as "the blood of the martyrs is the seed of the church." Although later attracted to sectarian thought, Tertullian combined reason and faith in a way that profoundly influenced the articulation of Christian doctrine.

Nelson Wesley Trout, bishop
Nelson Trout (1920–1996), born in Columbus, Ohio, attended the Evangelical Lutheran Theological Seminary in Columbus. Ordained in 1952, he served parishes in Montgomery, Alabama; Los Angeles, California; and Eau Claire, Wisconsin. Trout also served in staff positions with the American Lutheran Church, Lutheran Social Services of Dayton, Ohio, and the Columbus seminary. In 1983 Trout was elected bishop of the South Pacific District of the American Lutheran Church, the first African American to serve in such a capacity. *September 20*

Victor the Moor, martyr
Known also as Victor Maurus, this native of Mauritania was a Christian from his youth who served as a soldier in the Praetorian Guard. Under the persecution of Maximian, Victor died for his faith at Milan in 303. *May 8*

Rosa Jensey Young, teacher, missionary
Rosa Young (1874–1971), a laywoman, is considered the mother of black Lutheranism on the Alabama field. In 1915, following the advice given to her by Booker T. Washington, she sought financial assistance from the Lutheran Synodical Conference for her school in Rosebud, Alabama. The school was required to become a Lutheran school to receive funding, and Young (a Methodist at the time) was confirmed in the Lutheran church. In association with Nils Jules Bakke, she labored to establish the Lutheran church in the black belt of Alabama. During the 1920s three or four new congregations were established there each year.

PRAYERS

GENERAL

Lord God, you have surrounded us with so great a cloud of witnesses. Grant that we [encouraged by the example of your *servant/servants name*] may persevere in the course that is set before us, to be living signs of the gospel and at last, with all the saints, to share in your eternal joy; through your Son, Jesus Christ our Lord.

MARTYRS

Gracious Lord, in every age you have sent men and women who have given their lives for the message of your love. Inspire us with the memory of those martyrs for the gospel [like your *servant/servants name*] whose faithfulness led them in the way of the cross, and give us courage to bear full witness with our lives to your Son's victory over sin and death; through Jesus Christ our Lord.

MISSIONARIES

God of grace and might, we praise you for your *servant/servants name*, to whom you gave gifts to make the good news known. Raise up, we pray, in every country, heralds and evangelists of your kingdom, so that the world may know the immeasurable riches of our Savior, Jesus Christ our Lord.

RENEWERS OF THE CHURCH

Almighty God, we praise you for the men and women you have sent to call the Church to its tasks and renew its life [such as your *servant/servants name*]. Raise up in our own day teachers and prophets inspired by your Spirit, whose voices will give strength to your church and proclaim the reality of your kingdom; through your Son, Jesus Christ our Lord.

RENEWERS OF SOCIETY

Lord God, your Son came among us to serve and not to be served, and to give his life for the world. Lead us by his love to serve all those to whom the world offers no comfort and little help. Through us give hope to the hopeless, love to the unloved, peace to the troubled, and rest to the weary; through your Son, Jesus Christ our Lord.

OR

Holy and righteous God, you created us in your image. Grant us grace to contend fearlessly against evil and to make no peace with oppression. Help us [like your *servant/servants name*] to use our freedom to bring justice among people and nations, to the glory of your name; through your Son, Jesus Christ our Lord.

PASTORS AND BISHOPS

Almighty God, you have raised up faithful pastors and leaders of your church. May the memory of their lives be a source of joy for us and a bulwark of our faith, so that we may serve you and confess your name before the world; through your Son, Jesus Christ our Lord.

TEACHERS

O God of wisdom, in your goodness you provide faithful teachers for your church. By your Holy Spirit give all teachers insight into your word, holy lives as examples to us all, and the courage to know and do the truth; through your Son, Jesus Christ our Lord.

This Far by Faith

Psalms and Service Music
Hymns and Songs
Resources from the Tradition

PSALMS AND SERVICE MUSIC

Happy Are They

Psalm 1

1

Hap - py are they who trust in the LORD.

Oh, hap - py are they who trust, trust in the LORD.

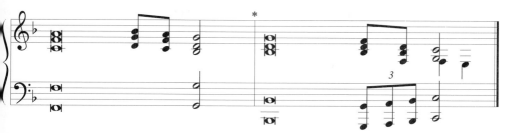

¹Happy are they who have not walked in the counsel | of the wicked,*
    nor lingered in the way of sinners, nor sat in the seats | of the scornful!
²Their delight is in the law | of the LORD,*
    and they meditate on his law | day and night.
³They are like trees planted by streams of water,
 bearing fruit in due season, with leaves that | do not wither;*
    everything they | do shall prosper.

⁴It is not so | with the wicked;*
    they are like chaff which the wind | blows away.
⁵Therefore the wicked shall not stand upright when | judgment comes,*
    nor the sinner in the council | of the righteous.
⁶For the LORD knows the way | of the righteous,*
    but the way of the wick- | ed is doomed.

Music: Rawn Harbor, refrain; *Psalter for Worship*, tone 37
Refrain © 1999 and tone © 1996 Augsburg Fortress

My God, My God

Psalm 22

My God, my God,

why have you for - sak - en me?

¹My God, my God,
  why have you for- | saken me*
    and are so far from my cry,
    and from the words of | my distress?
²O my God, I cry in the daytime,
  but you | do not answer;*
    by night as well, but I | find no rest.

³Yet you are the | Holy One,*
    enthroned upon the prais- | es of Israel.
⁴Our forefathers put their | trust in you;*
    they trusted, and you de- | livered them.
⁵They cried out to you and | were delivered;*
    they trusted in you
    and were not | put to shame.

⁶But as for me, I am a worm | and no man,*
    scorned by all
    and despised | by the people.
⁷All who see me laugh | me to scorn;*
    they curl their lips
    and wag | their heads, saying,
⁸"He trusted in the LORD;
  let him de- | liver him;*
    let him rescue him, if he de- | lights in him."

⁹Yet you are he
  who took me out | of the womb,*
    and kept me safe
    upon my | mother's breast.
¹⁰I have been entrusted to you
  ever since | I was born;*
    you were my God
    when I was still in my | mother's womb.
¹¹Be not far from me, for trou- | ble is near,*
  and there is | none to help.
¹²Many young bulls en- | circle me;*
    strong bulls of Ba- | shan surround me.
¹³They open wide their | jaws at me,*
  like a ravening and a | roaring lion.
¹⁴I am poured out like water;
  all my bones are | out of joint;*
    my heart within my breast is | melting wax.
¹⁵My mouth is dried out like a pot-sherd;
  my tongue sticks
  to the roof | of my mouth;*
    and you have laid me
    in the dust | of the grave.
¹⁶Packs of dogs close me in,
  and gangs of evildoers cir- | cle around me;*
    they pierce my hands and my feet,
    I can count | all my bones.

¹⁷They stare and gloat | over me;*
    they divide my garments among them;
    they cast lots | for my clothing.
¹⁸Be not far a- | way, O LORD;*
    you are my strength; hast- | en to help me.

¹⁹Save me | from the sword,*
    my life from the power | of the dog.
²⁰Save me from the | lion's mouth,*
    my wretched body
    from the horns | of wild bulls.
²¹I will declare your name | to my brethren;*
    in the midst of the congregation |
    I will praise you.
²²Praise the LORD, | you that fear him;*
    stand in awe of him,
    O offspring of Israel;
    all you of Jacob's | line, give glory.
²³For he does not despise
  nor abhor the poor in their poverty;
  neither does he hide his | face from them;*
    but when they cry to | him he hears them.
²⁴My praise is of him in the | great assembly;*
    I will perform my vows
    in the presence of those
    who | worship him.

²⁵The poor shall eat and be satisfied,
  and those who seek the | LORD
  shall praise him:*
    "May your heart | live forever!"
²⁶All the ends of the earth shall remember
  and turn | to the LORD,*
    and all the families of the nations
    shall | bow before him.
²⁷For kingship belongs | to the LORD;*
    he rules o- | ver the nations.
²⁸To him alone all who sleep in the earth
  bow | down in worship;*
    all who go down to the dust |
    fall before him.
²⁹My soul shall live for him;
  my descend- | ants shall serve him;*
    they shall be known
    as the | LORD's forever.
³⁰They shall come and make known
  to a people | yet unborn*
    the saving deeds that | he has done.

Music: Rawn Harbor, refrain; *Lutheran Book of Worship*, tone 7
Refrain © 1987 Rawn Harbor; tone © 1978 *Lutheran Book of Worship*

The Lord Is My Shepherd
Psalm 23

3

The LORD is my shep - herd; there is noth - ing I shall want.

¹The LORD is my shepherd;*
    I shall not | be in want.
²He makes me lie down | in green pastures*
    and leads me be- | side still waters.
³He re- | vives my soul*
    and guides me along right pathways |
    for his name's sake.

⁴Though I walk through the valley
    of the shadow of death,
    I shall | fear no evil;*

for you are with me;
    your rod and your staff,
    they | comfort me.
⁵You spread a table before me
    in the presence of those who | trouble me;*
    you have anointed my head with oil,
    and my cup is | running over.
⁶Surely your goodness and mercy
    shall follow me all the days | of my life,*
    and I will dwell in the house
    of the | LORD forever.

Music: Leon C. Roberts, refrain; *Psalter for Worship*, tone 37
Refrain © 1987 Leon C. Roberts; tone © 1996 Augsburg Fortress

Lift Up Your Heads

Psalm 24

Lift up your heads, O gates, and en-ter, O King, O King of glo-ry. King of glo-ry.

1. The earth is the LORD's and all | that is in it,*
   the world and all who | dwell therein.
2. For it is he who founded it up- | on the seas*
   and made it firm upon the rivers | of the deep.
3. "Who can ascend the hill | of the LORD*
   and who can stand in his | holy place?"
4. "Those who have clean hands and | a pure heart,*
   who have not pledged themselves to
   falsehood, nor sworn by what | is a fraud.
5. They shall receive a blessing | from the LORD*
   and a just reward
   from the God of | their salvation."

6. Such is the generation of | those who seek him,*
   of those who seek your face,
   O | God of Jacob.
7. Lift up your heads, O gates;
   lift them high, O ever- | lasting doors;*
   and the King of glory | shall come in.
8. "Who is this | King of glory?"*
   "The LORD, strong and mighty,
   the LORD, might- | y in battle."
9. Lift up your heads, O gates;
   lift them high, O ever- | lasting doors;*
   and the King of glory | shall come in.
10. "Who is he, this | King of glory?"*
    "The LORD of hosts, he is the | King of glory."

Music: Rawn Harbor, refrain; *Lutheran Book of Worship*, tone 3
Refrain © 1999 Augsburg Fortress; tone © 1978 *Lutheran Book of Worship*

Taste and See the Goodness of the Lord

Psalm 34

5

Taste and see the good-ness of the LORD.

Taste and see, taste and see.

¹I will bless the LORD | at all times;*
    his praise shall ever be | in my mouth.
²I will glory | in the LORD;*
    let the humble hear | and rejoice.
³Proclaim with me
the greatness | of the LORD;*
    let us exalt his | name together.
⁴I sought the Lord, and he | answered me*
    and delivered me out of | all my terror.
⁵Look upon him | and be radiant,*
    and let not your faces | be ashamed.
⁶I called in my affliction,
and | the Lord heard me*
    and saved me from | all my troubles.
⁷The angel of the LORD
encompasses | those who fear him,*
    and he will de- | liver them.
⁸Taste and see that the | LORD is good;*
    happy are they who | trust in him!

⁹Fear the LORD, you that | are his saints,*
    for those who fear | him lack nothing.
¹⁰The young lions lack and | suffer hunger,*
    but those who seek the LORD
    lack nothing | that is good.
¹¹Come, children, and lis- | ten to me;*
    I will teach you the fear | of the LORD.
¹²Who among | you loves life*
    and desires long life
    to en- | joy prosperity?

¹³Keep your tongue from | evil-speaking*
    and your lips from | lying words.
¹⁴Turn from evil | and do good;*
    seek peace | and pursue it.

¹⁵The eyes of the LORD
are up- | on the righteous,*
    and his ears are open | to their cry.
¹⁶The face of the LORD
is against those | who do evil,*
    to root out the remembrance of them |
    from the earth.
¹⁷The righteous cry,
and | the LORD hears them*
    and delivers them
    from | all their troubles.
¹⁸The LORD is near to the | brokenhearted*
    and will save those
    whose spir- | its are crushed.
¹⁹Many are the troubles | of the righteous,*
    but the LORD will deliver him
    out | of them all.
²⁰He will keep safe | all his bones;*
    not one of them | shall be broken.
²¹Evil shall | slay the wicked,*
    and those who hate the righteous |
    will be punished.
²²The LORD ransoms the life | of his servants,*
    and none will be punished
    who | trust in him.

Music: Rawn Harbor, refrain; *Psalter for Worship*, tone 27
Refrain © 1999 and tone © 1996 Augsburg Fortress

The Lord of Hosts Is with Us

Psalm 46

The LORD of hosts is with us, the God of Ja-cob our strong - hold, the God of Ja-cob our strong - hold.

[1]God is our ref- | uge and strength,*
    a very present | help in trouble.
[2]Therefore we will not fear, though the | earth be moved,*
    and though the mountains be toppled into the depths | of the sea;
[3]though its waters | rage and foam,*
    and though the mountains tremble | at its tumult.
[4]The LORD of | hosts is with us;*
    the God of Jacob | is our stronghold.

[5]There is a river whose streams make glad the cit- | y of God,*
    the holy habitation of | the Most High.
[6]God is in the midst of her; she shall not be | overthrown;*
    God shall help her at the | break of day.
[7]The nations make much ado, and the king- | doms are shaken;*
    God has spoken, and the earth shall | melt away.
[8]The LORD of | hosts is with us;*
    the God of Jacob | is our stronghold.

[9]Come now and look upon the works | of the LORD,*
    what awesome things he has | done on earth.
[10]It is he who makes war to cease in | all the world;*
    he breaks the bow, and shatters the spear, and burns the | shields with fire.
[11]"Be still, then, and know that | I am God;*
    I will be exalted among the nations; I will be exalted | in the earth."
[12]The LORD of | hosts is with us;*
    the God of Jacob | is our stronghold.

Music: Rawn Harbor, refrain; *Lutheran Book of Worship*, tone 9
Refrain © 1999 Augsburg Fortress; tone © 1978 *Lutheran Book of Worship*

Let the Peoples Praise You, O God

Psalm 67

Let the peo - ples praise you, O God, let

all the peo - ples praise you, O God.

[1]May God be merciful to | us and bless us,*
　　show us the light of his countenance, and | come to us.
[2]Let your ways be known | upon earth,*
　　your saving health a- | mong all nations.
[3]Let the peoples praise | you, O God;*
　　let all the | peoples praise you.
[4]Let the nations be glad and | sing for joy,*
　　for you judge the peoples with equity
　　and guide all the nations | upon earth.

[5]Let the peoples praise | you, O God;*
　　let all the | peoples praise you.
[6]The earth has brought | forth her increase;*
　　may God, our own God, give | us his blessing.
[7]May God give | us his blessing,*
　　and may all the ends of the earth stand in | awe of him.

Music: Rawn Harbor, refrain; *Psalter for Worship*, tone 26
Refrain © 1999 and tone © 1996 Augsburg Fortress

O Lord, Let Us See Your Kindness

Psalm 85

8

O LORD, let us see your kind-ness. O LORD, let us see your truth. O LORD, let us see your kind - ness.

We place our trust in you. you.

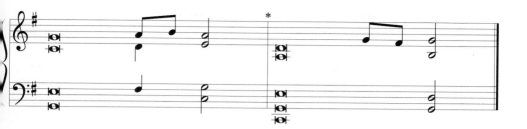

¹You have been gracious to your | land, O LORD;*
    you have restored the good for- | tune of Jacob.
²You have forgiven the iniquity | of your people*
    and blotted out | all their sins.
⁷Show us your mer- | cy, O LORD,*
    and grant us | your salvation.
⁸I will listen to what the LORD | God is saying,*
    for he is speaking peace to his faithful people
    and to those who turn their | hearts to him.
⁹Truly, his salvation is very near to | those who fear him,*
    that his glory may dwell | in our land.
¹⁰Mercy and truth have | met together;*
    righteousness and peace have | kissed each other.

¹¹Truth shall spring up | from the earth,*
    and righteousness shall look | down from heaven.
¹²The LORD will indeed | grant prosperity,*
    and our land will | yield its increase.
¹³Righteousness shall | go before him,*
    and peace shall be a pathway | for his feet.

Music: Rawn Harbor, refrain; *Psalter for Worship*, tone 52
Refrain © 1987 Rawn Harbor, tone © 1997 Augsburg Fortress

Come, Ring out Your Joy to the Lord

Psalm 95

9

Come, ring out your joy to the LORD!

Come, ring out your joy to the LORD!

ring out your joy to the LORD!

¹Come, let us sing | to the LORD;*
    let us shout for joy to the rock of | our salvation.
²Let us come before his presence | with thanksgiving*
    and raise a loud shout to | him with psalms.
³For the LORD | is a great God,*
    and a great king | above all gods.

⁴In his hand are the caverns | of the earth,*
    and the heights of the hills | are his also.
⁵The sea is his, | for he made it,*
    and his hands have molded | the dry land.
⁶Come, let us bow down and | bend the knee,*
    and kneel before the | LORD our Maker.
⁷For he is our God, and we are the people of his pasture
 and the sheep | of his hand.*
    Oh, that today you would hearken | to his voice!

⁸Harden not your hearts, as your forebears did | in the wilderness,*
    at Meribah, and on that day at Massah, when they | tempted me.
⁹They put me | to the test,*
    though they had | seen my works.
¹⁰Forty years long I detested that genera- | tion and said,*
    "This people are wayward in their hearts;
    they do not | know my ways."
¹¹So I swore | in my wrath,*
    "They shall not enter in- | to my rest."

Music: Rawn Harbor, refrain; *Psalter for Worship*, tone 22
Refrain © 1999 and tone © 1996 Augsburg Fortress

Let the Heavens Rejoice
Psalm 96

10

Let the heav-ens re-joice and the earth be glad,

re - joice, re - joice, be glad.

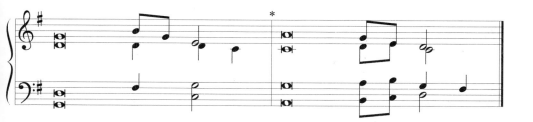

¹Sing to the LORD | a new song;*
    sing to the LORD, all | the whole earth.
²Sing to the LORD and | bless his name;*
    proclaim the good news
    of his salvation from | day to day.
³Declare his glory a- | mong the nations*
    and his wonders a- | mong all peoples.
⁴For great is the LORD and greatly | to be praised;*
    he is more to be feared | than all gods.

⁵As for all the gods of the nations, they | are but idols;*
    but it is the LORD who | made the heavens.
⁶Oh, the majesty and magnificence | of his presence!*
    Oh, the power and the splendor of his | sanctuary!
⁷Ascribe to the LORD, you families | of the peoples;*
    ascribe to the LORD hon- | or and power.
⁸Ascribe to the LORD the honor | due his name;*
    bring offerings and come in- | to his courts.
⁹Worship the LORD in the beau- | ty of holiness;*
    let the whole earth trem- | ble before him.

¹⁰Tell it out among the nations: "The | LORD is king!*
    He has made the world so firm that it cannot be moved;
    he will judge the peo- | ples with equity."
¹¹Let the heavens rejoice, and let the earth be glad;
    let the sea thunder and all | that is in it;*
    let the field be joyful and all that | is therein.
¹²Then shall all the trees of the wood shout for joy
    before the LORD | when he comes,*
    when he comes to | judge the earth.
¹³He will judge the | world with righteousness*
    and the peoples | with his truth.

Music: Rawn Harbor, refrain; *Psalter for Worship*, tone 54
Refrain © 1999 and tone © 1997 Augsburg Fortress

Bow Down before the Holy Mountain of God

Psalm 99

Bow down be-fore the ho-ly moun-tain of God, the ho-ly moun-tain of God.

[1]The LORD is king; let the | people tremble.*
  He is enthroned upon the cherubim;
  let | the earth shake.
[2]The LORD is | great in Zion;*
  he is high | above all peoples.
[3]Let them confess his name,
  which is | great and awesome;*
  he is the | Holy One.
[4]"O mighty King, lover of justice,
  you have | established equity;*
    you have executed justice
    and righteous- | ness in Jacob."
[5]Proclaim the greatness of the LORD our God
  and fall down be- | fore his footstool;*
  he is the | Holy One.

[6]Moses and Aaron among his priests,
  and Samuel among those
  who call up- | on his name,*
    they called upon the LORD,
    and he | answered them.
[7]He spoke to them out of the pil- | lar of cloud;*
  they kept his testimonies
  and the decree | that he gave them.
[8]O LORD our God,
  you answered | them indeed;*
    you were a God who forgave them,
    yet punished them for their | evil deeds.
[9]Proclaim the greatness of the LORD our God
  and worship him upon his | holy hill;*
    for the LORD our God is the | Holy One.

Music: Leon C. Roberts, refrain; *Lutheran Book of Worship*, tone 5
Refrain © 1999 Augsburg Fortress, tone © 1978 *Lutheran Book of Worship*

Indeed, How Good Is the Lord

Psalm 100

In - deed, how good is the LORD,

who is faith - ful from age to age.

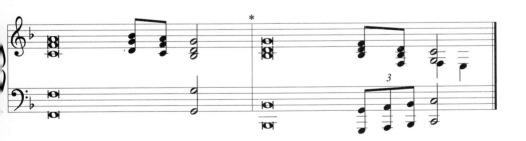

[1]Be joyful in the LORD, | all you lands;*
   serve the LORD with gladness
   and come before his presence | with a song.
[2]Know this: The LORD him- | self is God;*
   he himself has made us, and we are his;
   we are his people
   and the sheep | of his pasture.

[3]Enter his gates with thanksgiving;
   go into his | courts with praise;*
   give thanks to him and call up- | on his name.
[4]For the LORD is good;
   his mercy is | everlasting;*
   and his faithfulness endures
   from | age to age.

Music: Leon C. Roberts, refrain; *Psalter for Worship*, tone 37
Refrain © 1999 and tone © 1996 Augsburg Fortress

Lord, Send Out Your Spirit!

Psalm 104

13

LORD, send out your Spir - it!

LORD, send out your Spir - it!

LORD, send out your Spir- it! and re - new the face of the

earth.

²⁵O Lord, how manifold | are your works!*
  In wisdom you have made them all;
  the earth is full | of your creatures.
²⁶Yonder is the great and wide sea
 with its living things too man- | y to number,*
  creatures both | small and great.
²⁷There move the ships, and there is | that Leviathan,*
  which you have made for the | sport of it.
²⁸All of them | look to you*
  to give them their food | in due season.

²⁹You give it to them; they | gather it;*
  you open your hand,
  and they are filled | with good things.
³⁰You hide your face, and | they are terrified;*
  you take away their breath,
  and they die and return | to their dust.
³¹You send forth your Spirit, and they | are created;*
  and so you renew the face | of the earth.
³²May the glory of the Lord en- | dure forever;*
  may the Lord rejoice in | all his works.

³³He looks at the earth | and it trembles;*
  he touches the mountains | and they smoke.
³⁴I will sing to the Lord as long | as I live;*
  I will praise my God while I | have my being.
³⁵May these words | of mine please him;*
  I will rejoice | in the Lord.
³⁷Bless the Lord, | O my soul.*
  Hal- | lelujah!

Music: Rawn Harbor, refrain; *Lutheran Book of Worship*, tone 9
Refrain © 1987 Rawn Harbor; tone © 1978 *Lutheran Book of Worship*

I Will Call Upon the Name of the Lord

Psalm 116

I will call up - on the name of the LORD,

call up - on the name of the LORD.

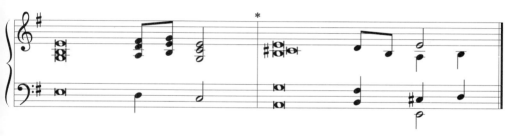

¹I love the LORD, because he has heard
  the voice of my | supplication,*
        because he has inclined his ear to me
        whenever I | called upon him.
²The cords of death entangled me;
  the grip of the grave took | hold of me;*
  I came to | grief and sorrow.
³Then I called
  upon the name | of the LORD:*
        "O LORD, I pray you, | save my life."

⁴Gracious is the | LORD and righteous;*
        our God is full | of compassion.
⁵The LORD watches o- | ver the innocent;*
        I was brought very low, |
        and he helped me.
⁶Turn again to your rest, | O my soul.*
        for the LORD has treat- | ed you well.
⁷For you have rescued
  my | life from death,*
        my eyes from tears,
        and my | feet from stumbling.
⁸I will walk in the presence | of the LORD*
        in the land | of the living.
⁹I believed, even when I said,
  "I have been brought | very low."*
        In my distress I said,
        "No one | can be trusted."

¹⁰How shall I re- | pay the LORD*
        for all the good things
        he has | done for me?
¹¹I will lift up the cup | of salvation*
        and call upon the name | of the LORD.
¹²I will fulfill my vows | to the LORD*
        in the presence of | all his people.
¹³Precious in the sight | of the LORD*
        is the death | of his servants.
¹⁴O LORD, I | am your servant;*
        I am your servant
        and the child of your handmaid;
        you have freed me | from my bonds.

¹⁵I will offer you the sacrifice |
  of thanksgiving*
        and call upon the name | of the LORD.
¹⁶I will fulfill my vows | to the LORD*
        in the presence of | all his people,
¹⁷in the courts of | the LORD's house,*
        in the midst of you, O Jerusalem. |
        Hallelujah!

Music: Leon C. Roberts, refrain; *Psalter for Worship*, tone 39
Refrain © 1999 and tone © 1996 Augsburg Fortress

The Lord Is My Strength
Psalm 118

The LORD is my strength, my strength and my song. The song.

¹Give thanks to the LORD, for | he is good;*
  his mercy en- | dures forever.
²Let Israel | now proclaim,*
  "His mercy en- | dures forever."
¹⁴The LORD is my strength | and my song,*
  and he has become | my salvation.
¹⁵There is a sound
  of exulta- | tion and victory*
  in the tents | of the righteous:
¹⁶"The right hand of the | LORD
  has triumphed!*
  The right hand of the LORD is exalted!
  The right hand of the | LORD
  has triumphed!"

¹⁷I shall not | die, but live,*
  and declare the works | of the LORD.
¹⁸The LORD has pun- | ished me sorely,*
  but he did not hand me o- | ver to death.
¹⁹Open for me the | gates of righteousness;*
  I will enter them;
  I will offer thanks | to the LORD.
²⁰"This is the gate | of the LORD;*
  he who is righ- | teous may enter."

²¹I will give thanks to you,
  for you | answered me*
  and have become | my salvation.
²²The same stone
  which the build- | ers rejected*
  has become the chief | cornerstone.
²³This is | the LORD's doing,*
  and it is marvelous | in our eyes.
²⁴On this day the | LORD has acted;*
  we will rejoice and be | glad in it.

²⁵Hosanna, | LORD, hosanna!*
  LORD, send us | now success.
²⁶Blessed is he
  who comes in the name | of the Lord;*
  we bless you
  from the house | of the LORD.
²⁷God is the LORD;
  he has | shined upon us;*
  form a procession with branches
  up to the horns | of the altar.
²⁸"You are my God, and | I will thank you;*
  you are my God, and I | will exalt you."
²⁹Give thanks to the LORD,
  for | he is good;*
  his mercy en- | dures forever.

Music: Leon C. Roberts, refrain; *Psalter for Worship*, tone 27
Refrain © 1999, tone © 1996 Augsburg Fortress

My Help Shall Come from the Lord

Psalm 121

16

My help shall come from the LORD who made heav-en and earth.

¹I lift up my eyes | to the hills;*
 from where is my | help to come?
²My help comes | from the LORD,*
 the maker of heav- | en and earth.
³He will not let your | foot be moved*
 and he who watches over you
 will not | fall asleep.

⁴Behold, he who keeps watch | over Israel*
 shall neither slum- | ber nor sleep;
⁵the LORD himself watches | over you;*
 the LORD is your shade at | your right hand,
⁶so that the sun shall not strike | you by day,*
 nor the | moon by night.
⁷The LORD shall preserve you | from all evil;*
 it is he who shall | keep you safe.
⁸The LORD shall watch over
your going out and your | coming in,*
 from this time forth for- | evermore.

Music: Leon C. Roberts, refrain; *Lutheran Book of Worship*, tone 4
Refrain © 1999 Augsburg Fortress, tone © 1978 *Lutheran Book of Worship*

Let Us Go Rejoicing

Psalm 122

Let us go re - joic- ing to the house of the LORD. Al- le - lu - ia! in- to the house of the LORD.

[*]

¹I was glad when they | said to me,*
 "Let us go to the house | of the LORD."
²Now our | feet are standing*
 within your gates, | O Jerusalem.
³Jerusalem is built | as a city*
 that is at unity | with itself;
⁴to which the tribes go up,
 the tribes | of the LORD,*
 the assembly of Israel,
 to praise the name | of the LORD.

⁵For there are the | thrones of judgment,*
 the thrones of the | house of David.
⁶Pray for the peace | of Jerusalem:*
 "May they pros- | per who love you.
⁷Peace be with- | in your walls*
 and quietness with- | in your towers.
⁸For my brethren and com- | panions' sake,*
 I pray for | your prosperity.
⁹Because of the house
 of the | LORD our God,*
 I will seek to | do you good."

Music: Rawn Harbor, refrain; *Lutheran Book of Worship*, tone 3
Refrain © 1987 Rawn Harbor; tone © 1978 *Lutheran Book of Worship*

Let My Prayer Arise before You

Psalm 141

18

Let my prayer a - rise be - fore you,

a - rise be - fore you like in - cense.

[1]O LORD, I call to you;
 come | to me quickly;*
  hear my voice when I | cry to you.
[2]Let my prayer be set forth
 in your | sight as incense,*
  the lifting up of my hands
  as the | evening sacrifice.

[3]Set a watch before my mouth, O LORD,
 and guard the door | of my lips;*
  let not my heart
  incline to any | evil thing.
[4]Let me not be occupied
 in wickedness with | evildoers,*
  nor eat of | their choice foods.
[8]But my eyes are turned to | you,
 Lord GOD;*
  in you I take refuge;
  do not strip me | of my life.

Music: Leon C. Roberts, refrain; *Lutheran Book of Worship*, tone 1
Refrain © 1999 Augsburg Fortress, tone © 1978 *Lutheran Book of Worship*

Let Everything Give Praise to the Lord

Psalm 150

19

Let ev - 'ry - thing give praise to the LORD.

Al - le - lu - ia!

[1]Hallelujah!
 Praise God in his | holy temple;*
  praise him
  in the firmament | of his power.
[2]Praise him for his | mighty acts;*
  praise him for his ex- | cellent greatness.
[3]Praise him with the blast |
 of the ram's horn;*
  praise him with | lyre and harp.

[4]Praise him with tim- | brel and dance;*
  praise him with | strings and pipe.
[5]Praise him with re- | sounding cymbals;*
  praise him with loud- | clanging cymbals.
[6]Let everything | that has breath*
  praise the Lord. | Hallelujah!

Music: Leon C. Roberts, refrain; *Psalter for Worship*, tone 37
Refrain © 1999 and tone © 1996 Augsburg Fortress

Kyrie

20

Lord, Have Mercy

1,3 Ky - ri - e e - le - i - son. Ky - ri - e e - le - i - son.
2 Chris - te e - le - i - son. Chris - te e - le - i - son.
1,3 Lord, ... have mer - cy. Lord, ... have mer - cy.
2 Christ, . . . have mer - cy. Christ, ... have mer - cy.

Ky - ri - e e - le - i - son. Ky - ri - e e - le - i - son.
Chris - te e - le - i - son. Chris - te e - le - i - son.
Lord, ... have mer - cy. Lord, ... have mer - cy.
Christ, . . . have mer - cy. Christ, ... have mer - cy.

Music: Dinah Reindorf; arr. *With One Voice,* 1995
Tune © 1987 Dinah Reindorf
Arr. © 1995 Augsburg Fortress

21

Lord, Have Mercy

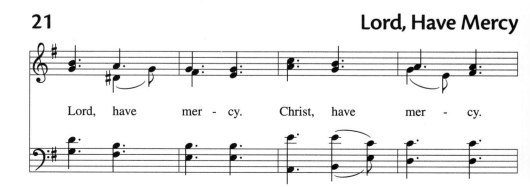

Lord, have mer - cy. Christ, have mer - cy.

Lord, have mer - cy; have mer - cy, O Lord.

Music: Avon Gillespie
Music © 1987 GIA Publications, Inc.

Lord, Have Mercy

Nkosi, Nkosi

22

Lord, have mer - cy; have mer - cy up - on us.
Nko - si, Nko - si, yi - ba nen - ce - ba.

Christ, have mer - cy; have mer - cy up - on us.
Kres - tu, Kres - tu, yi - ba nen - ce - ba.

Lord, have mer - cy; have mer - cy up - on us.
Nko - si, Nko - si, yi - ba nen - ce - ba.

Music: G. M. Kolisi
Music © 1984 Utryck, admin. Walton Music Corp.

Lord, Have Mercy

Señor, ten piedad

23

Ⅰ Lord, have mer-cy. Have
Se - ñor, ten pie- dad.

Ⅱ Lord, have mer-cy.
Se - ñor, ten pie- dad.

mer - cy on us, Christ.
Cris - to, ten pie - dad.

Have mer - cy on us, Christ.
Cris - to, ten pie - dad.

Lord, have mer- cy.
Se - ñor, ten pie- dad.

Lord,
Se - ñor,

Lord, have mer- cy, Lord.
Se - ñor, ten pie-dad, Se - ñor.

have mer- cy. Have mer- cy, Lord.
ten pie-dad. Ten pie-dad, Se - ñor.

Music: José Ruiz, b. 1956; arr. Orlando Laureano
Music © 1995 Augsburg Fortress

24

Glory to God

Refrain

Glo - ry to God. Glo - ry to God.

Glo - ry to God in the high - est.

Last time to coda ⊕

Glo - ry to God. Glo - ry to God, and

To stanzas 1, 2 | *To stanza 3*

peace to his peo - ple on all the earth. earth.

Text: International Consultation on English Texts
Music: Grayson Warren Brown; arr. Val Parker
Music © 1985 North American Liturgy Resources, admin. OCP Publications

25   Halle, Halle, Hallelujah

Hal - le, hal - le, hal - le - lu - jah!

Hal - le, hal - le, hal - le - lu - jah!

Hal - le - lu - jah!

Hal - le, hal - le, hal - le - lu - jah!

Hal - le - lu - jah! Hal - le - lu - jah!

Music: Caribbean traditional; arr. Mark Sedio, b. 1954
Arr. © 1995 Augsburg Fortress

Alleluia

Al - le - lu - ia, al - le - lu - ia. Al - le - lu - ia, al - le - lu - ia.

Al - le - lu - ia, al - le - lu - ia. Al - le - lu - ia, al - le - lu - ia.

Music: South African; arr. Gobingca Mxadana
Arr. © Gobingca Mxadana

Hallelujah

Hal - le - lu - jah, hal - le - lu - jah,

hal-le-lu-jah, hal-le-lu-jah, hal-le-lu-jah, hal-le-lu-jah.

Music: Fernando G. Allen
Music © 1987 Fernando G. Allen

28

Let the Vineyards Be Fruitful

Let the vine - yards be fruit - ful, Lord, and

fill to the brim our cup of bless - ing.

Gath- er a har-vest from the seeds that were sown, that

we may be fed with the bread of life.

Gath-er the hopes and dreams of all; u-nite them with the prayers we of-fer.

Grace our ta-ble with your pres-ence; give us a fore-taste of the feast to come.

Text: John Arthur, 1922-1980
Music: Tillis Butler and James Harris, *Detroit Folk Mass*

Text © 1978 *Lutheran Book of Worship*
Music © 1986 Fortress Press

29

Holy, Holy, Holy Lord

Ho- ly, ho - ly, ho - ly Lord,

God of pow- er and might,

heav'n and earth are full of your

glo - ry. Ho-

san - na in the high - est, ho -
san - na in the high - est.
Bless-ed is he who comes in the name of the Lord. Ho -
san - na in the high - est.

Text: International Consultation on English Texts
Music: Michael Hassell, b. 1952
Music © 1995 Augsburg Fortress

30   **Acclamations**

Christ has died. Christ is ris - en.
A - men. Come, Lord Je - sus.
A - men. Come, Ho - ly Spir - it.

Christ will come a - gain.
Come, Lord Je - sus, come.
Ho - ly Spir - it, come.

Music: Michael Hassell, b. 1952
Music © 1995 Augsburg Fortress

31   **Amen**

A - men, a - men, a - men.

Music: Michael Hassell, b. 1952
Music © 1995 Augsburg Fortress

Holy, Holy, Holy Lord

32

1 Ho - ly, ho - ly, ho - ly ho - ly,
2 Bless-ed is he who comes in the name . . . . . .

ho - ly Lord, God of pow-er and might,
of the Lord, in the name of the Lord.

heav-en and earth are full of your glo - ry.
Ho - san - na in . . . . the high - est,

Ho - san - na in the high - est.
ho - san - na in the high - est.

Text: International Consultation on English Texts
Music: Grayson Warren Brown; arr. Larry Adams
Music © 1979 Grayson Warren Brown, admin. by OCP Publications

Our Father, Who Art in Heaven

The Lord's Prayer

33

Our Fa - ther, who art in heav - en, hal - low-ed be

thy name, thy king - dom come, thy will be

done, on earth as it is in heav - en.

Give us this day our dai - ly bread; and for -

Let the Words of My Mouth

The Lord's Prayer

34

Let the words of my mouth, let the words of my mouth
and the med-i-ta-tions of my heart be ac-cept-a-ble in thy sight;
wilt thou teach me how to serve thee, wilt thou teach me how to pray?

Our Father, who art in heaven, hallowed be thy name,
Give us this day our dai - ly bread;
and lead us not into temptation, but deliver us from evil.

thy kingdom come, thy will be done, on earth as it is in heav-en.
and forgive us our trespasses, as we forgive those who tres - pass a - gainst us;
For thine is the kingdom, and the power, and the glory, for - ever and . . . ever. A - men . . .

Text: Ps. 19:14, Matt. 6:9-13, adapt.
Music: C. E. Leslie

Lamb of God

Lamb of God, you take a-way the sin of the world; have mer-cy on us. Lamb of God, you take a-way the sin of the world; have mer-cy on us. Lamb of God, you take a-way the sin of the world; grant us peace, grant us peace.

Text: International Consultation on English Texts
Music: Tillis Butler and James Harris, *Detroit Folk Mass*
Music © 1986 Fortress Press

36

O Lamb of God

O Lamb of God, you take a - way

the sin of the world;

have mer - cy and grant us peace,

we pray, O Lamb of God.

Text: traditional
Music: Grayson Warren Brown; arr. Larry Adams
Music © 1979 Grayson Warren Brown, admin. by OCP Publications

HYMNS AND SONGS

He Came Down   37

1 He came down that we may have love; he came down that we may have love;
2 He came down that we may have light; he came down that we may have light;
3 He came down that we may have peace; he came down that we may have peace;
4 He came down that we may have joy; he came down that we may have joy;

he came down that we may have love;
he came down that we may have light;
he came down that we may have peace;   hal - le - lu - jah for - ev - er - more.
he came down that we may have joy;

Text: Cameroon traditional
Music: HE CAME DOWN, Cameroon traditional; arr. John L. Bell, b. 1949
Arr. © 1986 Iona Community, admin. GIA Publications, Inc.

38

Soon and Very Soon

1 Soon and ver - y soon
2 No more cry - in' there,
3 No more dy - in' there,
4 Soon and ver - y soon
    we are goin' to see the King,

soon and ver - y soon
no more cry - in' there,
no more dy - in' there,
soon and ver - y soon
    we are goin' to see the King,

soon and ver - y soon
no more cry - in' there,
no more dy - in' there,
soon and ver - y soon
    we are goin' to see the King.

1, 2

Hal - le - lu - jah, hal - le - lu - jah, we're goin' to see the King!

Text: Andraé Crouch, b. 1945
Music: VERY SOON, Andraé Crouch, b. 1945

© 1976 Bud John Songs, Inc./Crouch Music, admin. EMI Christian Music Publishing

He's Right on Time

39

He may not come
when you want him
but he's right on time.

Anonymous, from North America

40 My Lord, What a Morning

Refrain

My Lord, what a morn-ing; my Lord, what a morn-ing; oh,

my Lord, what a morn-ing, when the stars be-gin to fall.

1 You'll hear the trum-pet sound,
2 You'll hear the sin-ner cry, to wake the na-tions un-der - ground,
3 You'll hear the Chris-tian shout,

Refrain

look-ing to my God's right hand, when the stars be-gin to fall.

Text: African American spiritual
Music: BURLEIGH, African American spiritual

I Want to Be Ready

Refrain

I want to be read - y, I want to be read - y,

I want to be read - y to walk in Je-ru-sa-lem just like John.

1 John said that Je - ru - sa - lem was four- square,
2 When Pe- ter was preach-ing at Pen - te - cost,
walk in Je-ru-sa-lem just like John,

Refrain

I know, good Lord, I'll meet you there,
oh, he was filled with the Ho - ly Ghost,
walk in Je-ru-sa-lem just like John.

Text: African American spiritual
Music: African American spiritual; arr. R. Nathaniel Dett, 1882-1943
Arr. © 1936 Paul A. Schmitt Music Co.; assigned to Belwin Mills, admin. CPP/Belwin Inc.

42

Come by Here

1 Come by here, Lord, come by here;
2 Some - one needs you, Lord, come by here;
3 Send a bless - ing, Lord, come by here;

come by here, Lord, come by here;
some - one needs you, Lord, come by here;
send a bless - ing, Lord, come by here;

come by here, Lord, come by here.
some - one needs you, Lord, come by here.
send a bless - ing, Lord, come by here.

Text: traditional
Music: KUM BA YAH, traditional; arr. Richard Smallwood
Arr. © 1975 Century Oak/Richwood Music

Come by Here   43

1 Come by here, my Lord, come by here; come by here, my Lord, come by here;
2 Some-one's cry - ing, Lord, come by here; some-one's cry - ing, Lord, come by here;
3 Some-one's sing - ing, Lord, come by here; some-one's sing - ing, Lord, come by here;
4 Some-one's pray- ing, Lord, come by here; some-one's pray - ing, Lord, come by here;
5 Some-one needs you, Lord, come by here; some - one needs you, Lord, come by here;

come by   here, my Lord, come by   here; O   Lord,   come by   here.
some-one's cry - ing, Lord, come by   here; O   Lord,   come by   here.
some-one's sing - ing, Lord, come by   here; O   Lord,   come by   here.
some-one's pray - ing, Lord, come by   here; O   Lord,   come by   here.
some-one needs you, Lord, come by   here; O   Lord,   come by   here.

Text: traditional
Music: KUM BA YAH, traditional

44   # Somebody's Knockin' at Your Door

Some-bod-y's knock-in' at your door; some-bod-y's knock-in' at your door;

O   sin-ner, why don't you an-swer? Some-bod-y's knock-in' at your door.

1 Knocks like   Je - sus.
2 Can't   you   hear him?
3 Je - sus   calls you.
4 Can't   you   trust him?

Some - bod - y's knock-in' at your door.

Knocks like   Je - sus.
Can't   you   hear him?
Je - sus   calls you.
Can't   you   trust him?

Some - bod - y's knock-in' at your door;

O sin-ner, why don't you an-swer? Some-bod-y's knock-in' at your door.

Text: African American spiritual
Music: African American spiritual; arr. Richard Proulx, b. 1937
Arr. © 1986 GIA Publications

Emmanuel

Em-man-u-el, Em-man-u-el,

his name is called Em-man-u-el;

God with us, re-vealed in us;

his name is called Em-man-u-el.

Text: Bob McGee, b. 1944
Music: McGEE, Bob McGee, b. 1944
© 1976 C.A. Music (div. of Christian Artists Corp.)

46 Freedom Is Coming

1 Oh, free - dom, oh, free - dom, oh,
2 Oh, Je - sus, oh, Je - sus, oh,

1 Free-dom is com - ing, free-dom is
2 Je - sus is com - ing, Je - sus is

free - dom. Oh,
Je - sus. Oh,

com - ing, free-dom is com - ing, oh, yes, I
com - ing, Je - sus is com - ing, oh, yes, I

free - dom, oh, free - dom, oh,
Je - sus, oh, Je - sus, oh,

know. Free-dom is com - ing, free-dom is
know. Je - sus is com - ing, Je - sus is

free - dom. Oh,
Je - sus.

com - ing, free-dom is com - ing, oh, yes, I
com - ing, Je - sus is com - ing, oh, yes, I

All Earth Is Hopeful
Toda la tierra

1 All earth is hope-ful, the Sav - ior comes at last!
2 Peo - ple of Is - rael, you heard the proph - et tell:
3 Moun-tains and val - leys will have to be pre - pared;
4 We first saw Je - sus a ba - by in a crib.

Fur - rows lie o - pen for God's cre - a - tive task: this, the
"A vir - gin moth - er will bear Em - man - u - el"; she con -
new high-ways o - pened, new pro - to - cols de - clared. Al - most
This same Lord Je - sus to - day has come to live in our

la - bor of peo - ple who strug - gle to see how
ceived him, "God with us," our broth - er, whose birth re -
here! God is near - ing, in beau - ty and grace! All
world; he is pres - ent, in neigh - bors we see our

1–3

God's trust and jus - tice set ev - 'ry - bod - y free.
stores hope and cour - age to chil - dren of this earth.
clear ev - 'ry gate - way, in haste, come out in haste!
Je - sus is with us, and

4

ev - er sets us free.

1 Toda la tierra espera al Salvador
  y el surco abierto, la obra del Señor;
  es el mundo que lucha por la libertad,
  reclama justicia y busca la verdad.

2 Dice el profeta al pueblo de Israel:
  "De madre virgen ya viene Emmanuel,"
  será "Dios con nosotros," hermano será,
  con él la esperanza al mundo volverá.

3 Montes y valles habrá que preparar;
  nuevos caminos tenemos que trazar.
  Él está ya muy cerca, venidlo a encontrar,
  y todas las puertas abrid de par en par.

4 En una cueva Jesús apareció,
  pero en el mundo está presente hoy.
  Vive en nuestros hermanos, con ellos está;
  y vuelve de nuevo a darnos libertad.

Text: Alberto Taulé, b. 1932; tr. Madeleine Forell Marshall, b. 1946
Music: TAULÉ, Alberto Taulé, b. 1932; arr. Skinner Chávez-Melo, 1944-1992
Spanish text and tune © 1972 Alberto Taulé, admin. OCP Publications
Tr. © 1995 Madeleine Forell Marshall, admin. Augsburg Fortress; arr. © Estate of Skinner Chávez-Melo

Let Justice Flow like Streams 48

1 Let   jus - tice flow   like   streams of   spark-ling wa - ter,   pure,
2 Let   righ-teous-ness roll   on   as   oth - ers' cares we   heed,
3 So   may God's plumb line, straight, de - fine   our   mea - sure true,

en - a - bling growth, re - fresh - ing life, a - bun - dant, cleans-ing, sure.
an   ev - er - flow - ing stream of faith trans-lat - ed   in - to deed.
and jus-tice, right, and   peace per-vade this world our   whole life through.

Text: Jane Parker Huber, b. 1926
Music: ST. THOMAS, Aaron Williams, 1731-1776
Text © 1984 Jane Parker Huber, admin. Westminster John Knox Press

49 On Jordan's Stormy Banks

1 On Jor-dan's storm-y banks I stand, and cast a wish-ful eye
2 All o'er those wide ex-tend-ed plains, shines one e-ter-nal day;
3 No chill-ing winds or pois'nous breath can reach that health-ful shore;
4 When shall I reach that hap-py place, and be for-ev-er blest?

to Ca-naan's fair and hap-py land, where my pos-ses-sions lie.
there God the Son for-ev-er reigns, and scat-ters night a-way.
sick-ness and sor-row, pain and death, are felt and feared no more.
When shall I see my Sav-ior's face, and in God's bo-som rest?

Refrain

I am bound for the prom-ised land, I am bound for the prom-ised land;

oh, who will come and go with me? I am bound for the prom-ised land.

Text: Samuel Stennett, 1727-1795
Music: PROMISED LAND, *Southern Harmony,* 1835; adapt. Rigdon M. McIntosh, 1836-1899; arr. Norman Johnson
Arr. © 1968 Singspiration Music, admin. Brentwood-Benson Music Publishing, Inc.

I Wonder As I Wander

1 I won - der as I wan - der, out un - der the sky, how
2 When Mar - y birthed . . Je - sus, all in a cow's stall, came
3 If Je - sus had . . . . want - ed for an - y wee thing, a
4 I won - der as I wan - der, out un - der the sky, how

Je - sus the Sav - ior did come for to die for
wise men and farm - ers and shep - herds and all, and
star in the sky or a bird on the wing, or
Je - sus the Sav - ior did come for to die for

poor ord' - n'ry peo - ple like you and like I. I
high from the heav - ens a star's light did fall; the
all of God's an - gels in heav'n for to sing, he
poor ord' - n'ry peo - ple like you and like I. I

won - der as I wan - der, out un - der the sky.
prom - ise of the a - ges it then did re - call.
sure - ly could have had it, 'cause he was the king.
won - der as I wan - der, out un - der the sky.

Text: Appalachian carol; collected by John Jacob Niles, 1892-1980
Music: I WONDER, Appalachian carol; adapt. John Jacob Niles, 1892-1980
© 1934 G. Schirmer, Inc. (ASCAP)

51 Jesus, What a Wonderful Child

Je - sus, Je - sus, oh, what a won-der-ful child.

Je - sus, Je - sus, so ho - ly, meek, and mild;

new life, new hope the child will bring.

Lis - ten to the an - gels sing,

"Glo - ry, glo - ry, glo - ry," let the heav - ens ring!

Finger snaps or claps on the off-beats may be used to fill the rests.

Text: African American traditional, alt.
Music: WONDERFUL CHILD, African American traditional; arr. Jeffrey Radford, b. 1953
Arr. © 1992 Pilgrim Press, from *The New Century Hymnal*

Go Tell It on the Mountain

52

Refrain

Go tell it on the moun - tain, o - ver the hills and ev - 'ry - where;

go tell it on the moun - tain that Je - sus Christ is born!

1 While shep-herds kept their watch-ing o'er si - lent flocks by night,
2 The shep-herds feared and trem - bled when, lo, a - bove the earth
3 Down in a lone - ly man - ger the hum - ble Christ was born;

Refrain

be - hold, through-out the heav-ens there shone a ho - ly light.
rang out the an - gel cho - rus that hailed our Sav - ior's birth.
and God sent us sal - va - tion that bless - ed Christ-mas morn.

Text: African American spiritual, refrain; John W. Work Jr., 1871-1925, stanzas, alt.
Music: GO TELL IT, African American spiritual

53   The Virgin Mary Had a Baby Boy

1 The vir - gin Mar - y had a ba - by boy, the
2 The an - gels sang . . . . when the ba - by was born, the
3 The shep - herds came . . . . where the ba - by was born, the

vir - gin Mar - y had a ba - by boy, the vir - gin Mar - y had a
an - gels sang . . when the ba - by was born, the an - gels sang. . . when the
shep - herds came . . where the ba - by was born, the shep - herds came . . where the

ba - by boy, and they say that his name is Je - sus.
ba - by was born, and they sang that his name is Je - sus.
ba - by was born, and they say that his name is Je - sus.

He come from the glo - ry, he come from the glo - rious king- dom.

Oh, yes, be- liev- er! Oh, yes, be- liev- er! He come from the

glo - ry, he come from the glo - rious king- dom.

Text: West Indian carol
Music: West Indian carol; arr. John Barnard, b. 1948
© 1945 Boosey and Company, Ltd, admin. Boosey and Hawkes, Inc.

54   # That Boy-Child of Mary

Refrain

That boy-child of Mar - y was born in a sta - ble,

a man-ger his cra - dle in Beth-le - hem.

1 What shall we call him, child of the man - ger?
2 His name is Je - sus, God ev - er with us,
3 How can he save us, how can he help us,
4 Gift of the Fa - ther, to hu - man moth - er,

Refrain

What name is giv - en in Beth-le - hem?
God giv - en for us in Beth-le - hem.
born here a - mong us in Beth-le - hem?
makes him our broth - er in Beth-le - hem.

5 One with the Father,
  he is our Savior,
  heaven-sent helper
  in Bethlehem.

6 Gladly we praise him,
  love and adore him,
  give ourselves to him
  in Bethlehem.

Text: Tom Colvin, b. 1925
Music: BLANTYRE, Malawi traditional; adapt. Tom Colvin, b. 1925
© 1969 Hope Publishing Co.

Mary Had a Baby

55

1 Mar - y had a ba - by, my Lord;
2 Where did . . . . she lay him, my Lord?
3 Laid him in a man - ger, my Lord;
4 What did . . . . she name him, my Lord?
5 Mar - y named him Je - sus, my Lord;

Mar - y had a ba - by, my Lord;
Where did . . . . she lay him, my Lord?
laid him in a mang - er, my Lord;
What did . . . . she name him, my Lord?
Mar - y named him Je - sus, my Lord;

Mar - y had a ba - by, Mar - y had a ba - by,
Where did . . . she lay him, where did . . . she lay him,
laid him in a man - ger, laid him in a man - ger,
What did . . . she name him, what did . . . she name him,
Mar - y named him Je - sus, Mar - y named him Je - sus,

Mar - y had a ba - by, my Lord.
where did . . . . she lay him, my Lord?
laid him in a man - ger, my Lord.
what did . . . . she name him, my Lord?
Mar - y named him Je - sus, my Lord.

Text: African American spiritual
Music: African American spiritual; arr. David N. Johnson, 1922-1987
Arr. © 1970 Augsburg Publishing House

Hush, Little Jesus Boy

Yesu, ulale

56

Leader / All

1 Hush, lit - tle Je - sus boy, hal - le - lu - jah.
1 Ye - su, u - la - le, ha - le - lu - ya.
2 Sleep, lit - tle Je - sus boy, hal - le - lu - jah.
2 La - la, ee Ye - su, ha - le - lu - ya.

Leader / All

Hush, lit - tle Je - sus boy, hal - le - lu - jah.
Ye - su, u - la - le, ha - le - lu - ya.
Sleep, lit - tle Je - sus boy, hal - le - lu - jah.
La - la, ee Ye - su, ha - le - lu - ya.

Leader / All

Dry your tears, Je - sus boy, hal - le - lu - jah.
Tu - li - a, mwa - na, ha - le - lu - ya.
Close your eyes, Je - sus boy, hal - le - lu - jah.
U - fu - mbe ma - cho, ha - le - lu - ya.

Leader / All

Dry your tears, Je - sus boy, hal - le - lu - jah.
Tu - li - a, mwa - na, ha - le - lu - ya.
Close your eyes, Je - sus boy, hal - le - lu - jah.
U - fu - mbe ma - cho, ha - le - lu - ya.

Leader / All

Sweet child of Mar - y, hal - le - lu - jah.
Mwa - na wa Ma - ri - a, ha - le - lu - ya.
Good seed of A - bra - ham, hal - le - lu - jah.
Mza - o wa I - bra - him, ha - le - lu - ya.

Leader / All

Strong son of Da - vid, hal - le - lu - jah.
Mwa - na wa Da - u - di, ha - le - lu - ya.
Great hope of I - saac, hal - le - lu - jah.
Ha - mu wa I - sa - ka, ha - le - lu - ya.

Trea - sure	of	Jo -	seph,	hal - le - lu - jah.
Shi - na	*la*	*Ye -*	*se,*	*ha - le - lu - ya.*
True heir	of	Ja -	cob,	hal - le - lu - jah.
Mri - thi	*wa*	*Ya - ko -*	*bo,*	*ha - le - lu - ya.*

Hal - le - lu-jah, hal - le - lu-jah, most ho - ly child, sweet in - deed.
Ha - le - lu - ya, ha - le - lu - ya, m - to - to wee, mwe - ma tu.

God has des-tined you peace to bring that we may con-fess and be-lieve in your name.
Ki - la a - na - ye - ku - a - mi - ni u - ta - mga - wi - a a - ma - ni - kuu.

Text: Ilyamba from *Membo ma Kiklisto*, anon.; tr. Howard S. Olson, b. 1922
Music: YESU ULALE, Ilyamba traditional

Feet o' Jesus

57

At the feet o' Jesus,
Sorrow like a sea.
Lordy, let yo' mercy
Come driftin' down on me.

At the feet o' Jesus
At yo' feet I stand.
O my little Jesus,
Please reach out yo' hand.

Langston Hughes, 1902-1967, "Feet o' Jesus"

There's a Star in the East

Rise Up, Shepherd, and Follow

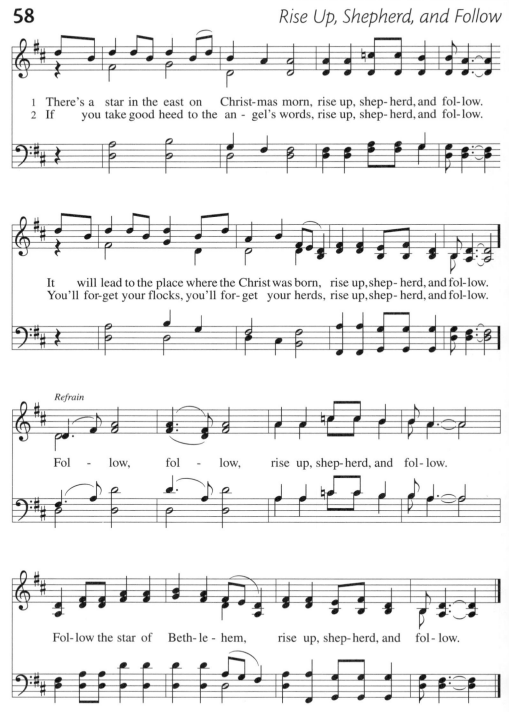

1 There's a star in the east on Christ-mas morn, rise up, shep-herd, and fol-low.
2 If you take good heed to the an - gel's words, rise up, shep-herd, and fol-low.

It will lead to the place where the Christ was born, rise up, shep- herd, and fol-low.
You'll for-get your flocks, you'll for- get your herds, rise up, shep- herd, and fol-low.

Refrain

Fol - low, fol - low, rise up, shep-herd, and fol-low.

Fol-low the star of Beth-le - hem, rise up, shep-herd, and fol-low.

Text: African American spiritual
Music: RISE UP, SHEPHERD, African American spiritual

Jesus, the Light of the World

We'll Walk in the Light

1 Hark! the her - ald an - gels sing, Je- sus, the Light of the world;
2 Joy - ful, all you na - tions, rise, Je- sus, the Light of the world;
3 Christ, by high - est heav'n a - dored, Je- sus, the Light of the world;
4 Hail the heav'n- born Prince of Peace! Je- sus, the Light of the world;

"Glo - ry to the new - born King," Je- sus, the Light of the world.
join the tri - umph of the skies; Je- sus, the Light of the world.
Christ, the ev - er - last - ing Lord! Je- sus, the Light of the world.
hail the Sun of righ- teous- ness! Je- sus, the Light of the world.

Refrain

We'll walk in the light, beau- ti- ful light, come where the dew- drops of mer- cy are bright.

Shine all a- round us by day and by night, Je- sus, the Light of the world.

Text: Charles Wesley, 1707-1788; addl. text "J.V.C."; adapt. George Elderkin
Music: JESUS, THE LIGHT OF THE WORLD, traditional; arr. George Elderkin

60   **Sister Mary**

Sis-ter Mar-y had - a but one child born in Beth-le-hem,

and-a ev-e-ry time the lit-tle ba - by cried, she

rocked him in a wea-ry land, she rocked him in a wea-ry land.

1 Oh,   three wise men   to Je - ru - sa - lem came,   they'd
2 King   Her - od   mar - velled; his heart . . . was   troub-led, ...
3 Oh,   three wise men   to . . . . Beth - le - hem came, . . . they'd
4 Sis - ter an - gel ap- peared to . . . . Jo   -   seph, . . . and

trav - eled ver - y far.   They said, "Where is he born
and his face was grim.   He said, "Tell me where the
trav - eled ver - y far.   They said, "Where is he born
gave him this com - mand: "A - rise now, take your

king of the Jews?   For we have seen his
child may be found;   I'll go and wor - ship
king of the Jews?   For we have seen his
wife and your child;   go flee in - to E - gypt

Refrain

star, for we have seen his star."
him, I'll go and wor - ship him."
star, for we have seen his star."
land, go flee in - to E - gypt land."

Text: African American spiritual
Music: African American spiritual, arr. *This Far by Faith*
Arr. © 1999 Augsburg Fortress

61 The Lord Is My Light

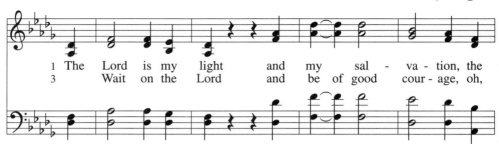

1 The Lord is my light and my sal - va - tion, the
3 Wait on the Lord and be of good cour - age, oh,

Lord is my light and my sal - va - tion, the Lord is my
wait on the Lord and be of good cour - age, . . . wait on the

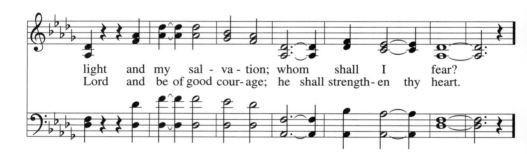

light and my sal - va - tion; whom shall I fear?
Lord and be of good cour - age; he shall strength - en thy heart.

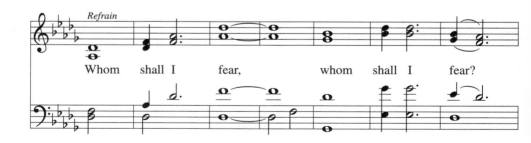

Refrain

Whom shall I fear, whom shall I fear?

The Lord is the strength of my life; whom shall I fear?

2 In the time of trou-ble, he shall hide me; oh, in the time of trou-ble, he shall hide me; in the time of trou-ble,

D.C. (to stanza 3)

he shall hide me; whom shall I fear?

Text: Psalm 27; adapt. Lillian Bouknight
Music: Lillian Bouknight; arr. Paul Gainer

I Heard the Voice of Jesus Say

Shine on Me

62

1 I heard the voice of Je - sus say, "Come
2 With pit - y - ing eyes the Prince of Peace be -

un - to me and rest, and rest; lay down, thou wea - ry
held our help - less grief, our grief; he saw, and oh, a -

one, lay down thy head up - on my breast."
maz - ing love! He came to our re - lief.

Refrain

Shine on me, shine on me, let the light from the

light - house   shine on   me.   Oh,   shine on   me,   shine   on

me,   let the   light from the   light-house   shine   on   me.

Text: Horatius Bonar, 1808-1889, adapt.
Music: traditional; arr. J. Jefferson Cleveland, 1937-1986 and Verolga Nix, b. 1933

We Are Marching in the Light of God

Siyahamba

63

We are march - ing in the light of God, we are march-ing in the
Si - ya - hamb' e - ku-kha-nyen' kwen- khos', si - ya - hamb' e - ku-kha-

light of God. We are march - ing in the light of God,
nyen' kwen-khos'. Si - ya - hamb' e - ku-kha - nyen' kwen-khos',

we are march-ing in the light of God.
si - ya - hamb' e - ku-kha-nyen' kwen - khos'.

we are march-ing in the light of, the light of God.
si - ya - hamb' e - ku-kha-nyen' kwen-, kha - nyen' kwen-khos'.

we are march-ing in the light of God.
si - ya - hamb' e - ku-kha-nyen' kwen - khos'.

We are march - ing   oo
Si - ya - ham - ba   oo

We are march-ing, march-ing, we are march-ing, march-ing,
Si - ya - ham - ba, ham-ba, si - ya - ham-ba, ham-ba,

Additional stanzas ad lib:
We are dancing . . .
We are praying . . .
We are singing . . .

Text: South African
Music: SIYAHAMBA, South African
© 1984 Utryck, admin. Walton Music Corp.

64

Shine, Jesus, Shine

Shine, Je-sus, shine, fill this land with the Fa-ther's glo-ry;

blaze, Spir-it, blaze, set our hearts on fire.

Flow, riv-er, flow, flood the na-tions with grace and mer-cy;

send forth your Word, Lord, and let there be light.

1 Lord, the light of your love is shin - ing, in the midst of the
2 As we gaze on your king - ly bright - ness, so our fac - es dis -

dark - ness, shin - ing; Je - sus, light of the world, shine up - on us,
play your like - ness, ev - er chang - ing from glo - ry to glo - ry,

set us free by the truth you now bring us.
mir - rored here, may our lives tell your sto - ry.

Shine on me, shine on me:
Shine on me, shine on me:

Text: Graham Kendrick
Music: SHINE, JESUS, SHINE, Graham Kendrick
© 1987 Make Way Music, admin. Integrity's Hosanna! Music in N., S., & C. America

65

This Little Light of Mine

1 This lit - tle light of mine,   I'm goin'- a let it shine;
2 Ev - 'ry - where I go,   I'm goin'- a let it shine;
3 Je - sus gave it to me,   I'm goin'- a let it shine;

oh,   oh,

this lit - tle light of mine,   I'm goin'- a let it shine;
ev - 'ry - where I go,   I'm goin'- a let it shine;
Je - sus gave it to me,   I'm goin'- a let it shine;

oh,

this lit - tle light of mine,   I'm goin'- a let it shine,
ev - 'ry - where I go,   I'm goin'- a let it shine,
Je - sus gave it to me,   I'm goin'- a let it shine,

oh,

let it shine, let it shine, let it shine.
let it shine, let it shine, let it shine.
let it shine, let it shine, let it shine.

Text: African American spiritual
Music: African American spiritual; arr. Horace Clarence Boyer, b. 1935
Arr. © 1992 Horace Clarence Boyer

I Want Jesus to Walk with Me

1 I want Je - sus to walk with me;
2 In my tri - als, Lord, walk with me;
3 When I'm in trou - ble, Lord, walk with me;

I want Je - sus to walk with me;
in my tri - als, Lord, walk with me;
when I'm in trou - ble, Lord, walk with me;

all a - long my pil - grim jour - ney,
when my heart is al - most break - ing,
when my head is bowed in sor - row,

Lord, I want Je - sus to walk with me.
Lord, I want Je - sus to walk with me.
Lord, I want Je - sus to walk with me.

Text: African American spiritual
Music: Sojourner, African American spiritual; arr. J. Jefferson Cleveland, 1937-1986 and Verolga Nix, b. 1933
Arr. © 1981 Abingdon Press, admin. The Copyright Company

67   # By the Waters of Babylon

By the wa-ters of Ba-by-lon where we sat down,

and there we wept when we re-mem-bered

Zi - on. By the wa-ters of For the wick-ed

car-ried us a-way, cap - tiv - i - ty re - quired from us a song.

How can we sing our ho-ly song in a strange land? For the wick-ed land? So let the words of my mouth and the med-i-ta-tions of my heart be ac-cept-a-ble in your sight, O God.

Text: Ps. 137:1-4, Ps. 19:14, adapt.
Music: Jamaican traditional; arr. Bread for the Journey
Arr. © 1997 Augsburg Fortress

68

That Priceless Grace

1 That price-less grace, that price-less grace, that price-less
2 That price-less blood, that price-less blood, that price-less
3 That pain-ful death, that pain-ful death, that pain-ful
4 That pre-cious word, that pre-cious word, that pre-cious

grace which gave me life: Je-sus' life is price-less grace.
blood which gave me life: Je-sus' blood is price-less grace.
death took sins a-way: Je-sus' death is price-less grace.
word which brought me light: Je-sus' word is price-less grace.

That price-less grace is life for me.

Text: Emmanuel F. Y. Grantson
Music: Ghanaian traditional; arr. James M. Capers, b. 1948
Text and arr. © 1999 Augsburg Fortress

What Can Wash Away My Sin?

Nothing but the Blood

69

1 What can wash a - way my sin? Noth-ing but the blood of Je - sus.
2 For my par-don this I see: noth-ing but the blood of Je - sus.
3 Noth-ing can for sin a - tone: noth-ing but the blood of Je - sus.
4 This is all my hope and peace: noth-ing but the blood of Je - sus.

What can make me whole a - gain? Noth-ing but the blood of Je - sus.
For my cleans-ing this my plea: noth-ing but the blood of Je - sus.
Naught of good that I have done: noth-ing but the blood of Je - sus.
This is all my righ-teous-ness: noth-ing but the blood of Je - sus.

Refrain

Oh, pre - cious is the flow that makes me bright as snow;

no oth - er fount I know: noth-ing but the blood of Je - sus.

Text: Robert Lowry, 1826-1899
Music: PLAINFIELD, Robert Lowry, 1826-1899

70

Lead Me, Guide Me

Refrain

Lead me, guide me, a - long the way;

for if you lead me, I can - not stray.

Lord, let me walk each day with thee.

Lead me, O Lord, lead me.

1 I am weak and I need thy strength and pow'r
2 Help me tread in the paths of righ - teous - ness,
3 I am lost if you take your hand from me,

to help me o - ver my weak - est hour.
be my aid when Sa - tan and sin op - press.
I am blind with - out . . . thy light to see.

Help me through the dark-ness thy face to see.
I am put - ting all . . . . my trust in thee.
Lord, just al - ways let me thy ser - vant be.

Refrain

Lead me, O Lord, lead me.

Text: Doris M. Akers, b. 1922
Music: Doris M. Akers, b. 1922; arr. Richard Smallwood
© 1953 Doris Akers, admin. Unichappell Music, Inc.

Alas! And Did My Savior Bleed

At the Cross

71

1 A - las! And did my Sav - ior bleed, and did my sov - 'reign die?
2 Was it for sins that I had done he groaned up - on the tree?
3 Well might the sun in dark - ness hide and shut its glo - ries in
4 Thus might I hide my blush - ing face while his dear cross ap - pears;
5 But tears of grief can - not re - pay the debt of love I owe;

Would he de - vote that sa - cred head for sin - ners such as I?
A - maz - ing pit - y, grace un - known, and love be - yond de - gree!
when God, the might - y mak - er, died for his own crea - tures' sin.
dis - solve my heart in thank - ful - ness, and melt my eyes to tears.
here, Lord, I give my - self a - way: it's all that I can do.

Refrain

At the cross, at the cross, where I first saw the light, and the

bur - den of my heart rolled a - way: it was there by faith I re -

ceived my sight, and now I am hap - py all the day.

Text: Isaac Watts, 1674-1748; Ralph E. Hudson, 1843-1901, refrain
Music: HUDSON, Ralph E. Hudson, 1843-1901

Down at the Cross

72

1 Down at the cross where my Sav - ior died, down where for cleans-ing from
2 I am so won - drous-ly saved from sin, Je - sus so sweet-ly a -
3 Oh, pre-cious foun - tain that saves from sin, I am so glad I have
4 Come to this foun - tain so rich and sweet; cast your poor soul at the

sin I cried; there to my heart was the blood ap - plied:
bides with-in; there at the cross where he took me in:
en - tered in; there Je - sus saves me and keeps me clean:
Sav - ior's feet; plunge in to - day, and be made com - plete:

Refrain

glo-ry to his name.
glo-ry to his name.
glo-ry to his name.   Glo-ry to his name,   glo-ry to his name!
glo-ry to his name.

There to my heart was the blood ap - plied: Glo-ry to his name.

Text: Elisha A. Hoffman, 1839-1929
Music: GLORY TO HIS NAME, John H. Stockton, 1813-1877

Jesus, Keep Me Near the Cross

Near the Cross

73

1. Je - sus, keep me near the cross, there's a pre - cious foun - tain;
2. Near the cross, a trem - bling soul, love and mer - cy found me;
3. Near the cross! O Lamb of God, bring its scenes be - fore me;
4. Near the cross I'll watch and wait, hop - ing, trust - ing ev - er,

free to all, a heal - ing stream flows from Cal - v'ry's moun - tain.
there the bright and Morn - ing Star sheds its beams a - round me.
help me walk from day to day with its shad - ows o'er me.
till I reach the gold - en strand just be - yond the riv - er.

Refrain

In the cross, in the cross be my glo - ry ev - er;

till my ran - somed soul shall find rest be - yond the riv - er.

Text: Fanny J. Crosby, 1820-1915
Music: NEAR THE CROSS, William H. Doane, 1832-1915

Days Are Filled with Sorrow and Care

Burdens Are Lifted at Calvary

1 Days are filled with sor-row and care, hearts are lone-ly and drear;
2 Cast your care on Je-sus to-day, leave your wor-ry and fear;
3 Trou-bled soul, the Sav-ior can see ev - 'ry heart-ache and tear;

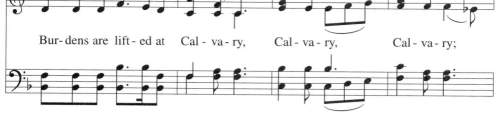

bur-dens are lift-ed at Cal - va - ry, Je-sus is ver - y near.

Refrain

Bur-dens are lift-ed at Cal - va - ry, Cal - va - ry, Cal - va - ry;

bur-dens are lift-ed at Cal - va - ry, Je-sus is ver - y near.
ver - y near.

Text: John M. Moore
Music: John M. Moore
© 1952 Singspiration Music/ASCAP, admin. Brentwood-Benson Music Publishing

75

I Know It Was the Blood

1 I know it was the blood, I know it was the blood,
2 It was my Sav-ior's blood, it was my Sav-ior's blood,
3 They pierced him in his side, they pierced him in his side,
4 He's com-ing back a-gain, he's com-ing back a-gain,

I know it was the blood for me.
it was my Sav-ior's blood for me.
they pierced him in his side for me.
he's com-ing back a-gain for me.

One day when I was lost, he died up-on the cross.
One day when I was lost, he died up-on the cross.
One day when I was lost, he died up-on the cross.
One day when I was lost, he died up-on the cross.

I know it was the blood for me.
It was my Sav-ior's blood for me.
They pierced him in his side for me.
He's com - ing back a - gain for me.

Text: traditional
Music: traditional; arr. James M. Capers, b. 1948
Arr. © 1999 Augsburg Fortress

Would You Be Free

There Is Power in the Blood

1 Would you be free from the bur - den of sin? There's
2 Would you be free from your pas - sion and pride? There's
3 Would you do ser - vice for Je - sus your king? There's

pow'r in the blood, pow'r in the blood. Would you o'er e - vil a
pow'r in the blood, pow'r in the blood. Come for a cleans-ing to
pow'r in the blood, pow'r in the blood. Would you live dai - ly his

vic - to - ry win? There's won - der - ful pow'r in the blood.
Cal - va - ry's tide. There's won - der - ful pow'r in the blood.
prais - es to sing? There's won - der - ful pow'r in the blood.

Refrain

There is pow'r, pow'r, won-der- work-ing pow'r in the
there is

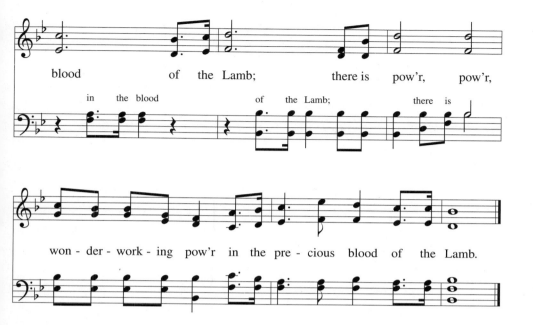

blood of the Lamb; there is pow'r, pow'r,

in the blood of the Lamb; there is

won - der - work - ing pow'r in the pre - cious blood of the Lamb.

Text: Lewis E. Jones, 1865-1936
Music: POWER IN THE BLOOD, Lewis E. Jones, 1865-1936

On a Hill Far Away

The Old Rugged Cross

1. On a hill far a-way stood an old rug-ged cross,
2. Oh, that old rug-ged cross so de-spised by the world,
3. In the old rug-ged cross, stained with blood so di-vine,
4. To the old rug-ged cross I will ev-er be true,

the em-blem of suf-f'ring and shame;
has a won-drous at-trac-tion for me;
a won-drous beau-ty I 'see;
its shame and re-proach glad-ly bear;

and I love that old cross where the dear-est and best
for the dear Lamb of God left his glo-ry a-bove,
for 'twas on that old cross Je-sus suf-fered and died,
Christ will call me some day to my home far a-way,

for a world of lost sin-ners was slain.
to . . . . bear it to dark Cal-va-ry.
to . . . . par-don and sanc-ti-fy me.
where his glo-ry for-ev-er I'll share.

Refrain

So I'll cher - ish the old rug - ged cross,
cross, the old rug - ged cross,

till my tro - phies at last I lay down;

I will cling to the old rug - ged cross,
cross, the old rug - ged cross,

and ex - change it some day for a crown.

Text: George Bennard, 1873-1958
Music: THE OLD RUGGED CROSS, George Bennard, 1873-1958

78 There Is a Fountain

1. There is a foun - tain filled with blood drawn
2. The dy - ing thief re - joiced to see that
3. Thou dy - ing Lamb, thy pre - cious blood shall
4. E'er since by faith I saw the stream thy
5. When this poor, fal - t'ring mor - tal tongue lies

from Im - man - uel's veins; and sin - ners, plunged be -
foun - tain in his day; and there have I, though
nev - er lose its pow'r till all the ran - somed
flow - ing wounds sup - ply; re - deem - ing love has
si - lent in the grave, then in a no - bler,

neath that flood, lose all their guilt - y stains: lose
vile as he, washed all my sins a - way: washed
church of God be saved, to sin no more: be
been my theme, and shall be till I die: and
sweet - er song I'll sing thy pow'r to save: I'll

all their guilt - y stains, lose all their guilt - y stains; and
all my sins a - way, washed all my sins a - way; and
saved, to sin no more, be saved, to sin no more; till
shall be till I die, and shall be till I die, re -
sing thy pow'r to save, I'll sing thy pow'r to save; then

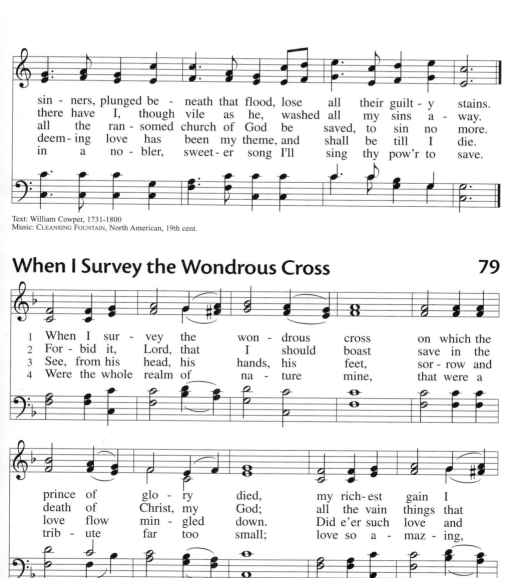

sin - ners, plunged be - neath that flood, lose all their guilt - y stains.
there have I, though vile as he, washed all my sins a - way.
all the ran - somed church of God be saved, to sin no more.
deem - ing love has been my theme, and shall be till I die.
in a no - bler, sweet - er song I'll sing thy pow'r to save.

Text: William Cowper, 1731-1800
Music: CLEANSING FOUNTAIN, North American, 19th cent.

When I Survey the Wondrous Cross   79

1 When I sur - vey the won - drous cross on which the
2 For - bid it, Lord, that I should boast save in the
3 See, from his head, his hands, his feet, sor - row and
4 Were the whole realm of na - ture mine, that were a

prince of glo - ry died, my rich - est gain I
death of Christ, my God; all the vain things that
love flow min - gled down. Did e'er such love and
trib - ute far too small; love so a - maz - ing,

count but loss and pour con - tempt on all my pride.
charm me most, I sac - ri - fice them to his blood.
sor - row meet, or thorns com - pose so rich a crown?
so di - vine, de - mands my soul, my life, my all.

Text: Isaac Watts, 1674-1748
Music: HAMBURG, Lowell Mason, 1792-1872

They Crucified My Lord
He Never Said a Mumbalin' Word

80

1 They cru - ci - fied my Lord, and he nev- er said a mum-ba-lin' word;
2 They nailed him to a tree, and he nev- er said a mum-ba-lin' word;
3 They pierced him in the side, and he nev- er said a mum-ba-lin' word;
4 The blood came stream-in' down, and he nev- er said a mum-ba-lin' word;
5 He hung his head and died, and he nev- er said a mum-ba-lin' word;

they cru - ci - fied my Lord, and he nev- er said a mum-ba-lin' word;
they nailed him to a tree, and he nev- er said a mum-ba-lin' word;
they pierced him in the side, and he nev- er said a mum-ba-lin' word;
the blood came stream-in' down, and he nev- er said a mum-ba-lin' word;
he hung his head and died, and he nev- er said a mum-ba-lin' word;

not a word, not a word, not a word.

Text: African American spiritual
Music: African American spiritual; arr. Carl Haywood, b. 1949
Arr. © 1992 Carl Haywood

mumbalin' = complaining

81

Were You There

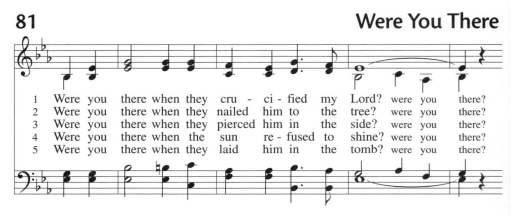

1 Were you there when they cru - ci - fied my Lord? were you there?
2 Were you there when they nailed him to the tree? were you there?
3 Were you there when they pierced him in the side? were you there?
4 Were you there when the sun re - fused to shine? were you there?
5 Were you there when they laid him in the tomb? were you there?

Were you there when they cru - ci - fied my Lord? were you there?
Were you there when they nailed him to the tree? were you there?
Were you there when they pierced him in the side? were you there?
Were you there when the sun re - fused to shine? were you there?
Were you there when they laid him in the tomb? were you there?

Refrain

Oh! some - times it caus - es me to

trem - ble, trem - ble, trem - ble. Were you

there when they cru - ci - fied my Lord? were you there?
there when they nailed him to the tree? were you there?
there when they pierced him in the side? were you there?
there when the sun re - fused to shine? were you there?
there when they laid him in the tomb? were you there?

Text: African American spiritual
Music: WERE YOU THERE, African American spiritual; arr. William Farley Smith, b. 1941
Arr. © 1989 The United Methodist Publishing House, admin. The Copyright Company

82
Oh, How He Loves You and Me

1 Oh, how he loves you and me.
2 Je - sus to Cal - v'ry did go

Oh, how he loves you and me;
his love for this world to show;

he gave his life, what more could he give?
what he did there brought hope from de - spair.

Refrain

Oh, how he loves you; oh, how he loves me;

oh, how he loves you and me!

Text: Kurt Kaiser, b. 1934
Music: PATRICIA, Kurt Kaiser, b. 1934

Jesu, Jesu, Fill Us with Your Love

83

Refrain

Je - su, Je - su, fill us with your love, show

us how to serve the neigh-bors we have from you.

1 Kneels at the feet of his friends, si - lent-ly wash-es their feet,
2 Neigh-bors are wealth-y and poor, var - ied in col - or and race,
3 These are the ones we will serve, these are the ones we will love;
4 Kneel at the feet of our friends, si - lent-ly wash-ing their feet:

Refrain

mas - ter who pours out him - self for them.
neigh-bors are near - by and far a - way.
all these are neigh - bors to us and you.
this is the way we will live with you.

Text: Tom Colvin, b. 1925
Music: CHEREPONI, Ghanaian folk tune; adapt. Tom Colvin, b. 1925; arr. Jane Marshall, b. 1924
Text and tune © 1969, arr. © 1982 Hope Publishing Co.

84 Where Charity and Love Prevail

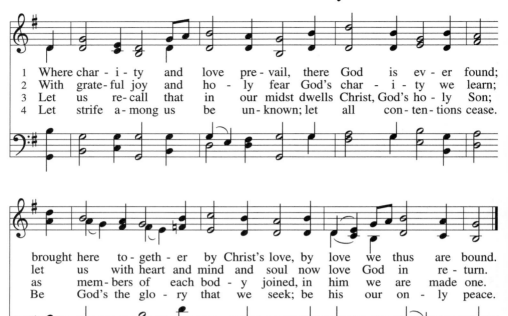

1 Where char - i - ty and love pre - vail, there God is ev - er found;
2 With grate - ful joy and ho - ly fear God's char - i - ty we learn;
3 Let us re - call that in our midst dwells Christ, God's ho - ly Son;
4 Let strife a - mong us be un - known; let all con - ten - tions cease.

brought here to - geth - er by Christ's love, by love we thus are bound.
let us with heart and mind and soul now love God in re - turn.
as mem - bers of each bod - y joined, in him we are made one.
Be God's the glo - ry that we seek; be his our on - ly peace.

5 For love excludes no race or clan
that names the Savior's name;
his family embraces all
whose Father is the same.

6 We now forgive each other's faults
as we our own confess,
that we may love each other well
in Christian gentleness.

Text: Latin hymn, 5th cent.; tr. Omer Westendorf, b. 1916, alt.
Music: MARTYRDOM, Hugh Wilson, 1764-1824
Text © 1960 World Library Publications, a division of J.S. Paluch Company, Inc.

85 Calvary

Refrain

Cal - va - ry, Cal - va - ry, Cal - va - ry,

Cal - va - ry, Cal - va - ry, Cal - va -

ry, sure - ly he died on Cal - va - ry.

1 Ev - 'ry time I think a - bout Je - sus, ev - 'ry time I
2 Sin - ner, do you love . . my Je - sus? Sin - ner, do you
3 Don't you hear him call - ing his Fa - ther? Don't you hear him
4 Don't you hear him say, "It is fin - ished!" Don't you hear him
5 Je - sus fur - nished my . . . sal - va - tion, Je - sus fur - nished

think a - bout Je - sus, ev - 'ry time I think a - bout
love . . . my Je - sus? Sin - ner, do you love . . . my
call - ing his Fa - ther? Don't you hear him call - ing his
say, "It is fin - ished!" Don't you hear him say, "It is
my . . . . sal - va - tion, Je - sus fur - nished my . . . . sal -

Refrain

Je - sus; sure - ly he died on Cal - va - ry.
Je - sus? Sure - ly he died on Cal - va - ry.
Fa - ther? Sure - ly he died on Cal - va - ry.
fin - ished!" Sure - ly he died on Cal - va - ry.
va - tion; sure - ly he died on Cal - va - ry.

Text: African American spiritual
Music: CALVARY, African American spiritual

King of My Life
Lead Me to Calvary

1. King of my life I crown thee now, thine shall the glo - ry be;
2. Show me the tomb where thou wast laid, ten - der - ly mourned and wept;
3. Let me, like Mar - y, through the gloom, come with a gift to thee;
4. May I be will - ing, Lord, to bear dai - ly my cross for thee,

lest I for-get thy thorn-crowned brow, lead me to Cal - va - ry.
an - gels in robes of light ar - rayed guard-ed thee whilst thou slept.
show to me now the emp - ty tomb, lead me to Cal - va - ry.
e - ven thy cup of grief to share; thou hast borne all for me.

Refrain

Lest I for-get Geth-sem - a- ne, lest I for-get thine ag - o - ny,

lest I for-get thy love for me, lead me to Cal-va - ry.

Text: Jennie Evelyn Hussey, 1874-1958
Music: William J. Kirkpatrick, 1838-1921

When Israel Was in Egypt's Land

Go Down, Moses

1 When Is-rael was in E-gypt's land,
2 The Lord told Mo-ses what to do,
3 The pillar of cloud shall clear the way, let my peo-ple go;
4 As Is-rael stood by the wa-ter-side,

op - pressed so hard they could not stand,
to lead the childr'n of Is - rael through, let my peo-ple go.
a fire by night, a shade by day,
at God's com-mand it did di-vide,

Refrain

Go down, Mo-ses, way down in E-gypt's land,

tell old Pha-raoh: Let my peo-ple go!

5 When they had reached the other shore,
  let my people go;
  they sang the song of triumph o'er,
  let my people go. *Refrain*

6 Oh, let us all from bondage flee,
  let my people go;
  and let us all in Christ be free,
  let my people go. *Refrain*

Text: African American spiritual
Music: TUBMAN, African American spiritual; arr. John W. Work Jr. 1871-1925

88

O Mary, Don't You Weep

Refrain

O Mar - y, don't you weep, don't you mourn,

O Mar - y, don't you weep, don't you mourn;

Pha-raoh's ar - my got drownd - ed, O Mar - y, don't you weep.

1 One of these morn - ings bright and fair, goin' - a
2 When I get to heav - en goin' - a sing and shout, ain't no -
3 When I get to heav - en goin' - a put on my shoes, goin' - a

take my   wings   and   cleave the air;   Pha-raoh's ar - my got
bod - y   there   goin' - a turn   me out;   Pha-raoh's ar - my got
run a - bout   and   spread the news;   Phar-aoh's ar - my got

Refrain

drownd - ed,   O   Mar - y, don't you weep.
drownd - ed,   O   Mar - y, don't you weep.
drownd - ed,   O   Mar - y, don't you weep.

Text: African American spiritual
Music: O MARY, African American spiritual; arr. William Farley Smith, b. 1941
Arr. © 1989 The United Methodist Publishing House, admin. The Copyright Company

89

The Lamb

1 The Lamb, the Lamb, O
2 The Lamb, the Lamb, one
3 The Lamb, the Lamb, as
4 He sighs, he dies, he
5 He rose, he rose, my

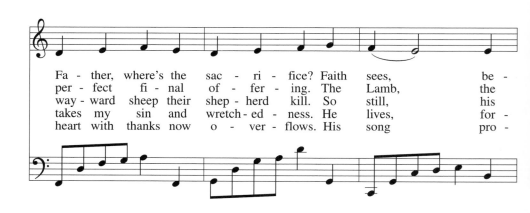

Fa - ther, where's the sac - ri - fice? Faith sees, be -
per - fect fi - nal of - fer - ing. The Lamb, the
way - ward sheep their shep - herd kill. So still, his
takes my sin and wretch - ed - ness. He lives, for -
heart with thanks now o - ver - flows. His song pro -

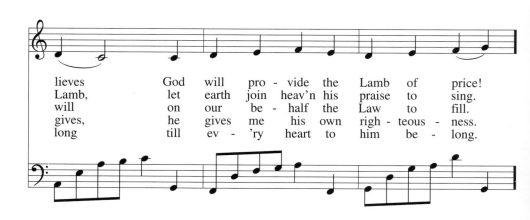

lieves God will pro - vide the Lamb of price!
Lamb, let earth join heav'n his praise to sing.
will on our be - half the Law to fill.
gives, he gives me his own righ - teous - ness.
long till ev - 'ry heart to him be - long.

Wor-thy is the Lamb whose death makes me his own! The

Lamb is reign-ing on his throne!

Text: Gerald Patrick Coleman
Music: THE LAMB, Gerald Patrick Coleman

They Crucified My Savior

He Rose

90

1. They cru-ci-fied my Sav-ior and nailed him to the tree,
2. Then Jo-seph begged his bod-y and laid it in the tomb,
3. Sister Mar-y, she came run-ning, a-look-ing for my Lord,
4. An an-gel came from heav-en and rolled the stone a-way,

they cru-ci-fied my Sav-ior and nailed him to the tree,
then Jo-seph begged his bod-y and laid it in the tomb,
sister Mar-y, she came run-ning, a-look-ing for my Lord,
an an-gel came from heav-en and rolled the stone a-way,

they cru-ci-fied my Sav-ior and nailed him to the tree,
then Jo-seph begged his bod-y and laid it in the tomb,
sister Mar-y, she came run-ning, a-look-ing for my Lord,
an an-gel came from heav-en and rolled the stone a-way,

and the Lord will bear my spir-it home.

Refrain

He rose, he rose, he rose from the dead,
he rose, he rose,

he rose, he rose, he rose from the dead,
he rose, he rose,

he rose, he rose, he rose from the dead,
he rose, he rose,

and the Lord will bear my spir-it home.

Text: African American spiritual
Music: HE ROSE, African American spiritual

91

Alleluia! Jesus Is Risen!

1 Al - le - lu - ia!   Je - sus is ris - en!
2 Walk - ing the way,   Christ in the cen - ter
3 Je - sus the vine,   we are the branch - es;
4 Weep - ing, be gone;   sor - row, be si - lent:
5 Cit - y of God,   Eas - ter for - ev - er,

Trum - pets re - sound - ing in glo - ri - ous light!
tell - ing the sto - ry to o - pen our eyes;
life in the Spir - it the fruit of the tree;
death put a - sun - der, and Eas - ter is bright.
gold - en Je - ru - sa - lem, Je - sus the Lamb,

Splen - dor, the Lamb,   heav - en for - ev - er!
break - ing our bread,   giv - ing us glo - ry:
heav - en to earth,   Christ to the peo - ple,
Cher - u - bim sing: "O grave, be o - pen!"
riv - er of life,   saints and arch - an - gels,

Oh, what a mir - a - cle God has in sight!
Je - sus our bless - ing, our con - stant sur - prise.
gift of the fu - ture now flow - ing to me.
Clothe us in won - der, a - dorn us in light.
sing with cre - a - tion to God the I Aм!

Je - sus is ris - en and we shall a - rise:

Give God the glo - ry! Al - le - lu - ia!

Text: Herbert F. Brokering, b. 1926
Music: EARTH AND ALL STARS, David N. Johnson, 1922-1987

Text © 1995 Augsburg Fortress
Music © 1969 *Contemporary Worship 1*, admin. Augsburg Fortress

Dancing before the Lord 92

Great is, O King,
Our happiness
In thy kingdom,
Thou, our king.

We dance before thee,
Our king,
By the strength
Of thy kingdom.

May our feet
Be made strong;
Let us dance before thee,
Eternal.

Give ye praise,
All angels,
To him above
Who is worthy of praise.

Anonymous, tr. Aylward Shorter, from *Prayer in the Religious Traditions of Africa*
© 1975 Oxford University Press

God Sent His Son

Because He Lives

1 God sent his Son, they called him Je - sus;
2 How sweet to hold a new - born ba - by;
3 And then one day I'll cross the riv - er;

he came to love, heal, and for - give;
and feel the pride and joy he gives,
I'll fight life's fi - nal war with pain;

he lived and died to buy my par - don,
but great - er still the calm as - sur - ance
and then as death gives way to vic - t'ry,

an emp - ty grave is there to prove my Sav - ior lives.
this child can face un - cer - tain days be - cause he lives.
I'll see the lights of glo - ry and I'll know he lives.

Refrain

Be - cause he lives I can face to - mor - row;

be - cause he lives all fear is gone;

be - cause I know he holds the fu - ture,

and life is worth the liv - ing just be - cause he lives.

Text: Gloria Gaither, b. 1942, William Gaither, b. 1936
Music: William Gaither, b. 1936

Low in the Grave He Lay

Up from the Grave He Arose

1 Low in the grave he lay, Je - sus my Sav - ior,
2 Vain - ly they watch his bed, Je - sus my Sav - ior;
3 Death can - not keep its prey, Je - sus my Sav - ior;

wait - ing the com - ing day, Je - sus my Lord.
vain - ly they seal the dead, Je - sus my Lord.
he tore the bars a - way, Je - sus my Lord.

Refrain

Up from the grave he a - rose, he a - rose, with a

might - y tri - umph o'er his foes; o'er his foes, he a -

rose a vic - tor o - ver death's do - main, and he

lives for - ev - er, with his saints to reign. He a -

rose! He a - rose! Hal - le - lu - jah! Christ a - rose!

He a- rose! He a - rose!

Text: Robert Lowry, 1826-1899
Music: CHRIST AROSE, Robert Lowry, 1826-1899

He Is Lord 95

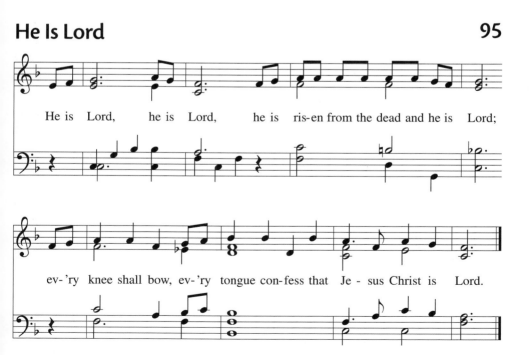

He is Lord, he is Lord, he is ris-en from the dead and he is Lord;

ev-'ry knee shall bow, ev-'ry tongue con-fess that Je - sus Christ is Lord.

Text: Philippians 2:10-11, adapt.
Music: HE IS LORD, traditional

96

Christ Has Arisen, Alleluia

1. Christ has a - ris - en, al - le - lu - ia.
2. For three long days the grave did its worst
3. The an - gel said to them, "Do not fear.
4. "Go spread the news: he's not in the grave.
5. Christ has a - ris - en to set us free.

Re - joice and praise him, al - le - lu - ia.
un - til its strength by God was dis - persed.
You look for Je - sus who is not here.
He has a - ris - en this world to save.
Al - le - lu - ia, to him prais - es be.

For our re - deem - er burst from the tomb,
He who gives life did death un - der - go,
See for your - selves the tomb is all bare.
Je - sus' re - deem - ing la - bors are done.
Je - sus is liv - ing! Let us all sing;

e - ven from death, dis - pel - ling its gloom.
and in its con - quest his might did show.
On - ly the grave cloths are ly - ing there."
E - ven the bat - tle with sin is won."
he reigns tri - um - phant, heav - en - ly king.

Refrain

Let us sing praise to him with end-less joy.

Death's fear-ful sting he has come to de-stroy.

Our sin for-giv-ing, al-le-lu-ia!

Je-sus is liv-ing, al-le-lu-ia!

Text: Bernard Kyamanywa, b. 1938; tr. Howard S. Olson, b. 1922
Music: MFURAHINI, HALELUYA, Tanzanian traditional
Tr. © 1977 Howard S. Olson

I Heard an Old, Old Story

Victory in Jesus

1 I heard an old, old sto - ry, how a Sav - ior came from glo - ry,
2 I heard a - bout his heal - ing, of his cleans - ing pow'r re - veal - ing,
3 I heard a - bout a man - sion he has built for me in glo - ry,

how he gave his life on Cal - va - ry to save a wretch like me;
how he made the lame to walk a - gain and caused the blind to see;
and I heard a - bout the streets of gold be - yond the crys - tal sea;

I heard a - bout his groan - ing, of his pre - cious blood's a - ton - ing,
and then I cried, "Dear Je - sus, come and heal my bro - ken spir - it,"
a - bout the an - gels sing - ing and the old re - demp - tion sto - ry,

how Je - sus saved me from my sins and won the vic - to - ry.
and some - how Je - sus came and brought to me the vic - to - ry.
and some sweet day I'll sing up there the song of vic - to - ry.

Refrain

Oh, vic-to-ry in Je-sus, my Sav-ior, for-ev-er!

He sought me and bought me with his re-deem-ing blood;

he loved me ere I knew him, and all my love is due him—

he plunged me to vic-to-ry be-neath the cleans-ing flood.

Text: Eugene M. Bartlett, 1885-1941
Music: HARTFORD, Eugene M. Bartlett, 1885-1941

98

Open Our Eyes, Lord

O - pen our eyes, Lord; we want to see

Je - sus, to reach out and touch

him, and say that we love him.

Text: Robert Cull, b. 1949
Music: Robert Cull, b. 1949
© 1976 Maranatha! Music, admin. The Copyright Company

How Lovely on the Mountains

Our God Reigns

1 How love-ly on the moun - tains are the feet of him
2 He had no state - ly form, he had no maj - es-ty,
3 It was our sin and guilt that bruised and wound-ed him;
4 Out of the tomb he came with grace and maj - es-ty;

who brings good news, good news;
that we should be drawn to him.
it was our sin that brought him down.
he is a - live, he is a - live.

an - nounc-ing peace, pro - claim - ing news of hap - pi - ness:
He was de - spised and we took no ac - count of him,
When we like sheep had gone a - stray, our Shep - herd came,
God loves us so; see Je - sus' hands, his feet, his side.

our God reigns, our God reigns.
yet now he reigns with the Most High.
and on his shoul - ders bore our shame.
Yes, we know, he is a - live.

Refrain

Our God reigns, our God reigns,

our God reigns, our God reigns.

Text: Leonard E. Smith, Jr.
Music: Our God Reigns, Leonard E. Smith, Jr.

We Praise Thee, O God

Revive Us Again

100

1 We praise thee, O God, for the Son of thy love,
2 We praise thee, O God, for thy Spir - it of light,
3 All glo - ry and praise to the Lamb that was slain,
4 Re - vive us a - gain, fill each heart with thy love,

for Je - sus who died and is now gone a - bove.
who has shown us our Sav - ior, and scat - tered our night.
who has borne all our sins and has cleansed ev - 'ry stain.
may each soul be re - kin - dled with fire from a - bove.

Refrain

Hal - le - lu - jah! Thine the glo - ry, hal - le - lu - jah! A - men.

Hal - le - lu - jah! Thine the glo - ry, re - vive us a - gain.

Text: William P. MacKay, 1837-1885
Music: Revive Us Again, John H. Husband, 1760-1825

Spirit of the Living God

Spir - it of the liv - ing God, fall fresh on me,

Spir - it of the liv - ing God, fall fresh on me.

Melt me, mold me, fill me, use me.

Spir - it of the liv - ing God, fall fresh on me.

Text: Daniel Iverson, 1890-1977
Music: Daniel Iverson, 1890-1977
© 1935 Birdwing Music, admin. EMI Christian Music Publishing

There's a Sweet, Sweet Spirit in This Place

Sweet, Sweet Spirit

There's a sweet, sweet Spir-it in this place,
and I know that it's the Spir-it of the Lord;
there are sweet ex-pres-sions on each face,
and I know they feel the pres-ence of the Lord.

Sweet Ho - ly Spir - it, sweet heav - en - ly Dove,

stay right here with us, fill - ing us with your love;

and for these bless - ings we lift our hearts in praise;

with - out a doubt we'll know that we have

been re - vived when we shall leave this place.

Text: Doris Akers, b. 1922
Music: SWEET, SWEET SPIRIT, Doris Akers, b. 1922
© 1962 Manna Music, Inc

Gracious Spirit, Heed Our Pleading

Njoo kwetu, Roho mwema

103

1 Gra-cious Spir - it,   heed our plead-ing,   fash - ion us all   a - new.
2 Come to   teach us,   come to   nour-ish   those who be-lieve in   Christ.
3 Guide our think-ing   and   our speak-ing   done in your ho - ly   name.
4 Not mere knowl-edge,   but   dis - cern-ment,   nor root-less lib - er - ty;
5 Keep us   fer - vent   in   our wit - ness;   un-swayed by earth's al - lure.

It's   your   lead-ing   that we're need-ing,   help   us   to fol - low   you.
Bless the   faith-ful,   may they flour-ish,   strength-ened by grace un - priced.
Mo - ti - vate all   in   their seek-ing,   free - ing from guilt and   shame.
turn   dis - qui - et   to   con - tent-ment,   doubt   in - to cer - tain-ty.
Ev - er   grant us   zeal-ous   fit - ness,   which you   a - lone as - sure.

Refrain/Kipokeo

Come,   come,   come, Ho - ly Spir - it,   come.
Njo - o,   njo - o,   njo - o,   Ro - ho   mwe - ma.

Come,   come,   come, Ho - ly Spir - it,   come.
Njo - o,   njo - o,   njo - o,   Ro - ho   mwe - ma.

1 *Njoo kwetu, Roho mwema, Mfariji wetu.*
  Tufundishe ya mbinguni, tuwe watu wapya. Kipokeo

2 *Utufanye waamini wa Yesu Mwokozi.*
  Tukaishi kikundini, kanisani mwako. Kipokeo

3 *Kwa huruma tubariki, tuishi na wewe.*
  Tukatende kila kitu kuongozwa nawe. Kipokeo

4 *Roho mwema, Mfariji, utupe hekima;*
  Tukiwaza na kutenda, yote yawe yako. Kipokeo

5 *Tudumishe tuwe hai na ukweli wako.*
  Tusivutwe na dunia, tushu'die neema. Kipokeo

Text: Wilson Niwagila; tr. Howard S. Olson, b. 1922
Music: NJOO KWETU, ROHO MWEMA, Wilson Niwagila; arr. Egil Hovland, b. 1924
Swahili text, trans., and tune © Lutheran Theological College, Makumira, Tanzania, admin. Augsburg Fortress
Arr. © Egil Hovland

Holy Spirit, Light Divine   104

1 Ho-ly Spir-it, light di-vine, shine up-on this heart of mine;
2 Ho-ly Spir-it, pow'r di-vine, cleanse this guilt-y heart of mine;
3 Ho-ly Spir-it, joy di-vine, cheer this sad-dened heart of mine;
4 Ho-ly Spir-it, all di-vine, dwell with-in this heart of mine;

chase the shades of night a - way, turn the dark-ness in-to day.
in your mer-cy pit-y me, from sin's bond-age set me free.
yield a sac-red, set-tled peace, let it grow and still in-crease.
cast down ev-'ry i-dol throne, reign su-preme, and reign a-lone.

Text: Andrew Reed, 1787-1862
Music: MERCY, Louis Moreau Gottschalk, 1829-1869; arr. Edwin P. Parker, 1836-1925

Oh, Let the Son of God Enfold You

Spirit Song

1 Oh, let the Son of God en - fold you with his Spir - it and his
2 Oh, come and sing this song with glad - ness as your hearts are filled with

love, let him fill your heart and sat - is - fy your soul.
joy, lift your hands in sweet sur - ren - der to his name.

Oh, let him have the things that hold you, and his Spir - it like a
Oh, give him all your tears and sad - ness, give him all your years of

dove will de - scend up - on your life and make you whole.
pain, and you'll en - ter in - to life in Je - sus' name.

Refrain

GM⁷   A/G   F♯m⁷   Bm⁷   Em⁷

Je - sus, O Je - sus, come and

A   DM⁷   C/E   D/F♯   GM⁷   A   A/G

fill your lambs. Je - sus, O

F♯m⁷   Bm⁷   Em⁷   Asus⁷   A⁷   D

Je - sus, come and fill your lambs.

Text: John Wimber
Music: John Wimber
© 1979 Mercy/Vineyard Publishing

Come, O Holy Spirit, Come
Wa wa wa Emimimo

106

Congregation

Come, O Ho-ly Spir-it, come,
Wa wa wa E-mi-mi-mo,

Come, al-might-y Spir-it,
Wa wa wa A-lag-ba-

Leader

Ho-ly Spir-it, come.
E - mi - o - lo - ye.

come,
ra,

Come, come, come.
Wa - o wa - o wa - o.

al-might-y Spir-it, come.
A - lag-ba-ra-me-ta.

O Spir-it, come.
E - mi-mi-mo.

Text: Nigerian traditional; tr. I-to Loh, b. 1936
Music: WA EMIMIMO, Samuel Solanke; arr. I-to Loh, b. 1936
Text and music © The Church of the Lord (Aldura)
Tr. © 1986 World Council of Churches and the Asian School of Music, Liturgy and the Arts

107

Holy Spirit, Descend

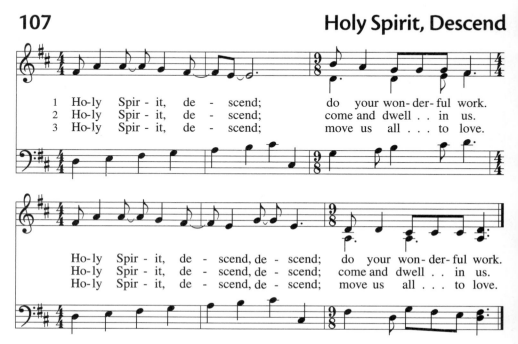

1 Ho-ly Spir-it, de - scend; do your won-der-ful work.
2 Ho-ly Spir-it, de - scend; come and dwell . . in us.
3 Ho-ly Spir-it, de - scend; move us all . . . to love.

Ho-ly Spir-it, de - scend, de - scend; do your won-der-ful work.
Ho-ly Spir-it, de - scend, de - scend; come and dwell . . in us.
Ho-ly Spir-it, de - scend, de - scend; move us all . . . to love.

Text: Emmanuel F. Y. Grantson
Music: NYAME NE SENSE, Ghanaian traditional; arr. This Far by Faith
Text and arr. © 1999 Augsburg Fortress

℗ It is indeed right and sal-u-tary that we should at all times and in all

plac - es of-fer thanks and praise to you, O Lord, holy Father, through

Christ our Lord. In the wonder and mystery of the Word

made flesh you have opened the eyes of faith to a new and radiant vision of your

glo - ry; that, beholding the God made visible, we may be drawn to love

the God whom we can-not see. And so, with the Church on earth and the

hosts of heav - en, we praise your name and join their un -

end - ing hymn:

It is indeed right and sal-u - tar - y that we should at all times and in all places offer thanks and praise to you, O Lord, ho-ly Fa-ther, al-might-y and ev - er-liv - ing God. You comforted your people with the promise of the Re - deem-er, through whom you will also make all things new in the day when he comes a-gain to judge the world in righ-teous-ness. And so, with the Church on earth and the hosts of heav - en, we praise your name and join their un-end - ing hymn:

Come, Thou Fount of Every Blessing 108

1 Come, thou Fount of ev-'ry bless-ing, tune my heart to sing thy grace;
2 Here I raise my Eb-en - e - zer, hith-er by thy help I'm come;
3 Oh, to grace how great a debt-or dai-ly I'm con-strained to be;

streams of mer - cy, nev-er ceas-ing, call for songs of loud-est praise.
and I hope, by thy good plea-sure, safe-ly to ar - rive at home.
let that grace now like a fet - ter bind my wan-d'ring heart to thee.

While the hope of end-less glo - ry fills my heart with joy and love,
Je - sus sought me when a strang-er, wan-d'ring from the fold of God;
Prone to wan - der, Lord, I feel it; prone to leave the God I love.

teach me ev - er to a-dore thee; may I still thy good-ness prove.
he, to res - cue me from dan-ger, in - ter-posed his pre-cious blood.
Here's my heart, oh, take and seal it; seal it for thy courts a - bove.

Text: Robert Robinson, 1735-1790
Music: NETTLETON, Wyeth's *Repository of Sacred Music,* Part II, 1813

109

I'm Goin'-a Sing

1 I'm goin'-a sing when the Spir-it says sing.
2 I'm goin'-a pray when the Spir-it says pray.
3 I'm goin'-a moan when the Spir-it says moan.
4 I'm goin'-a shout when the Spir-it says shout.

I'm goin'-a sing when the Spir-it says sing.
I'm goin'-a pray when the Spir-it says pray.
I'm goin'-a moan when the Spir-it says moan.
I'm goin'-a shout when the Spir-it says shout.

I'm goin'-a sing when the Spir-it says sing,
I'm goin'-a pray when the Spir-it says pray,
I'm goin'-a moan when the Spir-it says moan,
I'm goin'-a shout when the Spir-it says shout,

and o - bey the Spir-it of the Lord.
and o - bey the Spir-it of the Lord.
and o - bey the Spir-it of the Lord.
and o - bey the Spir-it of the Lord.

Text: African American spiritual
Music: I'M GOIN'-A SING, African American spiritual; arr. William Farley Smith, b. 1941
Arr. © 1989 The United Methodist Publishing House, admin. The Copyright Company

Joys Are Flowing like a River

Blessed Quietness

1 Joys are flow-ing like a riv-er since the Com-fort-er has come;
2 Bring-ing life and health and glad-ness all a-round, this heav'n-ly guest
3 Like the rain that falls from heav-en, like the sun-light from the sky,
4 See, a fruit-ful field is grow-ing, bless-ed fruit of righ-teous-ness;
5 What a won-der-ful sal-va-tion, where we al-ways see his face!

he a-bides with us for-ev-er, makes the trust-ing heart his home.
ban-ished un-be-lief and sad-ness, chang'd our wea-ri-ness to rest.
so the Ho-ly Ghost is giv-en, com-ing on us from on high.
and the streams of life are flow-ing in the lone-ly wil-der-ness.
What a per-fect hab-i-ta-tion, what a qui-et rest-ing place!

Refrain

Bless-ed qui-et-ness, ho-ly qui-et-ness—what as-sur-ance in my soul!

On the storm-y sea he speaks peace to me—how the bil-lows cease to roll!

Text: Marie P. Ferguson
Music: W. S. Marshall; arr. James M. Kirk

111   I've Just Come from the Fountain

Refrain

I've just come from the foun-tain, I've just come from the foun-tain, Lord, I've just come from the foun-tain, his name's so sweet. O Lord, I've sweet.

1 O broth-er, do you love Je-sus? Yes, yes, I do love my Je-sus.
2 O sis-ter, do you love Je-sus? Yes, yes, I do love my Je-sus.
3 O sin-ner, do you love Je-sus? Yes, yes, I do love my Je-sus.

Refrain

Broth-er, do you love Je-sus? His name's so sweet. O Lord, I've
Sis-ter, do you love Je-sus? His name's so sweet. O Lord, I've
Sin-ner, do you love Je-sus? His name's so sweet. O Lord, I've

Text: African American spiritual
Music: HIS NAME SO SWEET, African American spiritual; arr. James M. Capers, b. 1948
Arr. © 1995 Augsburg Fortress

Wash, O God, Our Sons and Daughters

112

1 Wash, O God, our sons and daugh-ters, where your cleans-ing wa-ters flow.
2 We who bring them long for nur - ture; by your milk may we be fed.
3 Oh, how deep your ho - ly wis - dom! Un - im - ag - ined, all your ways!

Num-ber them a - mong your peo - ple; bless as Christ blessed long a - go.
Let us join your feast, par - tak - ing cup of bless - ing, liv-ing bread.
To your name be glo - ry, hon - or! With our lives we wor-ship, praise!

Weave them gar-ments bright and spark-ling; com-pass them with love and light.
God, re - new us, guide our foot-steps; free from sin and all its snares,
We your peo - ple stand be - fore you, wa - ter-washed and Spir-it - born.

Fill, a - noint them; send your Spir - it, ho - ly dove and heart's de - light.
one with Christ in liv-ing, dy - ing, by your Spir - it, chil - dren, heirs.
By your grace, our lives we of - fer. Re - cre - ate us; God, trans-form!

Text: Ruth Duck, b. 1947
Music: BEACH SPRING, *The Sacred Harp*, Philadelphia, 1844; arr. *Lutheran Book of Worship*, 1978
Text © 1989 The United Methodist Publishing House, admin. The Copyright Company
Arr. © 1978 *Lutheran Book of Worship*

Have You Got Good Religion?

Certainly, Lord

113

1 Have you got good re - li - gion? Cer - t'nly, Lord! Have you got good re - li - gion? Cer - t'nly, Lord! Have you got good re - li - gion? Cer - t'nly, Lord! Cer - t'nly, cer - t'nly, cer - t'nly, Lord!

2 Have you been re - deemed? Cer - t'nly, Lord! Have you been re - deemed? Cer - t'nly, Lord! Have you been re - deemed? Cer - t'nly, Lord! Cer - t'nly, cer - t'nly, cer - t'nly, Lord!

3 Have you been to the wa - ter? Cer - t'nly, Lord! Have you been to the wa - ter? Cer - t'nly, Lord! Have you been to the wa - ter? Cer - t'nly, Lord! Cer - t'nly, cer - t'nly, cer - t'nly, Lord!

4 Have you been bap - tized? . . Cer - t'nly, Lord! Have you been bap - tized? . . Cer - t'nly, Lord! Have you been bap - tized? . . Cer - t'nly, Lord! Cer - t'nly, cer - t'nly, cer - t'nly, Lord!

Text: African American spiritual
Music: African American spiritual

114

Wade in the Water

Wade in the wa - ter, wade in the wa - ter, chil - dren,

wade in the wa-ter, God's a-goin'-a trou-ble the wa-ter.

Leader

All

1 See that host all dressed in white,
2 See that band all dressed in red, God's a-goin'-a trou-ble the
3 Look o-ver yon-der, what do I see?
4 If you don't be-lieve I've been re-deemed,

Leader

wa-ter.

the lead-er looks like the Is - ra - 'lite,
looks like the band that . . Mo - ses led,
the Ho - ly Ghost a - com-ing on me,
just fol-low me down to . . . Jor - dan's stream,

All

Refrain

God's a - goin'-a trou-ble the wa - ter.

Text: African American spiritual
Music: African American spiritual; arr. Carl Haywood, b. 1949
Arr. © 1992 Carl Haywood

115

I'm Going on a Journey

1 I'm go-ing on a jour-ney, and I'm start-ing to-day.

My head is wet, and I'm on my way.

God's mark is on me; it's on you, too.

God says he loves me, and he loves you, too!

2 I'm be-com-ing this day a saint of God.
3 There are oth - er saints who have said a-men.

It real-ly does-n't mat-ter what roads I trod.
They'll keep . . me . . faith-ful to my jour-ney's end.

Where-ev - er I go he's been there, too. God's
A - long . . the way I want to be the

love has touched me and will car-ry me through.
kind . . of per-son that . . God . . set free.

Text: Kenneth D. Larkin
Music: WET SAINTS, Edward V. Bonnemère, 1921-1996
© 1994 Augsburg Fortress

116

Free at Last

Refrain

All

Free at last, free at last, thank God al-might-y I'm free at last.

Leader

1 Sure-ly been 'buked, and sure-ly been scorned,
2 If you don't know that I been . . . re - deemed,

All   Leader

thank God al-might-y, I'm free at last, but
thank God al-might-y, I'm free at last, just

still my soul is-a heav-en - born,
fol - low me down to Jor-dan's stream,

thank God al - might - y, I'm free at last.
thank God al - might - y, I'm free at last.

Text: traditional
Music: African American spiritual; arr. J. Jefferson Cleveland, 1937-1986 and Verolga Nix, b. 1933
Arr. © 1981 Abingdon Press, admin. The Copyright Company

Take Me to the Water 117

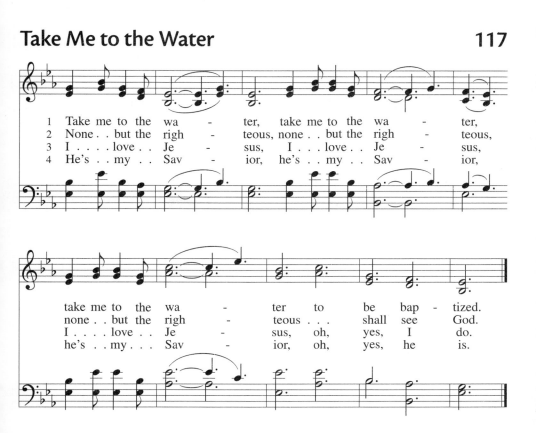

1 Take me to the wa - ter, take me to the wa - ter,
2 None . . but the righ - teous, none . . but the righ - teous,
3 I . . . . love . . Je - sus, I . . love . . Je - sus,
4 He's . . my . . Sav - ior, he's . . my . . Sav - ior,

take me to the wa - ter to be bap - tized.
none . . but the righ - teous . . . shall see God.
I . . . . love . . Je - sus, oh, yes, I do.
he's . . my . . . Sav - ior, oh, yes, he is.

Text: traditional
Music: African American spiritual; arr. Horace Clarence Boyer, b. 1935
Arr. © 1992 Horace Clarence Boyer

118

Blessed Assurance

1 Bless-ed as-sur-ance, Je-sus is mine! Oh, what a fore-taste of glo-ry di-vine!
2 Per-fect sub-mis-sion, per-fect de-light, vi-sions of rap-ture now burst on my sight;
3 Per-fect sub-mis-sion, all is at rest; I in my Sav-ior am hap-py and blest,

Heir of sal-va-tion, pur-chase of God, born of his Spir-it, washed in his blood.
an-gels de-scend-ing bring from a-bove ech-oes of mer-cy, whis-pers of love.
watch-ing and wait-ing, look-ing a-bove, filled with his good-ness, lost in his love.

Refrain

This is my sto-ry, this is my song, prais-ing my Sav-ior all the day long:

this is my sto-ry, this is my song, prais-ing my Sav-ior all the day long.

Text: Fanny J. Crosby, 1820-1915
Music: ASSURANCE, Phoebe P. Knapp, 1830-1908

Come, Let Us Eat

119

1 Come, let us eat, for now the feast is spread,
2 Come, let us drink, for now the wine is poured,
3 In . . . . his pres-ence now we meet and rest,
4 Rise, then, to spread a-broad God's might-y word,

come, let us eat, for now the feast is spread.
come, let us drink, for now the wine is poured.
in . . . . his pres-ence now we meet and rest.
rise, then, to spread a-broad God's might-y word.

Our Lord's bod-y let us take to-geth-er,
Je - sus' blood poured let us drink to-geth-er,
In the pres-ence of our Lord we gath-er,
Je - sus ris-en will bring in the king-dom,

our Lord's bod-y let us take to-geth-er.
Je - sus' blood poured let us drink to-geth-er.
in the pres-ence of our Lord we gath-er.
Je - sus ris-en will bring in the king-dom.

Text: Billema Kwillia, b. c. 1925, sts. 1-3; Gilbert E. Doan, b. 1930, st. 4, alt.; tr. Margaret D. Miller, b. 1927, sts. 1-3, alt.
Music: A VA DE, Billema Kwillia, b. c. 1925; arr. *Lutheran Book of Worship*, 1978
Text sts. 1-3 and tune © Lutheran World Federation; text st. 4 and arr. © 1972 *Contemporary Worship 4*, admin. Augsburg Fortress

Lord, I Hear of Showers of Blessings

Even Me

120

1 Lord, I hear of show'rs of bless-ings
2 Pass me not, O gen-tle Sav-ior,
3 Bread of heav - en, bread of heav-en,

thou art scat - t'ring full and free;
sin - ful though my heart may be;
ev - er let me feed on thee;

show'rs the thirst - y land re - fresh-ing,
I am long - ing for thy fa - vor,
Vine of heav - en, Vine of heav-en,

let some drops now fall on me!
while thou'rt bless - ing, oh, bless me!
let thy blood a - tone for me!

Refrain

Leader / All

E - ven me, yes! E - ven me!
E - ven me, yes! E - ven me!
E - ven me, yes! E - ven me!

Leader / All

E - ven me, Lord! E - ven me!
E - ven me, Lord! E - ven me!
E - ven me, Lord! E - ven me!

Let some drops now fall on me!
While thou'rt bless - ing, Lord, bless me!
Let thy blood a - tone for me!

Text: Elizabeth Conder, 1824-1919
Music: EVEN ME, William B. Bradbury, 1816-1868; arr. Roberta Martin, 1912-1969
Arr. © 1968 Roberta Martin, admin. Leonard Austin

121

This Is My Body

This is my bod-y giv-en up for you, this is my

blood poured out for you. This is my bod-y giv-en

up for you, this is my blood poured out for you.

Bod-y of Christ. A - men. Blood of Christ. A - men. Bod-y of Christ. A - men. Blood of Christ. A - men.

Text: traditional
Music: CAUSE OF OUR JOY, Edward V. Bonnemère, 1921-1996
Music © Amity Music Corp.

122   One Bread, One Body

One bread, one bod-y, one Lord of all;

one cup of bless-ing which we bless, and

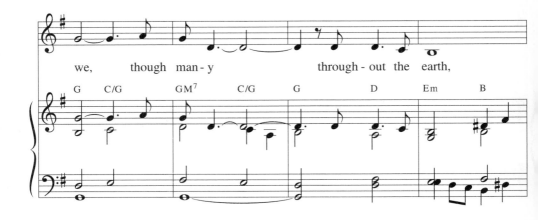

we, though man-y through-out the earth,

we are one bod - y in this one Lord.

Em   D   G   Em   A   D   G   C/G   G

1 Gen - tile   or   Jew,   ser - vant   or   free,
2 Man - y   the   gifts,   man - y   the   works,
3 Grain for   the   fields,   scat- tered and   grown,

Em   D   Em   D

Refrain

wom- an   or   man,   no   more.
one   in   the   Lord   of   all.
gath - ered to   one   for   all.

Em   F   Am   D

Text: John Foley, b. 1939
Music: ONE BREAD, ONE BODY, John Foley, b. 1939
© 1978, 1989 John B. Foley and New Dawn Music

123 Let Us Break Bread Together

1 Let us break bread to-geth-er on our knees; let us
2 Let us drink wine to-geth-er on our knees; let us

break bread to-geth-er on our knees.
drink wine to-geth-er on our knees.

Refrain

When I fall on my knees, with my face to the ris-ing

sun, O Lord, have mer-cy on me.

3 Let us praise God to-geth-er on our knees; let us

praise God to - geth - er on our knees.

Text: African American spiritual
Music: BREAK BREAD TOGETHER, African American spiritual; arr. *Contemporary Worship 4*, 1972
Arr. © 1972 *Contemporary Worship 4*, admin. Augsburg Fortress

Fill My Cup, Lord   124

Fill my cup, Lord, I lift it up, Lord. Come and
quench this thirst-ing of my soul. Bread of heav-en, feed me till I
want no more; fill my cup, fill it up and make me whole.

Text: Richard Blanchard, b. 1925
Music: FILL MY CUP, Richard Blanchard, b. 1925; arr. Eugene Clark
© 1964 Word Music, Inc.

125

Eat This Bread

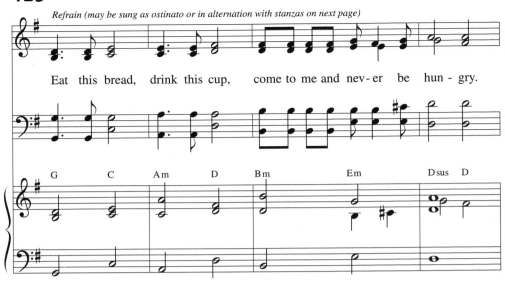

Refrain (may be sung as ostinato or in alternation with stanzas on next page)

Eat this bread, drink this cup, come to me and nev-er be hun-gry.

Eat this bread, drink this cup, trust in me and you will not thirst.

Text: John 6; adapt. Robert J. Batastini, b. 1942 and the Taizé Community
Music: BERTHIER, Jacques Berthier, 1923-1994
© 1984 Les Presses de Taizé, admin. GIA Publications, Inc.

126

Taste and See

Taste and see, taste and see the good - ness of the Lord. Oh, taste and see, taste and see the good - ness of the Lord, of the Lord.

1 I will bless the Lord at all times.
2 Glo - ri - fy the Lord with me.
3 Wor- ship . . . the Lord, all you peo - ple.

Text: Psalm 34, adapt.
Music: James E. Moore, Jr.
Music © 1983 GIA Publications, Inc.

127

Fill My Cup, Let It Overflow

Refrain

Fill my cup, let it o-ver-flow;   fill my cup, let it o-ver-flow;

fill my cup, let it o-ver-flow,   let it o-ver-flow with love.

1 Lord, let me be your in-stru-ment, spread-ing sun-shine in the land.
2 It's my de-sire to live for you   and   to al-ways walk up-right.

Refrain

Let all see your works in me; help me live the best I can.
Give me strength to face each day; stay with me through each dark night.

Text: Isaiah Jones Jr.
Music: Isaiah Jones Jr.
© 1970 Davike Music Co., admin. Fricon Entertainment

Now Behold the Lamb

128

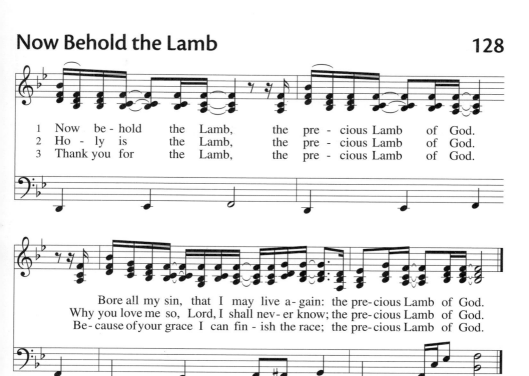

1 Now be - hold the Lamb, the pre - cious Lamb of God.
2 Ho - ly is the Lamb, the pre - cious Lamb of God.
3 Thank you for the Lamb, the pre - cious Lamb of God.

Bore all my sin, that I may live a - gain: the pre-cious Lamb of God.
Why you love me so, Lord, I shall nev- er know; the pre-cious Lamb of God.
Be- cause of your grace I can fin - ish the race; the pre-cious Lamb of God.

Text: Kirk Franklin
Music: Kirk Franklin; arr. Keith Hampton
© 1995 Lilly Mack Music

129

Now We Offer

Refrain

Now we of-fer you, our Fa-ther, with the bread and with the wine

all our joys and all our sor-rows, all our strug-gles and our time.

1 As the fields of wheat now grow-ing will be-come a ho-ly sign,
2 Like the grape put in the cel-lar, there to change in-to the wine,
3 In these gifts we see our one-ness through-out cit-y and the field,
4 All your peo-ple who are yearn-ing for the free-dom still a-head
5 We sing glo-ry to the Fa-ther and to Christ who lives a-bove,

so shall we re-veal you, Je-sus, that in us you now may shine.
all the poor on earth who suf-fer shed their sor-rows in this sign.
and we find a life of so-lace where the scars of strife are healed.
of-fer fruits of your cre-a-tion in these gifts of wine and bread.
and we praise the Ho-ly Spir-it for the gift to us of love.

Text: *Misa popular nicaragüense*; tr. Gerald Thorson, b. 1921
Music: TE OFRECEMOS, Nicaraguan folk tune; arr. Vernon Hamberg, b. 1948
Tr. © 1989 Lutheran World Federation
Arr. © 1989 Augsburg Fortress

Listen, God Is Calling

Refrain

Leader / All

Lis-ten, lis-ten, God is call-ing, through the Word in-vit-ing,

of-fer-ing for-give-ness, com - fort, and joy. joy.

Leader / All

1 Je - sus gave his man-date: share the good news
2 Let none be for-got-ten through-out the world.
3 Help us to be faith-ful, stand-ing stead-fast,

Leader / All / *Refrain*

that he came to save us and set us free.
In the tri-une name of God go and bap - tize.
walk-ing in your pre-cepts, led by your Word.

Text: Tanzanian traditional; tr. Howard S. Olson, b. 1922
Music: NENO LAKE MUNGU, Tanzanian tune; arr. Austin C. Lovelace, b. 1919
Tr. © Lutheran Theological College, Makumira, Tanzania
Arr. © Austin C. Lovelace

131 Lord, Let My Heart Be Good Soil

Lord, let my heart be good soil, o-pen to the seed of your word.

Lord, let my heart be good soil, where love can grow and peace is un-der-stood.

When my heart is hard, break the stone a-way. When my heart is cold,

warm it with the day. When my heart is lost, lead me on your way.

Lord, let my heart, Lord, let my heart, Lord, let my heart be good soil.

Text: Handt Hanson, b. 1950
Music: GOOD SOIL, Handt Hanson, b. 1950
© 1985 Prince of Peace/Changing Church, Inc.

Thy Word Is a Lamp

Thy word is a lamp un-to my feet and a light un-to my path.

1 When I feel a - fraid, think I've lost my way,
2 I will not for - get your love for me and yet my

still you're there right be - side me, and noth-ing will I fear as
heart for - ev - er is wan - der - ing. Je - sus, be my guide and

long as you are near. Please be near me to the end.
hold me to your side, and I will love you to the end.

Text: Amy Grant, b. 1960
Music: THY WORD, Michael W. Smith, b. 1957; arr. Keith Phillips

133 A Mighty Fortress Is Our God

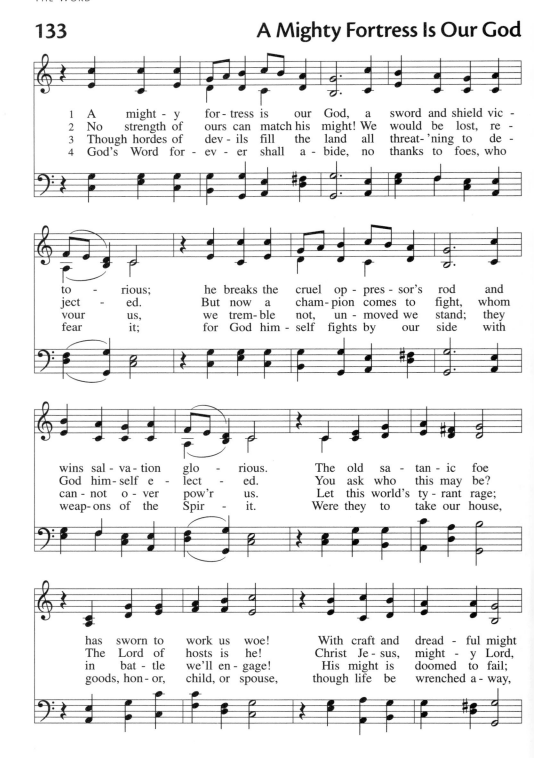

1 A might-y for-tress is our God, a sword and shield vic-
2 No strength of ours can match his might! We would be lost, re-
3 Though hordes of dev-ils fill the land all threat-'ning to de-
4 God's Word for-ev-er shall a-bide, no thanks to foes, who

to - rious; he breaks the cruel op-pres-sor's rod and
ject - ed. But now a cham-pion comes to fight, whom
vour us, we trem-ble not, un-moved we stand; they
fear it; for God him-self fights by our side with

wins sal-va-tion glo - rious. The old sa-tan-ic foe
God him-self e-lect - ed. You ask who this may be?
can-not o-ver pow'r us. Let this world's ty-rant rage;
weap-ons of the Spir - it. Were they to take our house,

has sworn to work us woe! With craft and dread-ful might
The Lord of hosts is he! Christ Je-sus, might-y Lord,
in bat-tle we'll en-gage! His might is doomed to fail;
goods, hon-or, child, or spouse, though life be wrenched a-way,

he arms him - self to fight. On earth he has no e - qual.
God's on - ly Son, a - dored. He holds the field vic - to - rious.
God's judg-ment must pre-vail! One lit - tle word sub-dues him.
they can - not win the day. The king-dom's ours for-ev - er!

Text: Martin Luther, 1483-1546; tr. *Lutheran Book of Worship*, 1978
Music: EIN FESTE BURG, Martin Luther, 1483-1546
Tr. © 1978 *Lutheran Book of Worship*

O Lord, Open My Eyes   134

O Lord, o - pen my eyes, let me see. O Lord,

o - pen my ears, let me hear. In your word there is

pow'r, in your word there is life. O Lord, o - pen my mouth, let me speak.

Text: Emmanuel F. Y. Grantson
Music: Ghanaian traditional, arr. *This Far by Faith*
Text and arr. © 1999 Augsburg Fortress

Come, We That Love the Lord

We're Marching to Zion

135

1. Come, we that love the Lord, and let our joys be known;
2. Let those refuse to sing who nev-er knew our God;
3. The hill of Zi-on yields a thou-sand sa-cred sweets
4. Then let our songs a-bound, and ev-'ry tear be dry;

join in a song with sweet ac-cord, join in a song with
but chil-dren of the heav'n-ly King, but chil-dren of the
be-fore we reach the heav'n-ly fields, be-fore we reach the
we're march-ing through Em-man-uel's ground, we're march-ing through Em-

sweet ac-cord and thus sur-round the throne, and thus sur-round the throne.
heav'n-ly King may speak their joys a-broad, may speak their joys a-broad.
heav'n-ly fields, or walk the gold-en streets, or walk the gold-en streets.
man-uel's ground, to fair-er worlds on high, to fair-er worlds on high.

Refrain

We're march-ing to Zi-on, beau-ti-ful, beau-ti-ful Zi-on:

we're march-ing up-ward to Zi-on, the beau-ti-ful cit-y of God.

Text: Isaac Watts, 1674-1748, stanzas; Robert Lowry, 1826-1899, refrain
Music: MARCHING TO ZION, Robert Lowry, 1826-1899

We Have Come into His House

136

1 We have come in-to his house and gath-ered in his name to
2 So for - get a - bout your-self and con-cen-trate on him and
3 Let us lift up ho - ly hands and mag - ni - fy his name and

wor - ship him. We have come in-to his house and
wor - ship him. So for - get a - bout your-self and
wor - ship him. Let us lift up ho - ly hands and

gath - ered in his name to wor - ship him. We have
con - cen - trate on him and wor - ship him. So for -
mag - ni - fy his name and wor - ship him. Let us

come in - to his house and gath - ered in his name to
get a - bout your-self and con - cen - trate on him and
lift up ho - ly hands and mag - ni - fy his name and

wor - ship Christ, the Lord; wor - ship him, Christ the Lord.

Text: Bruce Ballinger, b. 1945
Music: Bruce Ballinger, b. 1945
© 1976 Sound III, Inc, admin. MCA Music Publishing

137 Lord, This Day We've Come to Worship

1 Lord, this day we've come to wor-ship; Fa-ther, Son and Ho-ly Ghost,
2 In the pow'r of re-sur-rec-tion we have come to praise the Lord,
3 May your word en-rich our spir-it, give us strength to do your will,
4 As we meet our bless-ed Sav-ior at the ta-ble of the Lord,
5 Cel-e-brate the re-sur-rec-tion in the church and sing his praise,

grace us with your bless-ed pre-sence; bless-ed Sav-ior, be our host.
cel-e-brate his bless-ed sup-per, and to learn his ho-ly word.
show the king-dom we'll in-her-it, when at last our voice is still.
may his bod-y bro-ken for us strength and com-fort, Lord, af-ford.
till we come to true per-fec-tion: Serve the Lord through all our days.

Refrain

Al - le - lu - ia, al - le - lu - ia,

al - le - lu - ia, praise the Lord! Al - le - lu - ia,

al - le - lu - ia, al - le - lu - ia, praise the Lord!

Text: Richard C. Dickinson
Music: GLORIOUS NAME, B. B. McKinney, 1886-1952
Text © 1995 Richard C. Dickinson
Music © 1942, 1970 Broadman Press

Come, All You People

Uyai mose

1 Come, all you peo - ple, come and praise the Most High;
1 U - ya - i mo - se, ti - na - ma - te Mwa - ri;
2 Come, all you peo - ple, come and praise the Sav - ior;
3 Come, all you peo - ple, come and praise the Spir - it;

come, all you peo - ple, come and praise the Most High;
u - ya - i mo - se, ti - na - ma - te Mwa - ri;
come, all you peo - ple, come and praise the Sav - ior;
come, all you peo - ple, come and praise the Spir - it;

come, all you peo - ple, come and praise the Most High;
u - ya - i mo - se, ti - na - ma - te Mwa - ri;
come, all you peo - ple, come and praise the Sav - ior;
come, all you peo - ple, come and praise the Spir - it;

come now and wor - ship the Lord.
u - ya - i mo - se Zvi - no.
come now and wor - ship the Lord.
come now and wor - ship the Lord.

Percussion
Handclap or Blocks

*The polyrhythmic pattern of 3 beats
against 2 beats is integral to this song.*

Text: Alexander Gondo, st. 1; tr. I-to Loh, b. 1936; *With One Voice*, 1995, sts. 2-3
Music: UYAI MOSE, Alexander Gondo
© 1986 World Council of Churches

139

What a Blessing

Refrain

What a bless - ing, what a bless - ing,

to be here in the ser - vice of the Lord.

We are thank-ful for an - oth - er chance to wor - ship God,

we've come to praise his ho - ly name.

1 Praise him, we've come to praise him,
2 Thank him, we've come to thank him,

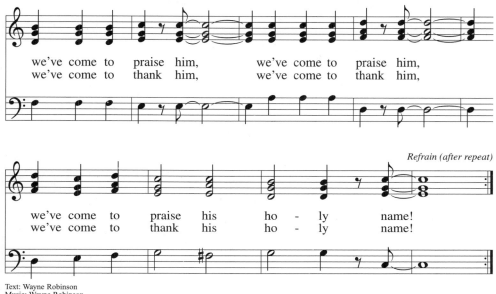

we've come to praise him, we've come to praise him,
we've come to thank him, we've come to thank him,

Refrain (after repeat)

we've come to praise his ho - ly name!
we've come to thank his ho - ly name!

Text: Wayne Robinson
Music: Wayne Robinson
© 1994 Wayne Robinson

Jesus, We Are Gathered

Yesu, tawa pano

140

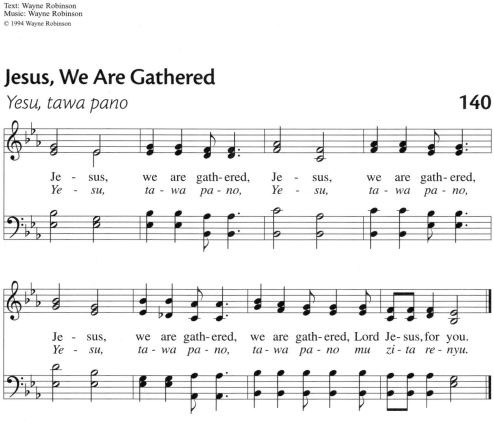

Je - sus, we are gath-ered, Je - sus, we are gath-ered,
Ye - su, ta - wa pa - no, Ye - su, ta - wa pa - no,

Je - sus, we are gath-ered, we are gath-ered, Lord Je - sus, for you.
Ye - su, ta - wa pa - no, ta - wa pa - no mu zi - ta re - nyu.

Text: Patrick Matsikenyiri
Music: YESU, TAWA PANO, Patrick Matsikenyiri
© WGRG The Iona Community (Scotland), admin. GIA Publications, Inc.

Come and Go with Me to My Father's House

141

In My Father's House

1 Come and go with me to my Fa-ther's house, to my Fa-ther's house,
2 It's not ve-ry far to my Fa-ther's house, to my Fa-ther's house,
3 Je - sus is the way to my Fa-ther's house, to my Fa-ther's house,
4 Je - sus is the light in my Fa-ther's house, in my Fa-ther's house,

to my Fa-ther's house. Come and go with me
to my Fa-ther's house. It's not ve - ry far
to my Fa-ther's house. Je - sus is the way
in my Fa-ther's house. Je - sus is the light

to my Fa-ther's house, where there's joy, joy, joy!
to my Fa-ther's house, where there's joy, joy, joy!
to my Fa-ther's house, where there's joy, joy, joy!
in my Fa-ther's house, where there's joy, joy, joy!

5 All is peace and love   6 We will dance and sing   7 We will praise the Lord
in my Father's house . . .   in my Father's house . . .   in my Father's house . . .

Text: traditional
Music: traditional; arr. Charles High
Arr. © 1978 Word of God Music, admin. The Copyright Company

In the Name of the Father

The Trinity

In the name of the Fa - ther, in the name of the Son,

in the name of the Spir - it,

Lord, now we come. Lord, now we come.

Text: James M. Capers, b. 1948
Music: James M. Capers, b. 1948
© 1999 Augsburg Fortress

143   # The Lord Is in His Holy Temple

The Lord is in his ho-ly tem-ple; the
Lord is in his ho-ly tem-ple. Keep
si-lence, keep si-lence, keep si-lence, keep
si-lence, keep si-lence, keep si-lence be-

Text: Habakkuk 2:20
Music: Glenn Burleigh
Music © 1988 Glenn Burleigh, Burleigh Inspirations Music

Jesus Ose

144

Je-sus o-see, yey! Yey, yey o! Je-sus o-see, yey! Yey, yey o!

Je-sus o, yey! Je-sus o, yey, yey!

Literal translation: Jesus has won the good battle. This Jesus is good, yes! Jesus, Jesus is good.

Text: Ghanaian traditional
Music: Ghanaian traditional; transcribed Emmanuel F. Y. Grantson

Jesus, We Want to Meet

145

1 Je - sus, we want to meet on this thy ho - ly day.
2 We kneel in awe and fear on this thy ho - ly day,
3 Thy bless - ing, Lord, we seek on this thy ho - ly day.
4 Our minds we ded - i - cate on this thy ho - ly day,

We gath - er round thy throne on this thy ho - ly day.
pray God to teach us here on this thy ho - ly day.
Give joy of thy vic - to - ry on this thy ho - ly day.
heart and soul con - se - crate on this thy ho - ly day.

Thou art our heav'n - ly friend, hear our prayers as they as - cend,
Save us and cleanse our hearts, lead and guide our acts of praise,
Through grace a - lone are we saved, in thy flock may we be found.
Ho - ly Spir - it, make us whole, bless the ser - mon in this place,

look in - to our hearts and minds to - day, on this thy ho - ly day.
and our faith from seed to flow - er raise, on this thy ho - ly day.
Let the mind of Christ a - bide in us on this thy ho - ly day.
and . . . as we go . . . . lead us, Lord: on this thy ho - ly day.

Text: A. T. Olajide Olude, b. 1908; tr. Biodun Adebesin, b. 1928; versification Austin C. Lovelace, b. 1919
Music: NIGERIA, A. T. Olajide Olude, b. 1908
Tr. and versification © 1964 Abingdon Press, admin. The Copyright Company

I Can Hear My Savior Calling

Where He Leads Me

146

1 I can hear my Sav - ior call-ing, I can hear my Sav - ior call-ing,
2 I'll go with him through the gar-den, I'll go with him through the gar-den,
3 I'll go with him through the judg-ment, I'll go with him through the judg-ment,
4 He will give me grace and glo-ry, he will give me grace and glo-ry,

I can hear my Sav - ior call-ing, "Take thy cross and fol-low, fol-low me."
I'll go with him through the gar-den, I'll go with him, with him all the way.
I'll go with him through the judg-ment, I'll go with him, with him all the way.
he will give me grace and glo-ry, and go with me, with me all the way.

Refrain

Where he leads me I will fol-low, where he leads me I will fol-low,

where he leads me I will fol-low, I'll go with him, with him all the way.

Text: E. W. Blandy
Music: NORRIS, John S. Norris, 1844-1907

I Shall Not Be Moved

Refrain

I shall not be, I shall not be moved. I shall not be, I shall not be moved;

like a tree plant-ed by the wa - ter, I shall not be moved.
be moved.

1 When my cross is heav - y, I shall not be moved,
2 The church of God is march - ing, I shall not be moved, the
3 Je - sus is our cap - tain, I shall not be moved,
4 Fight - ing sin and Sa - tan, I shall not be moved,

when my cross is heav - y, I shall not be moved;
church of God is march - ing, I shall not be moved;
Je - sus is our cap - tain, I shall not be moved;
fight - ing sin and Sa - tan, I shall not be moved;

Refrain

like a tree plant-ed by the wa - ter, I shall not be moved.
be moved.

Text: African American spiritual
Music: African American spiritual

148

Glory, Glory, Hallelujah!

1 Glo - ry, glo - ry, hal - le - lu - jah!
2 I feel bet - ter, so much bet - ter,
3 Feel like shout - ing, "Hal - le - lu - jah!"
4 I am climb - ing Ja - cob's lad - der,
5 Ev - 'ry round goes higher and high - er,

since I laid my bur - den down.
since I laid my bur - den down.
since I laid my bur - den down.
since I laid my bur - den down.
since I laid my bur - den down.

Glo - ry, glo - ry, hal - le - lu - jah!
I feel bet - ter, so much bet - ter,
Feel like shout - ing, "Hal - le - lu - jah!"
I am climb - ing Ja - cob's lad - der,
Ev - 'ry round goes higher and high - er,

since I laid my bur - den down.
since I laid my bur - den down.
since I laid my bur - den down.
since I laid my bur - den down.
since I laid my bur - den down.

Text: African American spiritual
Music: African American spiritual; arr. Carl Haywood, b. 1949

Seek Ye First

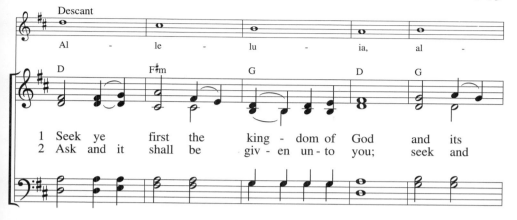

Descant

Al - le - lu - ia, al -

1 Seek ye first the king - dom of God and its
2 Ask and it shall be giv - en un - to you; seek and

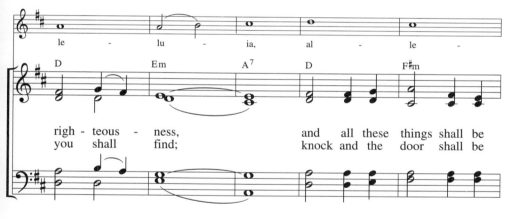

le - lu - ia, al - le -

righ - teous - ness, and all these things shall be
you shall find; knock and the door shall be

lu - ia, al - le - lu - ia.

add - ed un - to you. Al - le - lu, al - le - lu - ia.
o - pened un - to you. Al - le - lu, al - le - lu - ia.

Text: Matt. 6:33, 7:7, adapt.
Music: LAFFERTY, Karen Lafferty, b. 1948

150   Pass Me Not, O Gentle Savior

1 Pass me not, O gen - tle Sav - ior,   hear my hum - ble   cry;
2 Let me at thy throne of mer - cy   find a sweet re - lief;
3 Trust-ing on - ly in thy mer - it,   would I seek thy   face;
4 Thou, the spring of all my com - fort,   more than life to   me,

while on oth - ers thou art call - ing,   do not pass me by.
kneel-ing there in deep con-tri - tion,   help my un - be - lief.
heal my wound-ed, bro-ken spir - it,   save me by thy grace.
whom have I on earth be-side thee?   Whom in heav'n but thee?

Refrain

Sav - ior, Sav - ior, hear my hum - ble cry;

while on oth - ers thou art call - ing, do not pass me by.

Text: Fanny J. Crosby, 1820-1915
Music: PASS ME NOT, William H. Doane, 1832-1915

He Leadeth Me

151

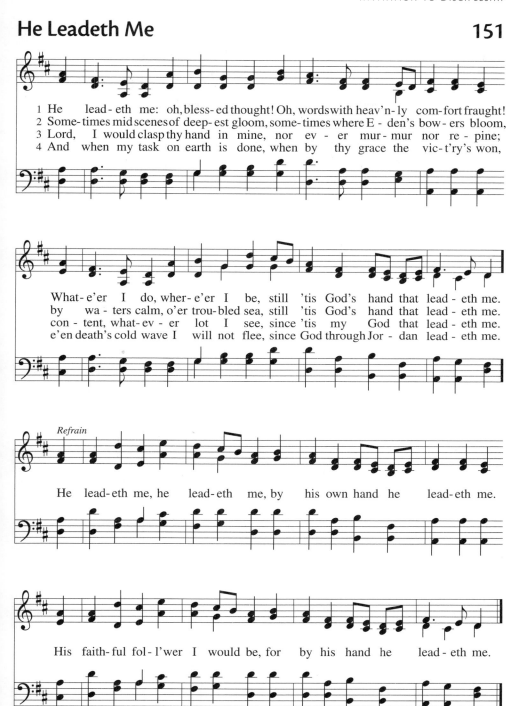

1 He lead - eth me: oh, bless - ed thought! Oh, words with heav'n-ly com-fort fraught!
2 Some-times mid scenes of deep-est gloom, some-times where E - den's bow-ers bloom,
3 Lord, I would clasp thy hand in mine, nor ev - er mur - mur nor re - pine;
4 And when my task on earth is done, when by thy grace the vic-t'ry's won,

What-e'er I do, wher-e'er I be, still 'tis God's hand that lead - eth me.
by wa - ters calm, o'er trou-bled sea, still 'tis God's hand that lead - eth me.
con - tent, what-ev - er lot I see, since 'tis my God that lead - eth me.
e'en death's cold wave I will not flee, since God through Jor - dan lead - eth me.

Refrain

He lead-eth me, he lead-eth me, by his own hand he lead-eth me.

His faith-ful fol - l'wer I would be, for by his hand he lead - eth me.

Text: Joseph H. Gilmore, 1834-1918, alt.
Music: HE LEADETH ME, William B. Bradbury, 1816-1868

152

Have Thine Own Way, Lord

1 Have thine own way, Lord, have thine own way.
2 Have thine own way, Lord, have thine own way.
3 Have thine own way, Lord, have thine own way.
4 Have thine own way, Lord, have thine own way.

Thou art the pot - ter, I am the clay.
Search me and try me, Mas - ter, to - day.
Wound - ed and wea - ry, help me, I pray.
Hold o'er my be - ing ab - so - lute sway.

Mold me and make me af - ter thy will,
Pur - er than snow, Lord, wash me just now,
Pow - er, all pow - er sure - ly is thine.
Fill with thy Spir - it till all shall see

while I am wait - ing, yield - ed and still.
as in thy pres - ence hum - bly I bow.
Touch me and heal me, Sav - ior di - vine.
Christ on - ly, al - ways, liv - ing in me.

Text: Adelaide A. Pollard, 1862-1934
Music: ADELAIDE, George C. Stebbins, 1846-1945

Guide My Feet

1 Guide my feet
2 Hold my hand
3 Stand by me while I run this race.
4 I'm your child
5 Search my heart

Yes, my Lord!

Guide my feet
Hold my hand
Stand by me while I run this race.
I'm your child
Search my heart

Yes, my Lord!

Guide my feet
Hold my hand
Stand by me while I run this race,
I'm your child
Search my heart

for I don't want to run this race in vain.

Text: African American spiritual
Music: African American spiritual; arr. *This Far by Faith*
Arr. © 1999 Augsburg Fortress

You Have Come Down to the Lakeshore

154

Tú has venido a la orilla

1 You have come down to the lake - shore seek-ing
2 You know full well what I have, Lord: nei - ther
3 You need my hands, my ex - haus - tion, work-ing
4 You who have fished oth - er wa - ters; you, the

nei - ther the wise nor the wealth - y, but on - ly
trea - sure nor weap-ons for con - quest, just these my
love for the rest of the wea - ry— a love that's
long - ing of souls that are yearn - ing: O lov - ing

ask - ing for me to fol - low.
fish - nets and will for work - ing.
will - ing to go on lov - ing.
Friend, you have come to call me.

Refrain/Estribillo

Sweet Lord, you have looked in - to my eyes;
Se - ñor: me_has mi - ra - do_a los o - jos;

kind-ly smil - ing, you've called out my name.
son - ri - en - do, has di - cho mi nom - bre;

On the sand I have a - ban-doned my small boat;
en la_a - re - na he de - ja - do mi bar - ca;

now with you, I will seek oth- er seas.
jun - to_a ti bus - ca - ré o - tro mar.

1 *Tú has venido_a la_orilla;*
no_has buscado ni_a sabios, ni_a ricos;
tan sólo quieres que yo te siga. Estribillo

2 *Tú sabes bien lo que tengo:*
en mi barca no_hay oro ni_espadas;
tan sólo redes y mi trabajo. Estribillo

3 *Tú necesitas mis manos,*
mi cansancio que_a otros descanse,
amor que quiera seguir amando. Estribillo

4 *Tú, Pescador de_otros mares,*
ansia_eterna de_almas que_esperan.
Amigo bueno, que_así me llamas. Estribillo

Text: Cesáreo Gabarain, 1936-1991; tr. Madeleine Forell Marshall, b. 1946
Music: PESCADOR DE HOMBRES, Cesáreo Gabarain, 1936-1991

Spanish text and music © 1979 Ediciones Paulinas, admin. OCP Publications
Tr. © Editorial Avance Luterano

155   Softly and Tenderly Jesus Is Calling

1 Soft - ly and ten - der - ly Je - sus is call - ing,
2 Why should we tar - ry when Je - sus is plead - ing,
3 Oh, for the won - der - ful love he has prom - ised,

call - ing for you and for me. See, on the por - tals he's
plead-ing for you and for me? Why should we lin - ger and
prom-ised for you and for me! Though we have sinned, he has

wait-ing and watch-ing, watch-ing for you and for me.
heed not his mer - cies, mer - cies for you and for me?
mer - cy and par - don, par - don for you and for me.

Refrain

"Come home, come home! You who are wea-ry, come
Come home, come home!

home." Ear - nest - ly, ten - der - ly,

Je - sus is call - ing, call-ing, "O sin-ner, come home!"

Text: Will Thompson, 1847-1909
Music: THOMPSON, Will Thompson, 1847-1909

Come to Jesus 156

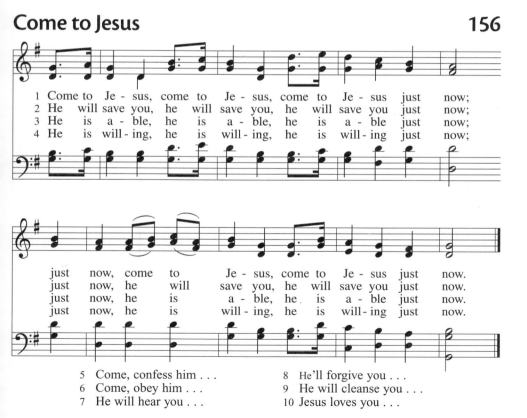

1 Come to Je - sus, come to Je - sus, come to Je - sus just now;
2 He will save you, he will save you, he will save you just now;
3 He is a - ble, he is a - ble, he is a - ble just now;
4 He is will - ing, he is will - ing, he is will - ing just now;

just now, come to Je - sus, come to Je - sus just now.
just now, he will save you, he will save you just now.
just now, he is a - ble, he is a - ble just now.
just now, he is will - ing, he is will - ing just now.

5 Come, confess him . . .   8 He'll forgive you . . .
6 Come, obey him . . .   9 He will cleanse you . . .
7 He will hear you . . .   10 Jesus loves you . . .

Text: traditional
Music: traditional

157 # God Be with You till We Meet Again

1 God be with you till we meet a - gain; by his
2 God be with you till we meet a - gain; 'neath his
3 God be with you till we meet a - gain; when life's
4 God be with you till we meet a - gain; keep love's

coun - sels guide, up - hold you, with his sheep se - cure - ly
wings se - cure - ly hide you, dai - ly man - na still proper - ils thick con - found you, put his arms un - fail - ing
ban - ner float - ing o'er you, smite death's threat - 'ning wave be-

fold you;
vide you;   God be with you till we meet a - gain.
'round you;
fore you;

Refrain

Till we meet, till we meet, till we meet at Je - sus' feet;

till we meet, till we meet a - gain, till we meet,

till we meet, till we meet, God be with you till we meet a - gain.

till we meet, till we meet a - gain,

Text: Jeremiah E. Rankin, 1828-1904
Music: GOD BE WITH YOU, William G. Tomer, 1833-1896

Hallelujah! We Sing Your Praises

Hal - le - lu - jah! We sing your prais - es, all our hearts are filled with glad - ness. Hal - le - lu - jah! We sing your prais - es, all our hearts are filled with glad - ness.

1 Christ the Lord to us said: I am wine, I am bread,
2 Now he sends us all out, strong in faith, free of doubt,

I am wine, I am bread, give to all who thirst and hun - ger.
strong in faith, free of doubt. Tell to all the joy - ful gos - pel.

Text: South African
Music: HALELUYA! PELO TSO RONA, South African
Text and arr. © 1984 Utryck, admin. Walton Music Corp.

Take the Name of Jesus with You

Precious Name

159

1 Take the name of Je - sus with you, child of sor - row and of woe;
2 Take the name of Je - sus ev - er as a shield from ev - 'ry snare;
3 Oh, the pre-cious name of Je - sus! How it thrills our souls with joy,
4 At the name of Je - sus bow-ing, fall - ing pros - trate at his feet,

it will joy and com-fort give you; take it then, wher-e'er you go.
if temp-ta-tions 'round you gath - er, breathe that ho - ly name in prayer.
when his lov-ing arms re - ceive us, and his songs our tongues em-ploy!
King of kings in heav'n we'll crown him, when our jour-ney is com-plete.

Refrain

Pre - cious name, oh, how sweet!
Pre - cious name, oh, how sweet!

Hope of earth and joy of heav'n. Pre - cious name,
Pre - cious name,

oh, how sweet! Hope of earth and joy of heav'n.
oh, how sweet, how sweet!

Text: Lydia Baxter, 1809-1874
Music: PRECIOUS NAME, William H. Doane, 1832-1915

God Be with You

160

God be with you, God be with you,

God be with you, un-til we meet a - gain;

God be with you, God be with you,

God be with you, un-til we meet a - gain.

Text: Thomas A. Dorsey, 1899-1993
Music: Thomas A. Dorsey, 1899-1993; arr. Horace Clarence Boyer, b. 1935

161

Go, My Children, with My Blessing

1 "Go, my chil - dren, with my bless - ing, nev - er a - lone.
2 "Go, my chil - dren, sins for - giv - en, at peace and pure.
3 "Go, my chil - dren, fed and nour - ished, clos - er to me.
4 "I the Lord will bless and keep you, and give you peace.

Wak - ing, sleep - ing, I am with you, you are my own.
Here you learned how much I love you, what I can cure.
Grow in love and love by serv - ing, joy - ful and free.
I the Lord will smile up - on you, and give you peace.

In my love's bap - tis - mal riv - er I have made you mine for - ev - er.
Here you heard my dear Son's sto - ry, here you touched him, saw his glo - ry.
Here my Spir - it's pow - er filled you, here his ten - der com - fort stilled you.
I the Lord will be your Fa - ther, Sav - ior, Com - fort - er and Broth - er.

Go, my chil - dren, with my bless - ing, you are my own."
Go, my chil - dren, sins for - giv - en, at peace and pure."
Go, my chil - dren, fed and nour - ished, joy - ful and free."
Go, my chil - dren, I will keep you, and give you peace."

Text: Jaroslav J. Vajda, b. 1919
Music: AR HYD Y NOS, Welsh
Text © 1983 Jaroslav J. Vajda

May God Bless Us

Bwana awabariki

162

May God bless us and keep us; may God bless us and keep us;
Bwa - na a - wa - ba - ri - ki, Bwa - na a - wa - ba - ri - ki,

may God bless us and keep us ev - er - more.
Bwa - na a - wa - ba - ri - ki mi - le - le.

Leader

All

Re - vere the Lord; may God bless us and keep us.
U - ki - mcha Bwa - na; Bwa - na a - wa - ba - ri - ki.

Text: Numbers 6:24, adapt.
Music: African

We Shall Not Be Alone

163

Be in the fleeting word, our Father, the stumbling effort.
Touch mind and heart and life,
that as we move from this place
into the way that we must take,
we shall not be alone,
but feel thy presence beside us, all the way.

164

Great Day!

Refrain

Great day! Great day, the righteous marching. Great day!

1 **2** Leader

1 Char-
2 This

God's going to build up Zion's walls. God's going to build up Zion's walls.

-iot rode on the mountain-top,
is the day of ... jubilee,

My
The

God's going to build up Zion's walls.

Refrain

God spoke and the chariot did stop,
Lord has set his ... people free,

God's going to build up Zion's walls.

Text: African American spiritual
Music: GREAT DAY, African American spiritual; arr. J. Jefferson Cleveland, 1937-1986
Arr. © 1981 Abingdon Press, admin. The Copyright Company

In the Morning When I Rise

Give Me Jesus

1 In the morn-ing when I rise, in the morn-ing when I rise,
2 Dark . . . mid-night was my cry, dark . . . mid-night was my cry,
3 Just a-bout the break of day, just a-bout the break of day,
4 Oh, . . . when I come to die, oh, . . . when I come to die,
5 And . . . when I want to sing, and . . . when I want to sing,

in the morn-ing when I rise, give me Je - sus.
dark . . . mid-night was my cry, give me Je - sus.
just a-bout the break of day, give me Je - sus.
oh, . . . when I come to die, give me Je - sus.
and . . . when I want to sing, give me Je - sus.

Refrain

Give me Je - sus, give me Je - sus.

You may have all the rest, give me Je - sus.

Text: African American spiritual
Music: GIVE ME JESUS, African American spiritual; arr. L. L. Fleming, b. 1936
Arr. © 1973 Augsburg Publishing House

166

Oh, I Woke Up This Morning

1 Oh, I woke up this morn - ing with my mind, and it was
2 Can't hate your neigh - bor in your mind, when you keep it
3 Makes you love ev - 'ry - bod - y with your mind, when you keep it
4 The dev - il can't catch you in your mind, when you keep it
5 Je - sus, the cap - tain in your mind, when you keep it

stayed, stayed on Je - sus, woke up this morn - ing with my
stayed, stayed on Je - sus, can't hate your neigh - bor in your
stayed, stayed on Je - sus, love ev - 'ry - bod - y with your
stayed, stayed on Je - sus, dev - il can't catch you in your
stayed, stayed on Je - sus, Je - sus, the cap - tain in your

mind, and it was stayed, stayed on Je - sus,
mind, when you keep it stayed, stayed on Je - sus,
mind, when you keep it stayed, stayed on Je - sus,
mind, when you keep it stayed, stayed on Je - sus,
mind, when you keep it stayed, stayed on Je - sus,

woke up this morn - ing with my mind, and it was
can't hate your neigh - bor in your mind, when you keep it
love ev - 'ry - bod - y with your mind, when you keep it
dev - il can't catch you in your mind, when you keep it
Je - sus, the cap - tain in your mind, when you keep it

stayed, stayed on Je - sus, hal - le - lu, hal - le - lu, hal - le -

lu, hal - le - lu, hal - le - lu - jah.

Text: African American spiritual
Music: African American spiritual

Jesus in the Morning 167

1 Je - sus, Je - sus, Je - sus in the morn-ing, Je - sus in the noon-time;
2 Praise him, praise him, praise him in the morn-ing, praise him in the noon-time;
3 Love him, love him, love him in the morn-ing, love him in the noon-time;
4 Serve him, serve him, serve him in the morn-ing, serve him in the noon-time;
5 Je - sus, Je - sus, Je - sus in the morn-ing, Je - sus in the noon-time;

Je - sus, Je - sus, Je - sus when the sun goes down.
praise him, praise him, praise him when the sun goes down.
love him, love him, love him when the sun goes down.
serve him, serve him, serve him when the sun goes down.
Je - sus, Je - sus, Je - sus when the sun goes down.

Text: African American spiritual
Music: African American spiritual

My Soul Does Magnify the Lord
Magnificat

1 My soul does mag-ni-fy the Lord;
2 From this day all will call me blessed:
3 His mer-cy touch-es those who love,
4 He cast the might-y from their thrones,

my spir-it sings of God, my Sav-ior,
from now through all the com-ing ag-es.
and those who serve . . . one an-oth-er.
and he has lift-ed up the low-ly.

for he has looked with love and fa-vor
The Lord has done great things for me and
And with great strength he has scat-tered all the
He fills the hun-gry with good things while

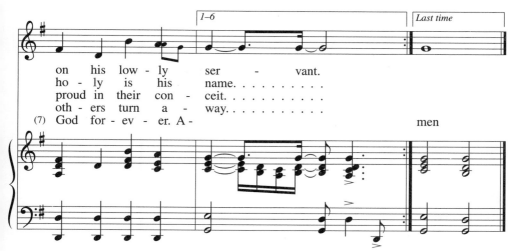

on   his   low - ly   ser -   vant.
ho - ly   is   his   name. . . . .
proud in their con - ceit. . . . .
oth - ers turn a - way. . . . .
(7) God for - ev - er. A-   men

5 He comes to all who seek his love,
for he remembers the promise
that he had made to Abraham and
to the children of God.

6 All glory be to God on high,
and to his Son, God the Savior,
and to the Spirit of life and truth that
burns within our hearts.

7 Just as it was, it is today,
and it shall last through all tomorrows,
and so my soul magnifies the Lord; praise
God forever. Amen

Text: Grayson Warren Brown; based on Luke 1:46-55
Music: Grayson Warren Brown
© 1992 Grayson Warren Brown, admin. OCP Publications

A Prayer at Evening

169

Lord, I sing your praise,
the whole day through until the night.
Dad's nets are filled,
I have helped him.
We have drawn them in,
stamping the rhythm with our feet,
the muscles tense.
We have sung your praise.
On the beach, there were our mammies,
who bought the blessing out of the nets,
out of the nets into their basins.
They rushed to the market,
returned and bought again.

Lord, what a blessing is the sea
with fish in plenty.
Lord, that is the story of your grace.
Nets tear, and we succumb
because we cannot hold them.
Lord, with your praise
we drop off to sleep.
Carry us through the night,
make us fresh for the morning.
Hallelujah for the day!
And blessing for the night!
Amen

Anonymous from Ghana, tr. Aylward Shorter, *Prayer in the Religious Traditions of Africa*
© 1975 Oxford University Press

170

If I Have Wounded Any Soul Today

1 If I have wound-ed an - y soul to - day,
2 If I have ut - tered i - dle words or vain,
3 If I have been per - verse, or hard, or cold,
4 For - give the sins I have con - fessed to thee;

if I have caused one foot to go a - stray,
if I have turned a - side from want or pain,
if I have longed for shel - ter in the fold
for - give the se - cret sins I do not see;

if I have walked in my own will - ful way,
lest I of - fend some oth - er through the strain,
when thou hast giv - en me some fort to hold,
oh, guide me, love me, and my keep - er be.

dear Lord, for - give.
dear Lord, for - give.
dear Lord, for - give.
A - men, a - men.

Text: C. M. Battersby
Music: AN EVENING PRAYER, Charles H. Gabriel, 1856-1932

Swing Low, Sweet Chariot

Refrain

Swing low, sweet char-i-ot, com-ing for to car-ry me home. Swing low, sweet char-i-ot, com-ing for to car-ry me home.

1 I looked o-ver Jor-dan, and what did I see,
2 If you get . . . there . . . be-fore . . . I do,
3 The bright-est . . . day . . . that ev-er I saw,
4 I'm some-times . . up, . . . I'm some-times down,

com-ing for to car-ry me home? A band of an-gels
com-ing for to car-ry me home; tell all my friends I'm
com-ing for to car-ry me home; when Je-sus washed my
com-ing for to car-ry me home; but still my soul feels

Refrain

com-ing af-ter me, com-ing for to car-ry me home.
com-ing . . . too, com-ing for to car-ry me home.
sins . . . a-way, com-ing for to car-ry me home.
heav-en-ly . . . bound, com-ing for to car-ry me home.

Text: African American spiritual
Music: SWING LOW, African American spiritual

If When You Give the Best of Your Service

He Understands; He'll Say, "Well Done"

1. If when you give the best of your ser - vice,
   tell - ing the world that the Sav - ior is come;
   be not dis - mayed when friends don't be - lieve you;
   he un - der - stands; he'll say, "Well done."

2. Mis - un - der - stood, the Sav - ior of sin - ners
   hung on the cross; he was God's on - ly Son;
   oh, hear him call his Fa - ther in heav - en,
   "not . . . my will, but thine be done."

3. So when this life of la - bor is end - ed,
   and the re - ward of the race you have run;
   oh! the sweet rest pre - pared for the faith - ful
   will be his blest and fi - nal "Well done."

4. But if you try and fail in your try - ing,
   hands sore and scarred from the work you've be - gun;
   take up your cross, run quick - ly to meet him;
   he'll un - der - stand; he'll say, "Well done."

Text: Lucie E. Campbell 1885-1963
Music: Lucie E. Campbell, 1885-1963

When upon Life's Billows

173

Count Your Blessings

Refrain

Count your bless-ings, name them one by one;
Count your man-y bless-ings, name them one by one;

count your bless-ings, see what God has done!
count your man-y bless-ings, see what God has done!

Count your bless-ings, name them one by one;
Count your man-y bless-ings,

and it will sur-prise you what the Lord has done.

Text: Johnson Oatman Jr., 1856-1922
Music: Edwin O. Excell, 1851-1921

174

Deep River

Refrain

Deep riv-er, my home is o-ver Jor-dan,
deep riv-er, Lord, I want to cross o-ver in-to camp-ground.

1 Oh, don't you want to go to that gos-pel feast,
2 Oh, when I get to heav-en, I'll take my seat,

that prom-ised land where all is peace? Oh,
and cast my crown at Je-sus' feet. Oh,

Refrain

Text: African American spiritual
Music: Deep River, African American spiritual; arr. J. Jefferson Cleveland, 1937-1986
Arr. © 1981 Abingdon Press, admin. The Copyright Company

Steal Away

175

Refrain

Steal a-way, steal a-way, steal a-way to Je-sus!

Steal a-way, steal a-way home, I ain't got long to stay here.

1 My Lord calls me, he calls me by the thun-der;
2 Green trees are bend-ing, poor sin - ners stand a - trem-bling;
3 Tomb-stones are burst-ing, poor sin - ners stand a - trem-bling;
4 My Lord calls me, he calls me by the light-ning;

Refrain

the trum-pet sounds with-in-a my soul, I ain't got long to stay here.

Text: African American spiritual
Music: STEAL AWAY, African American spiritual

Some Glad Morning When This Life Is O'er

I'll Fly Away

176

1 Some glad morn - ing when this life is o'er,
2 When the shad - ows of this life have grown,
3 Just a few more wea - ry days and then,

to a home on
like a bird from
to a land where

fly a - way, fly a - way; to a land where

God's ce - les - tial shore,
pris - on bars has flown, I'll fly a - way.
joys shall nev - er end, fly a - way, fly a - way.

Refrain

I'll fly a - way, oh glo - ry, I'll fly a - way;
fly a - way, fly a - way, in the morn - ing;

when I die, hal- le - lu - jah by and by, I'll fly a- way.

fly a- way, fly a- way.

Text: Albert E. Brumley
Music: I'LL FLY AWAY, Albert E. Brumley
© 1932, 1980 Albert E. Brumley, admin. Integrated Copyright Group

O God, Save Me　　　　　　　　　　　　　177

Our house stood within a few rods of the Chesapeake Bay, whose broad bosom was ever white with sails from every quarter of the habitable globe. Those beautiful vessels, robed in white, and so delightful to the eyes of freemen, were to me so many shrouded ghosts, to terrify and torment me with thoughts of my wretched condition.

I have often, in the deep stillness of a summer's Sabbath, stood all alone upon the banks of that noble bay, and traced, with saddened heart and tearful eye, the countless number of sails moving off to the mighty ocean. The sight of these always affected me powerfully. My thoughts would compel utterance; and there, with no audience but the Almighty, I would pour out my soul's complaint in my rude way with an apostrophe to the multitude of ships.

"You are loosed from your moorings, and free. I am fast in my chains, and am a slave! You move merrily before the gentle gale, and I sadly before the bloody whip. You are freedom's swift-winged angels, that fly around the world; I am confined in bonds of iron. Oh, that I were free! Oh, that I were one of your gallant decks, and under your protecting wing. Alas! betwixt me and you the turbid waters roll. Go on, go on; Oh, that I could also go! Could I but swim! If I could fly! Oh, why was I born a man, of whom to make a brute! The glad ship is gone: she hides in the dim distance. I am left in the hell of unending slavery.

"O God, save me! God, deliver me! Let me be free!—Is there any God? Why am I a slave? I will run away. I will not stand it. Get caught or get clear, I'll try it. I had as well die with ague as with fever. I have only one life to lose. I had as well be killed running as die standing. Only think of it: one hundred miles north, and I am free! Try it? Yes! God helping me, I will. It cannot be that I shall live and die a slave. I will take to the water. This very bay shall yet bear me into freedom."

Frederick Douglass, 1817-1895, *The Life and Times of Frederick Douglass Written by Himself*, 1893

178

Do, Lord, Remember Me

1 Do, Lord,   do, Lord,   do, Lord, re-mem-ber me;
2 When I'm   in trou - ble,   do, Lord, re-mem-ber me,
3 When I   am dy - ing,   do, Lord, re-mem-ber me,
4 I've got a home in glory land,   do, Lord, re-mem-ber me,

have mer - cy

do, Lord,   do, Lord,   do, Lord, re-mem-ber me;
when I'm   in trou - ble,   do, Lord, re-mem-ber me,
when I   am dy - ing,   do, Lord, re-mem-ber me,
I've got a home in glory land,   do, Lord, re-mem-ber me,

sing the song, chil - dren

do, Lord,   do, Lord,   do, Lord, re-mem-ber me;
when I'm   in trou - ble,   do, Lord, re-mem-ber me;
when I   am dy - ing,   do, Lord, re-mem-ber me;
I've got a home in glory land,   do, Lord, re-mem-ber me;

sing-ing

1–3

do, Lord, re - mem - ber me.

Last time

oh glo - ry

Text: African American spiritual
Music: DITMUS, African American spiritual; arr. William Farley Smith, b. 1941
Arr. © 1989 The United Methodist Publishing House, admin. The Copyright Company

Shall We Gather at the River

1 Shall we gath - er at the riv - er, where bright an - gel feet have trod,
2 On the mar - gin of the riv - er, wash - ing up its sil - ver spray,
3 Ere we reach the shin - ing riv - er, lay we ev - 'ry bur - den down;
4 Soon we'll reach the shin - ing riv - er, soon our pil - grim - age will cease;

with its crys - tal tide for - ev - er flow-ing by the throne of God?
we will walk and wor - ship ev - er, all the hap - py gold - en day.
grace our spir - its will de - liv - er, and pro - vide a robe and crown.
soon our hap - py hearts will quiv - er with the mel - o - dy of peace.

Refrain

Yes, we'll gath - er at the riv - er, the beau - ti - ful, the beau - ti - ful riv - er;

gath - er with the saints at the riv - er that flows by the throne of God.

Text: Robert Lowry, 1826-1899
Music: HANSON PLACE, Robert Lowry, 1826-1899

180   Oh, When the Saints Go Marching In

1. Oh, when the saints go march-ing in, oh, when the
2. Oh, when the Lord in glo-ry comes, oh, when the
3. Oh, when the new world is re-vealed, oh, when the
4. Oh, when they gath-er 'round the throne, oh, when they

saints go march-ing in, O Lord, I want to be in that
Lord in glo-ry comes, O Lord, I want to be in that
new world is re-vealed, O Lord, I want to be in that
gath-er 'round the throne, O Lord, I want to be in that

num-ber when the saints go march-ing in.
num-ber when the Lord in glo-ry comes.
num-ber when the new world is re-vealed.
num-ber when they gath-er 'round the throne.

5. Oh, when they crown him King of kings,
oh, when they crown him King of kings,
O Lord, I want to be in that number
when they crown him King of kings.

6. And on that hallelujah day,
and on that hallelujah day,
O Lord, I want to be in that number
on that hallelujah day.

Text: African American spiritual
Music: African American spiritual; arr. Jeffrey Rickard
Arr. © 1994 Selah Publishing Co.

To Go to Heaven

181

Leader

1 To go to heav - en   my heart is long - ing.
2 The peace of heav - en   all else ex - cel - ling:
3 The God who loves us   as no one oth - er
4 Why de - lay long - er?   This is the best day

How shall I get there   with - out pro - long - ing?
the place ce - les - tial   where God is dwell - ing.
has sent us Je - sus   to be our broth - er.
to fol - low Je - sus,   who is the true way.

Refrain
All

The way is Je - sus.   He chang - es nev - er.

The Sav - ior wants you   with him for - ev - er.

Text: Ndilivako Ndelwa; tr. Howard S. Olson, b. 1922
Music: KULE MBINGUNI NATAKA KWENDA, Tanzanian
Text © 1977 Howard S. Olson
Music © Lutheran Theological College, Makumira, Tanzania

182   **Ride On, King Jesus**

Ride on, King Je-sus, no one can-a hin-der me.

Ride on, King Je-sus, ride on, no one can-a hin-der me.

1 King Je-sus rides a milk-white horse, no one works like him,
2 I know that my re-deem-er lives, no one works like him,

the riv-er Jor-d'n he did cross, no one works like him. Oh,
and of his bless-ing free-ly gives, no one works like him. Oh,

Text: African American spiritual
Music: African American spiritual; arr. Hezekiah Brinson Jr., b. 1958
Arr. © 1990 Hezekiah Brinson, Jr.

I Must Tell Jesus

1. I must tell Je-sus all of my tri - als; I can-not bear these bur-dens a - lone; in my dis-tress he kind-ly will help me, he ev - er loves and cares for his own.

2. I must tell Je-sus all of my trou - bles; he is a kind, com-pas-sion-ate friend; if I but ask him, he will de-liv - er, make of my trou - bles quick-ly an end.

3. Tempt-ed and tried, I need a great Sav - ior, one who can help my bur-dens to bear; I must tell Je - sus, I must tell Je - sus; he all my cares and sor - rows will share.

4. Oh, how the world to e - vil al - lures me! oh, how my heart is tempt-ed to sin; I must tell Je - sus, and he will help me o - ver the world the vic - t'ry to win.

Refrain

I must tell Je - sus, I must tell Je - sus! I can-not bear my bur-dens a - lone.

I must tell Je - sus, I must tell Je - sus! Je-sus can help me, Je-sus a - lone.

Text: Elisha A. Hoffman, 1839-1919
Music: ORWIGSBURG, Elisha A. Hoffman, 1839-1919

184

Wonderful Grace of Jesus

1 Won-der-ful grace of Je-sus, great-er than all my sin;
2 Won-der-ful grace of Je-sus, reach-ing to all the lost,
3 Won-der-ful grace of Je-sus, reach-ing the most de - filed,

how shall my tongue de - scribe it, where shall its praise be - gin?
by it I have been par - doned, saved to the ut - ter - most.
by its trans-form - ing pow - er I now am God's dear child.

Tak - ing a - way my bur - den, set - ting my spir - it free—
Chains have been torn a - sun - der, giv - ing me lib - er - ty—
Pur - chas-ing peace and heav - en for all e - ter - ni - ty—

the won - der - ful grace of Je - sus reach - es me.
the won - der - ful grace of Je - sus reach - es me.
the won - der - ful grace of Je - sus reach - es me.

Text: Haldor Lillenas, 1885-1959
Music: WONDERFUL GRACE, Haldor Lillenas, 1885-1959

185

There Is a Balm in Gilead

Refrain

There is a balm in Gil-e-ad to make the wound-ed whole;

there is a balm in Gil-e-ad to heal the sin-sick soul.

1 Some-times I feel dis - cour-aged and think my work's in vain,
2 If you can - not preach like Pe - ter, if you can - not pray like Paul,
3 Don't ev - er be dis - cour-aged, for Je - sus is your friend;

Refrain

but then the Ho - ly Spir - it re - vives my soul a - gain.
you can tell the love of Je - sus and say, "He died for all."
and if you lack for knowl-edge he'll ne'er re - fuse to lend.

Text: African American spiritual
Music: BALM IN GILEAD, African American spiritual

Come, Ye Disconsolate

186

1 Come, ye dis - con - so - late, wher - e'er ye lan - guish;
2 Joy of the des - o - late, light of the stray - ing,
3 Here see the Bread of life; see wa - ters flow - ing

come to the mer - cy - seat, fer - vent - ly kneel.
hope of the pen - i - tent, fade - less and pure;
forth from the throne of God, pure from a - bove.

Here bring your wound - ed hearts, here tell your an - guish;
here speaks the Com - fort - er, ten - der - ly say - ing,
Come to the feast of love; come, ev - er know - ing

earth has no sor - row that heav'n can - not heal.
"Earth has no sor - row that heav'n can - not cure."
earth has no sor - row but heav'n can re - move.

Text: Thomas Moore, 1779-1852, sts. 1-2, Thomas Hastings, 1784-1872, st. 3
Music: CONSOLATOR, Samuel Webbe, 1740-1816

God Forgave My Sin in Jesus' Name

Freely, Freely

1 God for-gave my sin in Je - sus' name, I've been born a - gain in
2 All ... pow'r is giv'n in Je - sus' name, in ... earth and heav'n in

Je - sus' name, and in Je - sus' name I come to you, to share his
Je - sus' name, and in Je - sus' name I come to you, to share his

Refrain

love as he told me to. He said, "Free - ly, free - ly
pow'r as he told me to.

you have re - ceived, free - ly, free - ly give. Go in my

name, and be - cause you be - lieve, oth - ers will know that I live."

Text: Carol Owens, b. 1931
Music: FREELY, FREELY, Carol Owens, b. 1931
© 1972 Bud John Songs, Inc., admin. by EMI Christian Music Publishing

I Was Sinking Deep in Sin

Love Lifted Me

1 I was sink-ing deep in sin, far from the peace-ful shore, ver-y deep-ly
2 All my heart to him I give, ev-er to him I'll cling, in his bless-ed
3 Souls in dan-ger, look a-bove, Je-sus com-plete-ly saves; he will lift you

stained with-in, sink-ing to rise no more; but the mas-ter of the sea
pres-ence live, ev-er his prais-es sing; love so might-y and so true
by his love out of the an-gry waves; he's the mas-ter of the sea,

heard my de-spair-ing cry, from the wa-ters lift-ed me, now safe am I.
mer-its my soul's best songs; faith-ful lov-ing ser-vice, too, to him be-longs.
bil-lows his will o-bey; he your Sav-ior true will be: be saved to-day.

Refrain

Love lift-ed me! Love lift-ed me! When noth-ing
e - ven me! e - ven me!

1 else could help, love lift-ed me. *2* love lift-ed me.

Text: James Rowe, 1865-1933
Music: SAFETY, Howard E. Smith, 1863-1918

189

Heal Me, O Lord

Heal me, O Lord, and I shall be healed, save me and I shall be saved; saved; for thou art my praise, save me and I shall be saved.

Text: Steven Eulberg; based on Jeremiah 17:14
Music: Steven Eulberg
Text and music © 1990 Steven B. Eulberg, published by Owl Mountain Music

God Has Smiled on Me

190

Refrain

God has smiled on me, he has set me free.

God has smiled on me, he's been good to me.

1 God is the source of all my joy, and fills me with his love;
2 A light un-to my path is he, my strength when I would fall;

Refrain

the grace that I em-ploy, he sends down from a-bove.
he guides each day for me, God is my all in all.

Text: Isaiah Jones Jr.; Hezekiah Brinson Jr., b. 1958, refrain
Music: Isaiah Jones Jr.; arr. Hezekiah Brinson Jr.
Text and music © 1973 Davike Music Co., admin. Fricon Entertainment

191

I'm So Glad Jesus Lifted Me

1 I'm so glad
2 Satan had me bound,
3 When I was in trouble,

Je - sus lift - ed me.

I'm so glad
Satan had me bound,
When I was in trouble,

Je - sus lift - ed me.

I'm so glad
Satan had me bound,
When I was in trouble,

Je - sus lift - ed me,

sing - ing glo - ry, hal - le - lu - jah! Je - sus lift - ed me.

Text: African American spiritual
Music: JESUS LIFTED ME, African American spiritual; arr. *With One Voice*, 1995
Arr. © 1995 Augsburg Fortress

My Hope Is Built on Nothing Less

192

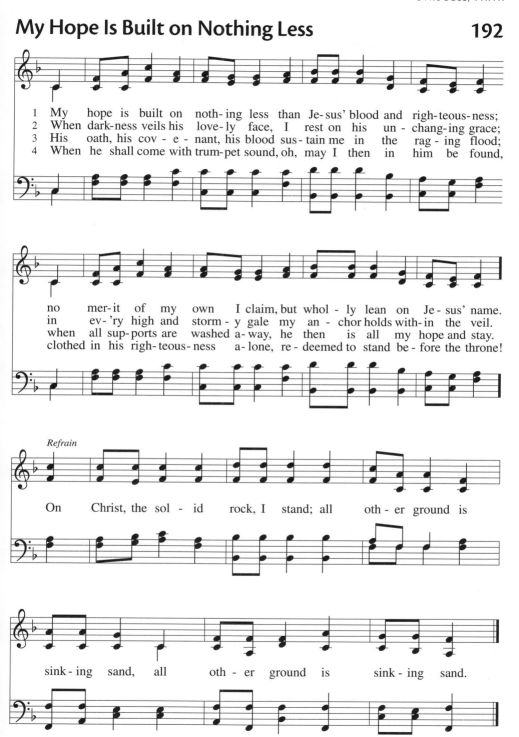

1 My hope is built on noth-ing less than Je-sus' blood and righ-teous-ness;
2 When dark-ness veils his love-ly face, I rest on his un - chang-ing grace;
3 His oath, his cov - e - nant, his blood sus-tain me in the rag - ing flood;
4 When he shall come with trum-pet sound, oh, may I then in him be found,

no mer-it of my own I claim, but whol - ly lean on Je - sus' name.
in ev-'ry high and storm - y gale my an - chor holds with-in the veil.
when all sup-ports are washed a-way, he then is all my hope and stay.
clothed in his righ-teous-ness a-lone, re - deemed to stand be - fore the throne!

Refrain

On Christ, the sol - id rock, I stand; all oth - er ground is

sink - ing sand, all oth - er ground is sink - ing sand.

Text: Edward Mote, 1797-1874, alt.
Music: THE SOLID ROCK, William B. Bradbury, 1816-1868

193

Precious Lord, Take My Hand

1 Pre - cious Lord, take my hand, lead me on, let me stand,
2 When my way grows . . drear, pre - cious Lord, lin - ger near,
3 When the dark - ness ap - pears and the night draws . . near,

I am tired, I am weak, I am worn.
when my life is . . . al - most . . gone,
and the day is . . . past and . . gone,

Through the storm, through the night, lead me on to the light,
hear my cry, hear my call, hold my hand lest I fall.
at the riv - er I stand, guide my feet, hold my hand.

take my hand, pre - cious Lord, lead me home.
Take my hand, pre - cious Lord, lead me home.
Take my hand, pre - cious Lord, lead me home.

Text: George N. Allen, 1812-1877; adapt. Thomas A. Dorsey, 1899-1993
Music: PRECIOUS LORD, Thomas A. Dorsey, 1899-1993, based on MAITLAND, George N. Allen
© 1938 Unichappell Music, Inc.

When Peace, Like a River

It Is Well with My Soul

1 When peace, like a riv - er, at - tend - eth my way; when
2 Though Sa - tan should buf - fet, though tri - als should come, let
3 He lives—oh, the bliss of this glo - ri - ous thought; my
4 And Lord, haste the day when our faith shall be sight, the

sor - rows, like sea bil - lows, roll; what - ev - er my lot, thou hast
this blest as - sur - ance con - trol, that Christ hath re - gard - ed my
sin, not in part, but the whole, is nailed to his cross and I
clouds be rolled back as a scroll, the trum - pet shall sound and the

taught me to say, it is well, it is well with my soul.
help - less es - tate, and hath shed his own blood for my soul.
bear it no more. Praise the Lord, praise the Lord, O, my soul!
Lord shall de - scend; e - ven so it is well with my soul.

Refrain

It is well with my soul, it is well, it is well with my soul.
it is well with my soul,

Text: Horatio G. Spafford, 1828-1888
Music: It Is Well, Philip P. Bliss, 1838-1876

195

Yield Not to Temptation

1 Yield not to temp-ta - tion, for yield-ing is sin;
2 Shun e - vil com-pan - ions, bad lan-guage dis - dain;
3 God saves us in tri - al, God gives us the crown;

each vic - t'ry will help you some oth - er to win;
God's name hold in rev - 'rence, nor take it in vain;
through faith we shall con - quer, though of - ten cast down;

fight val - iant - ly on - ward, dark pas - sions sub - due.
be thought-ful and ear - nest, kind - heart - ed and true.
Christ Je - sus our Sav - ior our strength will re - new.

Look ev - er to Je - sus, he'll car - ry you through.
Look ev - er to Je - sus, he'll car - ry you through.
Look ev - er to Je - sus, he'll car - ry you through.

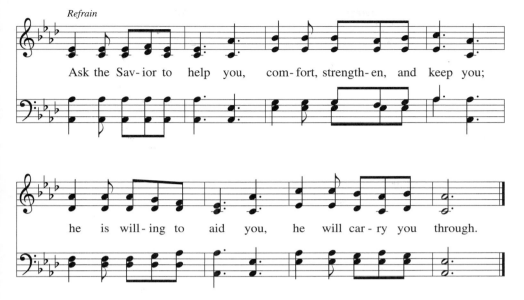

Ask the Sav-ior to help you, com-fort, strength-en, and keep you;
he is will-ing to aid you, he will car-ry you through.

Text: Horatio R. Palmer, 1834-1907
Music: PALMER, Horatio R. Palmer, 1834-1907

Help Me   196

Help me, help me.
Every day, every day, Lord, help me.
I ask my Lord for help in mind,
to be like Jesus now.
Help me, help me, Lord; I am thine.
Help me, help me, Christ, God's friend.
Help me, help me, Jesus, I am thine.
Help me say, the Lord is mine.
Help me say, Lord, I am thine.
Help me, help me, O Lord.
Help me to come to thee when you call.
Help me to say, Lord, thou art all.

C. G. Brown, observations of Elder C. H. Mason, Chief Apostle in *The History and Life Work of Elder C. H. Mason*

197

We've Come This Far by Faith

Refrain

We've come this far by faith,

lean-ing on the Lord; trust-ing in his ho-ly

word, he's nev-er failed us yet.

Oh, we can't turn back, we've come this far by

faith. We've come this far by faith.

Hymn continues on next page

1 Just re-mem-ber the good things God has
2 Don't be dis-cour-aged with trou-ble in your

done, things that seemed im-pos-si-ble; oh,
life; he'll bear your ... bur - dens, and

praise him for the vic - t'ries he has won.
move ... all the dis - cord and strife.

Refrain

Oh! We've

Text: Albert A. Goodson
Music: Albert A. Goodson
© 1965, 1993 Manna Music

When the Storms of Life Are Raging

Stand by Me

1 When the storms of life are rag-ing, stand by me;
2 In the midst of trib-u-la-tion, stand by me;
3 In the midst of faults and fail-ures, stand by me;
4 In the midst of per-se-cu-tion, stand by me;
5 When I'm grow-ing old and fee-ble, stand by me;

when the storms of life are rag-ing, stand by me;
in the midst of trib-u-la-tion, stand by me;
in the midst of faults and fail-ures, stand by me;
in the midst of per-se-cu-tion, stand by me;
when I'm grow-ing old and fee-ble, stand by me;

when the world is toss-ing me like a ship up-on the sea;
when the hosts of hell as-sail, and my strength be-gins to fail,
when I do the best I can, and my friends mis-un-der-stand,
when my foes in battle ar-ray un-der-take to stop my way,
when my life be-comes a burden, and I'm near-ing chil-ly Jordan,

thou who rul-est wind and wa-ter, stand by me.
thou who nev-er lost a bat-tle, stand by me.
thou who know-est all a-bout me, stand by me.
thou who saved . . Paul and Si-las, stand by me.
O thou Lil-y of the Val-ley, stand by me.

Text: Charles A. Tindley, 1851-1933
Music: STAND BY ME, Charles A. Tindley, 1851-1933; arr. J. Jefferson Cleveland, 1937-1986 and Verolga Nix, b. 1933
Arr. © 1981 Abingdon Press, admin. The Copyright Company

199   'Tis the Old Ship of Zion

Refrain

'Tis the old ship of Zi-on, 'tis the old ship of Zi-on,

'tis the old ship of Zi-on, get on board, get on board.

1. It has land-ed many a thou-sand, it has land-ed many a thou-sand,
2. Ain't no dan-ger in the wa-ter, ain't no dan-ger in the wa-ter,
3. It was good for my dear moth-er, it was good for my dear moth-er,
4. It was good for my dear fa-ther, it was good for my dear fa-ther,
5. It will take you home to glo-ry, it will take you home to glo-ry,

Refrain

it has land-ed many a thou-sand, get on board, get on board.
ain't no dan-ger in the wa-ter, get on board, get on board.
it was good for my dear moth-er, get on board, get on board.
it was good for my dear fa-ther, get on board, get on board.
it will take you home to glo-ry, get on board, get on board.

Text: African American spiritual
Music: YARMOUTH, African American spiritual

Be Not Dismayed Whate'er Betide

God Will Take Care of You

1 Be not dis-mayed what-e'er be-tide, God will take care of you;
2 Through days of toil when heart doth fail, God will take care of you;
3 All you may need he will pro-vide, God will take care of you;
4 No mat-ter what may be the test, God will take care of you;

be - neath his wings of love a - bide, God will take care of you.
when dan - gers fierce your path as - sail, God will take care of you.
noth - ing you ask will be de - nied, God will take care of you.
lean, wea - ry one, up - on his breast, God will take care of you.

Refrain

God will take care of you, through ev - 'ry day, o'er all the way;

God will take care of you, God will take care of you.
take care of you.

Text: Civilla D. Martin, 1869-1948
Music: MARTIN, W. Stillman Martin, 1862-1935

201

The Blood that Jesus Shed for Me

1 The blood that Je - sus shed for me,
2 It soothes my doubts and calms my fears,

'way back on Cal - va - ry; the blood that gives me strength from
and it dries all my tears; the blood that gives me strength from

day to day, it will nev - er lose its power.
day to day, it will nev - er lose its power.

Refrain

It reach-es to the high - est moun - tain.

It flows to the low - est val - ley.

The blood that gives me strength from day to day,

it will nev - er lose its power.

Text: Andraé Crouch, b. 1945
Music: THE BLOOD, Andraé Crouch, b. 1945
© 1966, 1994 Manna Music

A Pastor's Prayer for a Son on Drugs   202

Most heavenly Father, I come to you, first saying, "Thank you for letting me rise to a new day." I thank you for being merciful to me and my family. Thank you for watching over us while we slumbered in the cool of the night. Lord, I thank you.

Father, I am asking you to please look down from heaven and help the son of a heartbroken mother. His name is Joe, Lord. You know him, and you know that crack has possessed his mind and body. Lord, please deliver him from the demon of drugs. Loose him from Satan's grip. Restore him to manhood and a good life. Satan has robbed too many black men of character, employment and self-respect.

O Lord, I am not just praying for brother Joe, I'm praying and asking your help for a good many men and women. Lord, please deliver brother Joe just as you delivered Jonah from the belly of the whale. I thank you, Father, in the name of your Son, Jesus. Amen

Lloyd Preston Terrell, b. 1950, a pastor in Newark, New Jersey
© 1993 Lloyd Preston Terrell, *Pray, Pastor, Pray!* Columbus, GA: Brentwood Christian Press

Holy Is Our God
Santo es nuestro Dios

203

Ho - ly, ho - ly, ho - ly, ho - ly, ho - ly, ho - ly is our God,
San - to, san - to, san - to, san - to, san - to, san - to es nues - tro Dios,

God, the Lord of earth and heav - en. Ho - ly, ho - ly is our God.
Se - ñor de to - da la tie - rra. San - to, san - to es nues - tro Dios.

Ho - ly, ho - ly, ho - ly, ho - ly, ho - ly, ho - ly is our God,
San - to, san - to, san - to, san - to, san - to, san - to es nues - tro Dios,

God, the Lord of all of his - t'ry. Ho - ly, ho - ly is our God.
Se - ñor de to - da la his - to - ria. San - to, san - to es nues - tro Dios.

Who ac - com - pa - nies our peo - ple, who
Que a - com - pa - ña a nues - tro pue - blo, que

Text: Guillermo Cuéllar, *Misa popular salvadoreña*, 1986; tr. Linda McCrae
Music: CUÉLLAR, Guillermo Cuéllar; arr. Diana Kodner

I Believe in God

Nasadiki

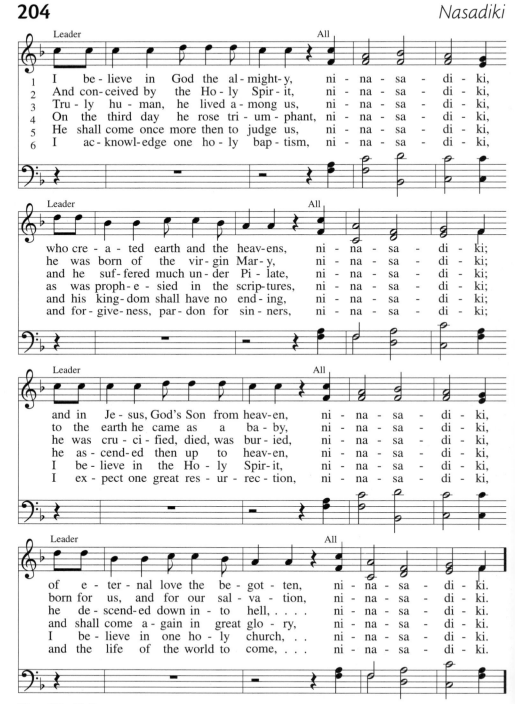

1. I be-lieve in God the al-might-y, ni - na - sa - di - ki,
2. And con-ceived by the Ho-ly Spir-it, ni - na - sa - di - ki,
3. Tru-ly hu-man, he lived a-mong us, ni - na - sa - di - ki,
4. On the third day he rose tri-um-phant, ni - na - sa - di - ki,
5. He shall come once more then to judge us, ni - na - sa - di - ki,
6. I ac-knowl-edge one ho-ly bap-tism, ni - na - sa - di - ki,

who cre-a-ted earth and the heav-ens, ni - na - sa - di - ki;
he was born of the vir-gin Mar-y, ni - na - sa - di - ki;
and he suf-fered much un-der Pi-late, ni - na - sa - di - ki;
as was proph-e-sied in the scrip-tures, ni - na - sa - di - ki;
and his king-dom shall have no end-ing, ni - na - sa - di - ki;
and for-give-ness, par-don for sin-ners, ni - na - sa - di - ki;

and in Je-sus, God's Son from heav-en, ni - na - sa - di - ki,
to the earth he came as a ba-by, ni - na - sa - di - ki,
he was cru-ci-fied, died, was bur-ied, ni - na - sa - di - ki,
he as-cend-ed then up to heav-en, ni - na - sa - di - ki,
I be-lieve in the Ho-ly Spir-it, ni - na - sa - di - ki,
I ex-pect one great res-ur-rec-tion, ni - na - sa - di - ki,

of e-ter-nal love the be-got-ten, ni - na - sa - di - ki.
born for us, and for our sal-va-tion, ni - na - sa - di - ki.
he de-scend-ed down in-to hell, ... ni - na - sa - di - ki.
and shall come a-gain in great glo-ry, ni - na - sa - di - ki.
I be-lieve in one ho-ly church, . . ni - na - sa - di - ki.
and the life of the world to come, . . . ni - na - sa - di - ki.

Ninasadiki = I believe

Text: based on the Nicene Creed; tr. composite
Music: NASADIKI, S. C. Ochieng Okeyo, *Kariobangi Mass*
© S.C. Ochieng Okeyo

The Ten Commandments   205

I am the Lord your God. You shall have no other gods.

You shall not take the name of the Lord your God in vain.

Remember the sabbath day, to keep it holy.

Honor your father and your mother.

You shall not kill.

You shall not commit adultery.

You shall not steal.

You shall not bear false witness against your neighbor.

You shall not covet your neighbor's house.

You shall not covet your neighbor's wife, or his manservant,
or his maidservant, or his cattle, or anything that is your neighbor's.

From Exodus 20:1-7, trans. *The Small Catechism by Martin Luther in Contemporary English*
© 1960, 1968 Augsburg Publishing House, Board of Publications of the Lutheran Church in America, and Concordia Publishing House

We Are Often Tossed and Driven

We'll Understand It Better By and By

1 We are of - ten tossed and driv'n on the rest - less sea of time,
2 We are of - ten des - ti - tute of the things that life de - mands,
3 Tri - als dark on ev - 'ry hand, and we can - not un - der - stand,
4 Temp - ta - tions, hid - den snares of - ten take us un - a - wares,

som - ber skies and howl - ing tem - pest oft suc - ceed a bright sun - shine;
want of food and want of shel - ter, thirst - y hills and bar - ren lands;
all the ways that God would lead us to that bless - ed prom - ised land;
and our hearts are made to bleed for many a thought - less word or deed;

in that land of per - fect day, when the mists have rolled a - way,
we are trust - ing in the Lord, and ac - cord - ing to his word,
but he guides us with his eye and we'll fol - low till we die;
and we won - der why the test when we try to do our best;

we will un - der - stand it bet - ter by and by, by and by.
we will un - der - stand it bet - ter by and by, by and by.
for we'll un - der - stand it bet - ter by and by, by and by.
but we'll un - der - stand it bet - ter by and by, by and by.

By and by when the morn - ing comes,

when the saints of God are gath - ered home,

we'll tell the sto - ry, how we've o - ver - come;

for we'll un - der - stand it bet - ter by and by, by and by.

Text: Charles A. Tindley, 1851-1933
Music: BY AND BY, Charles A. Tindley, 1851-1933; arr. F. A. Clark

207 Satan, We're Going to Tear Your Kingdom Down

1 Sa-tan, we're going to tear your king-dom down.
2 Sa-tan, we're going to pray your king-dom down.
3 Sa-tan, we're going to sing your king-dom down.
4 Sa-tan, the cross has torn your king-dom down.

Sa-tan, we're going to tear your king-dom down.
Sa-tan, we're going to pray your king-dom down.
Sa-tan, we're going to sing your king-dom down.
Sa-tan, the cross has torn your king-dom down.

You've been build-ing your king-dom all o-ver this world;

1–3 *4*

Sa-tan, we're going to tear your king-dom down.
Sa-tan, we're going to pray your king-dom down.
Sa-tan, we're going to sing your king-dom down.
Sa-tan, the cross has torn your king-dom down.

Text: traditional
Music: traditional; arr. James M. Capers, b. 1948
Arr. © 1999 Augsburg Fortress

Oh, Freedom

208

1 Oh, free-dom, oh, free-dom,
2 No more moan-ing, no more moan-ing,
3 There'll be sing-ing, there'll be sing-ing,
4 There'll be shout-ing, there'll be shout-ing,
5 There'll be pray-ing, there'll be pray-ing,

oh, free-dom o-ver me,
no more moan-ing o-ver me,
there'll be sing-ing o-ver me,
there'll be shout-ing o-ver me,
there'll be pray-ing o-ver me,

me, o-ver me,

Refrain

and be-fore I'd be a slave, I'll be bur-ied in my grave,

and go home to my Lord, and be free.

Text: African American spiritual
Music: African American spiritual; arr. Evelyn Davidson White

209

We've Come a Long Way, Lord

Refrain

We've come a long way, Lord, a might-y long way,

we've come a long way, Lord, a might-y long way.

We've borne our bur-dens in the heat of the day,

but we know the Lord has made the way,

we've come a long way, Lord, a might-y long way.

1 I've been in the val - ley and I prayed night and day,
2 I've had hard .. tri - als each and ev - 'ry ... day,

I've been in the val - ley and I prayed night and day;
I've had hard .. tri - als each and ev - 'ry ... day;

I've been in the val - ley and I prayed night and day,
I've had hard ... tri - als each and ev - 'ry .... day,

and I know the Lord has made the way.
but I know the Lord has made the way.

Refrain (after repeat)

We've come a long way, Lord, a might-y long way.
We've come a long way, Lord, a might-y long way.

Text: traditional; adapt. Kenneth Morris
Music: traditional; arr. Kenneth Morris
Text adapt. and arr. © 1968 Martin and Morris Music, Inc.

210

I've Got a Robe

1 I've got a robe,   you've got a robe, all of God's chil-dren got a   robe.
2 I've got . . shoes,   you've got . . shoes, all of God's chil-dren got . . shoes.
3 I've got . . wings,   you've got . . wings, all of God's chil-dren got . . wings.
4 I've got a crown,   you've got a crown, all of God's chil-dren got a   crown.

When I   get   to   heav - en   goin' to   put   on   my   robe,
When I   get   to   heav - en   goin' to   put   on   my   shoes,
When I   get   to   heav - en   goin' to   put   on   my   wings,
When I   get   to   heav - en   goin' to   put   on   my   crown,

goin' to   shout all   o - ver God's heav-en,   heav-en,   heav-en.
goin' to   walk all   o - ver God's heav-en,   heav-en,   heav-en.
goin' to   fly   all   o - ver God's heav-en,   heav-en,   heav-en.
goin' to   shout all   o - ver God's heav-en,   heav-en,   heav-en.

Ev-'ry-bod-y   talk-in' 'bout   heav-en   ain't   go - in'   there;
Ev-'ry-bod-y   talk-in' 'bout   heav-en   ain't   go - in'   there;
Ev-'ry-bod-y   talk-in' 'bout   heav-en   ain't   go - in'   there;
Ev-'ry-bod-y   talk-in' 'bout   heav-en   ain't   go - in'   there;

heav-en, heav-en, goin' to shout all o - ver God's heav-en.
heav-en, heav-en, goin' to walk all o - ver God's heav-en.
heav-en, heav-en, goin' to fly all o - ver God's heav-en.
heav-en, heav-en, goin' to shout all o - ver God's heav-en.

5 I've got a harp, you've got a harp,
all of God's children got a harp.
When I get to heaven goin' to play my harp,
goin' to play all over God's heaven, heaven, heaven.
Ev'rybody talkin' 'bout heaven ain't goin' there;
heaven, heaven, goin' to play all over God's heaven.

6 I've got a song, you've got a song,
all of God's children got a song.
When I get to heaven goin' to sing my song,
goin' to sing all over God's heaven, heaven, heaven.
Ev'rybody talkin' 'bout heaven ain't goin' there;
heaven, heaven, goin' to sing all over God's heaven.

7 I've got a prayer, you've got a prayer,
all of God's children got a prayer.
When I get to heaven goin' to pray my prayer,
goin' to pray all over God's heaven, heaven, heaven.
Ev'rybody talkin' 'bout heaven ain't goin' there;
heaven, heaven, goin' to pray all over God's heaven.

Text: African American spiritual
Music: African American spiritual

A Slave Woman's Prayer   211

O Lord, bless my master. When he calls upon thee to damn his soul, do not hear him, do not hear him, but hear me—save him—make him know he is wicked, and he will pray to thee.

I am afraid, O Lord, I have wished him bad wishes in my heart—keep me from wishing him bad—though he whips me and beats me sore, tell me of my sins, and make me pray more to thee—make me more glad for what thou hast done for me, a poor Negro.

Stephen Hays, a minister in upstate New York, reported this prayer by an anonymous slave woman in his *The Praying African*, tract no. 92 in *Publications of the American Tract Society*, vol. 3, New York: The American Tract Society, 1832 (?).

212

Don't Be Worried

Refrain

Don't be wor - ried on ac - count of the wick - ed.

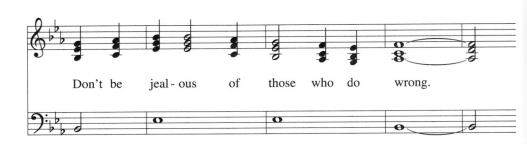

Don't be jeal - ous of those who do wrong.

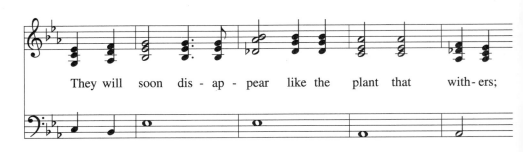

They will soon dis - ap - pear like the plant that with - ers;

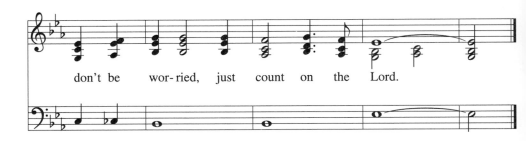

don't be wor - ried, just count on the Lord.

Text: Grayson Warren Brown, b. 1948; based on Psalm 37
Music: Grayson Warren Brown, b. 1948; arr. Grayson Warren Brown, Val Parker, and Larry Adams
© 1992 Grayson Warren Brown, admin. OCP Publications

213

We Shall Overcome

1 We shall o - ver - come, we shall o - ver - come,
2 We'll walk hand in hand, we'll walk hand in hand,
3 We shall all have peace, we shall all have peace,
4 We shall see the Lord, we shall see the Lord,
5 We are not a - fraid, we are not a - fraid,
6 God is on our side, God is on our side,

we shall o - ver - come some - day. Oh,
we'll walk hand in hand some - day. Oh,
we shall all have peace some - day. Oh,
we shall see the Lord some - day. Oh,
we are not a - fraid to - day. Oh,
God is on our side to - day. Oh,

deep in our hearts we do be - lieve we shall o - ver - come some - day.
deep in our hearts we do be - lieve we'll walk hand in hand some - day.
deep in our hearts we do be - lieve we shall all have peace some - day.
deep in our hearts we do be - lieve we shall see the Lord some - day.
deep in our hearts we do be - lieve we are not a - fraid to - day.
deep in our hearts we do be - lieve God is on our side to - day.

Text: traditional
Music: African American spiritual; arr. J. Jefferson Cleveland, 1937-1986
Arr. © 1981 Abingdon Press, admin. The Coypright Company

In Christ There Is No East or West   214

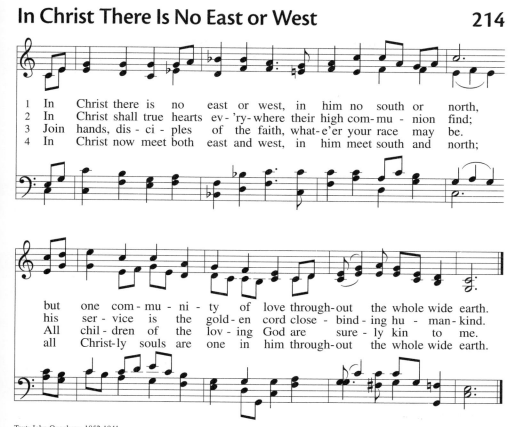

1 In Christ there is no east or west, in him no south or north,
2 In Christ shall true hearts ev-'ry-where their high com-mu - nion find;
3 Join hands, dis-ci - ples of the faith, what-e'er your race may be.
4 In Christ now meet both east and west, in him meet south and north;

but one com-mu-ni-ty of love through-out the whole wide earth.
his ser-vice is the gold-en cord close-bind-ing hu-man-kind.
All chil-dren of the lov-ing God are sure-ly kin to me.
all Christ-ly souls are one in him through-out the whole wide earth.

Text: John Oxenham, 1852-1941
Music: MCKEE, African American spiritual; arr. Harry T. Burleigh, 1866-1949

Give Us Grace   215

Give us grace, O God, to dare to do the deed
which we well know cries to be done.
Let us not hesitate because of ease,
or the words of men's mouths, or our own lives.
Mighty causes are calling us—
the freeing of women, the training of children,
the putting down of hate and murder and poverty—
all these and more.
But they call with voices
that mean work and sacrifice and death.
Mercifully grant us, O God, the spirit of Esther, that we say:
I will go unto the King and if I perish, I perish—Amen.

W. E. B. DuBois, 1868-1963
From *Prayers for Dark People*, Herbert Aotheker, ed.
© 1980 University of Massachusetts Press

216 # Give Me a Clean Heart

Give me a clean heart so I may serve thee.

Lord, fix my heart so that I may be used by thee.

For I'm not wor - thy of all these bless - ings.

Give me a clean heart and I'll fol-low thee.

Text: Margaret J. Douroux, b. 1941
Music: Margaret J. Douroux, b. 1941; arr. Albert D. Tessier
© 1970 Margaret J. Douroux

217

Bind Us Together, Lord

Refrain

Bind us to-geth-er, Lord, bind us to-geth-er with cords that can-not be bro - ken. Bind us to-geth-er, Lord, bind us to-geth-er, Lord; bind us to-geth-er in love.

1 There is on-ly one God. There is on-ly one King.
2 You are the fam-'ly of God. You are the prom-ise di - vine.

There is on-ly one Bod-y; that is why we can sing.
You are God's cho-sen de-sire, . . you are the glo-rious new wine.

Text: Bob Gillman, b. 1946
Music: BIND US TOGETHER, Bob Gillman, b. 1946
© 1977 Kingsway Thankyou Music, admin. Integrity's Hosanna! Music in N., S., and C. America

Behold, What Manner of Love

218

Be-hold, what man-ner of love the Fa-ther has giv-en un-to us;

be-hold, what man-ner of love the Fa-ther has giv-en un-to us,

that we should be called the chil-dren of God,

that we should be called the chil-dren of God.

* May be sung as a two-part round

Text: 1 John 3:1; adapt. Patricia van Tine
Music: THEIMER, Patricia van Tine

219

For All the Faithful Women

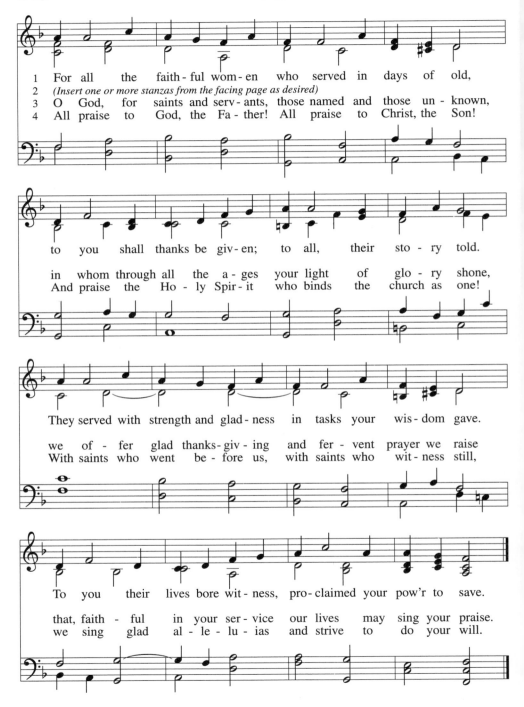

1 For all the faith-ful wom-en who served in days of old,
2 *(Insert one or more stanzas from the facing page as desired)*
3 O God, for saints and serv-ants, those named and those un-known,
4 All praise to God, the Fa-ther! All praise to Christ, the Son!

to you shall thanks be giv-en; to all, their sto-ry told.
in whom through all the a-ges your light of glo-ry shone,
And praise the Ho-ly Spir-it who binds the church as one!

They served with strength and glad-ness in tasks your wis-dom gave.
we of-fer glad thanks-giv-ing and fer-vent prayer we raise
With saints who went be-fore us, with saints who wit-ness still,

To you their lives bore wit-ness, pro-claimed your pow'r to save.
that, faith-ful in your ser-vice our lives may sing your praise.
we sing glad al-le-lu-ias and strive to do your will.

Miriam

5 We praise your name for Miriam
who sang triumphantly
while Pharaoh's vaunted army
lay drowned beneath the sea.
As Israel marched to freedom,
her chains of bondage gone,
so may we reach the kingdom
your mighty arm has won.

Deborah

6 All praise for that brave warrior
who fought at your command.
You made her Israel's savior
when foes oppressed the land.
As Deborah stood with valor
upon that battlefield,
may we, in evil's hour,
truth's sword with boldness wield.

Hannah

7 To Hannah, praying childless
before the throne of grace,
you gave a son and called him
to serve before your face.
Grant us her perseverance;
Lord, teach us how to pray
and trust in your deliv'rance
when darkness hides our way.

Ruth

8 For Ruth who left her homeland
and ventured forth in faith,
who pledged to serve and worship
Naomi's God till death,
we praise you, God of Israel
and pray for hearts set free
to bind ourselves to others
in love and loyalty.

Mary, Mother of Our Lord

9 We sing of Mary, mother,
fair maiden, full of grace.
She bore the Christ, our brother,
who came to save our race.
May we, with her, surrender
ourselves to your command
and lay upon your altar
our gifts of heart and hand.

Martha and Mary

10 We sing of busy Martha
who toiled with pot and pan
while Mary sat in silence
to hear the word again.
Christ, keep our hearts attentive
to truth that you declare,
and strengthen us for service
when work becomes our prayer.

The Woman at the Well

11 Recall the outcast woman
with whom our Lord conversed:
Christ gave her living water
to quench her deepest thirst.
Like hers, our hearts are yearning;
Christ offers us his word.
Then may our lips be burning
to witness to our Lord.

Mary Magdalene

12 We praise the other Mary
who came at Easter dawn
and near the tomb did tarry,
but found her Lord was gone.
But, as with joy she saw him
in resurrection light,
may we by faith behold him,
the day who ends our night.

Dorcas

13 Lord, hear our praise of Dorcas
who served the sick and poor.
Her hands were cups of kindness,
her heart an open door.
Send us, O Christ, your Body,
where people cry in pain,
and touch them with compassion
to make them whole again.

Text: Herman G. Stuempfle Jr., b. 1923
Music: BARONITA, Doreen Potter, 1925-1980
Text © 1993, 1997 GIA Publications
Music © 1975 Hope Publishing Co.

What a Fellowship, What a Joy Divine

Leaning on the Everlasting Arms

220

1 What a fel - low-ship, what a joy di - vine, lean-ing on the ev-er- last-ing arms;
2 Oh, how sweet to walk in this pil-grim way, lean-ing on the ev-er- last-ing arms;
3 What have I to dread, what have I to fear, lean-ing on the ev-er- last-ing arms;

what a bless-ed-ness, what a peace is mine, lean-ing on the ev-er- last-ing arms.
oh, how bright the path grows from day to day, lean-ing on the ev-er- last-ing arms.
I have bless-ed peace with my Lord so near, lean-ing on the ev-er- last-ing arms.

Refrain

Lean - ing, lean - ing, safe and se-cure from all a-larms;

Lean-ing on Je - sus, lean-ing on Je - sus,

lean - ing, lean - ing, lean-ing on the ev - er- last-ing arms.

lean-ing on Je - sus, lean-ing on Je - sus,

Text: Elisha Hoffman, 1838-1929
Music: SHOWALTER, Anthony J. Showalter, 1858-1924

We Are All One in Christ
Somo uno en Cristo

221

We are all one in Christ, we are one bod-y, all one
So - mos u - no en Cris - to, so - mos u - no. So - mos

peo-ple out of man-y. man-y.
u - no, u - no so - lo. so - lo.

There is one God, and on-ly one Lord; there is one
Un so - lo Dios, un so - lo Se - ñor, u - na so - la

faith, one ho-ly love. There is one bap-tism; there is one
fe, un so - lo_a - mor. Un so - lo bau - tis - mo, un so - lo_Es-

Spir - it, who is God the com-fort - er.
pí - ri - tu, y_e - se_es el con - so - la - dor.

Text: traditional; tr. Gerhard Cartford, b. 1923
Music: SOMOS UNO, traditional
Tr. © 1998 Augsburg Fortress

222 God the Sculptor of the Mountains

1 God   the sculp-tor of the moun - tains,
2 God   the nui - sance to the Pha - raoh,
3 God   the dress - er of the vine - yard,
4 God   the un - ex - pect - ed in - fant,

God   the mill - er of the sand,
God   the cleav - er of the sea,
God   the plant - er of the wheat,
God   the calm, de - ter - mined youth,

God   the jewel - er of the heav - ens,
God   the pil - lar in the dark - ness,
God   the reap - er of the har - vest,
God   the ta - ble - turn - ing proph - et,

God   the pot - ter of the land:
God   the bea - con of the free:
God   the source of all we eat:
God   the re - sur - rect - ed truth:

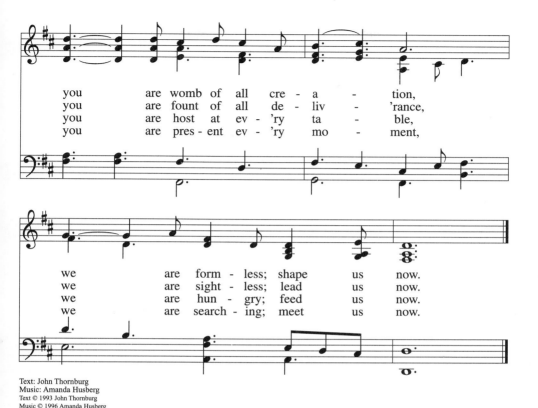

you are womb of all cre - a - tion,
you are fount of all de - liv - 'rance,
you are host at ev - 'ry ta - ble,
you are pres - ent ev - 'ry mo - ment,

we are form - less; shape us now.
we are sight - less; lead us now.
we are hun - gry; feed us now.
we are search - ing; meet us now.

Text: John Thornburg
Music: Amanda Husberg
Text © 1993 John Thornburg
Music © 1996 Amanda Husberg

We Believe 223

We believe in the one high God, who out of love created the beautiful world and everything good in it. He created man and woman, and wanted them to be happy in the world. God loves the world and every nation and tribe on earth. God promised in the book of his word, the Bible, that he would save the world and all the nations and tribes.

We believe that God made good his promise by sending his Son, Jesus Christ, a man in the flesh, a Jew by tribe, born poor in a little village, who left his home and was always on safari doing good, curing people by the power of God, teaching about God and humankind, showing that the meaning of religion is love. He was rejected by his people, tortured, nailed hands and feet to a cross, and died. He lay buried in the grave, but the hyenas did not touch him. On the third day he rose from the grave. He ascended to the skies. He is the Lord.

We believe that all our sins are forgiven through him. All who have faith in him must be sorry for their sins, be baptized in the Holy Spirit of God, live the rules of love, and share the bread together in love, to announce the good news to others until Jesus comes again. We are waiting for him. He is alive. He lives. This we believe.

Anonymous, from the Masai people

224

Help Me, Jesus

Help me, Je- sus, to love my neigh-bor as my-self.

Help me, Je- sus, to love my neigh-bor as my-self.

He does-n't care 'bout the col- or of your

skin or what re - li - gion you've been in. Help me,

Je-sus, to love my neigh-bor as my-self.

Text: Edward V. Bonnemère, 1921-1996
Music: Edward V. Bonnemère, 1921-1996
© 1968 Edward V. Bonnemère, admin. Augsburg Fortress

I Believe I'll Testify

225

1 I be-lieve I'll tes - ti - fy   while I have a chance,
2 I be-lieve I'll clap my hands   while I have a chance,
3 I be-lieve I'll sing this song   while I have a chance,
4 I be-lieve I'll shout for God   while I have a chance,

I be-lieve I'll tes - ti - fy   while I have a chance,
I be-lieve I'll clap my hands   while I have a chance,
I be-lieve I'll sing this song   while I have a chance,
I be-lieve I'll shout for God   while I have a chance,

I be-lieve I'll tes - ti - fy   while I have a chance,
I be-lieve I'll clap my hands   while I have a chance,
I be-lieve I'll sing this song   while I have a chance,
I be-lieve I'll shout for God   while I have a chance,

for I may not have a chance an - y - more.
for I may not have a chance an - y - more.
for I may not have a chance an - y - more.
for I may not have a chance an - y - more.

Text: traditional
Music: traditional; arr. James M. Capers, b. 1948
Arr. © 1999 Augsburg Fortress

You Are the Seed

Sois la semilla

226

1 You are the seed that will grow a new sprout; you're a star that will
2 You are the flame that will light-en the dark, so re-splen-dent with
3 You are the life that will nur-ture the plant; you're the waves in a

shine in the night; you are the yeast and a small grain of salt, a
hope, faith and love; you are the shep-herds to lead the whole world to
tur-bu-lent sea; yes-ter-day's yeast is be-gin-ning to rise, a

bea-con to glow in the dark. You are the dawn that will bring a new day;
wa-ters and pas-tures of peace. "You are the friends that I chose for my-self,
new loaf of bread it will yield. There is no place for a cit-y to hide,

you're the wheat that will bear gold-en grain; you are a sting and a
you're the word that I want to pro-claim. You are the new reign of
there's no moun-tain can cov-er its might; let your light shine so that

soft, gen - tle touch, to wit - ness where - ev - er you go.
God built on rock, where jus - tice and truth are at home."
your lov - ing works give hon - or and glo - ry to God.

Refrain/Estribillo

Go, my friends, go to the world, pro - claim the great love of
Be, my friends, a loy - al wit - ness, from the dead Christ a -
Id, a - mi - gos, por el mun - do, a - nun - cian - do_el a -
Sed, a - mi - gos, mis tes - ti - gos de mi re - su - rrec -

God; mes - sen - gers to tell the way of life,
rose; "Lo, I'll be with you for - ev - er - more,
mor; men - sa - je - ros de la vi - da,
ción. Id lle - van - do mi pre - sen - cia;

peace and par - don for all.
de la paz y_el per - dón.

till the end of the world."
con vo - so - tros es - toy.

Text: Cesáreo Gabarain, 1936-1991; tr. Raquel Gutiérrez-Achon, b. 1927 and Skinner Chávez-Melo, 1944-1992, alt.
Music: ID Y ENSEÑAD, Cesáreo Gabarain, 1936-1991; arr. Skinner Chávez-Melo, 1944-1992

How to Reach the Masses

Lift Him Up

227

1 How to reach the mass - es, those of ev - 'ry birth, for an
2 Oh, the world is hun - gry for the liv - ing bread; lift the
3 Lift him up by liv - ing as a Chris - tian ought; let the

an - swer Je - sus gave a key: "And I, when I am lift - ed
Sav - ior up for them to see. Trust him, and do not doubt the
world in you the Sav - ior see. Then all will glad - ly fol - low

up from the earth, will draw all peo - ple to me."
words that he said; "I'll draw all peo - ple to me."
him who once taught: "I'll draw all peo - ple to me."

Refrain

Lift him up, lift him up.
Lift the pre - cious Sav - ior up, lift the pre - cious Sav - ior up.

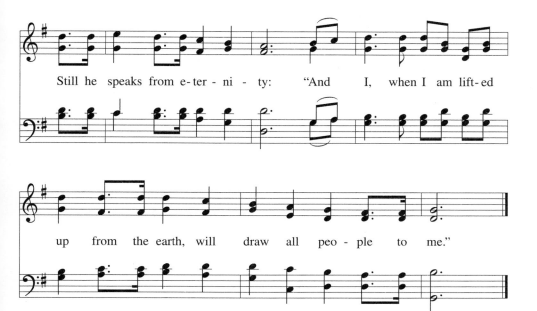

Still he speaks from e-ter-ni-ty: "And I, when I am lift-ed

up from the earth, will draw all peo-ple to me."

Text: Johnson Oatman, Jr., 1856-1926, alt.
Music: LIFT HIM UP, B. B. Beall

228

I Love to Tell the Story

1 I love to tell the sto - ry of un - seen things a - bove,
2 I love to tell the sto - ry: how pleas- ant to re - peat
3 I love to tell the sto - ry, for those who know it best
4 I love to tell the sto - ry, of how, from heav'n a - bove

of Je - sus and his glo - ry, of Je - sus and his love.
what seems, each time I tell it, more won- der- ful - ly sweet!
seem hun - ger- ing and thirst-ing to hear it like the rest.
our Lord and Sav- ior Jes - us was sent to show God's love

I love to tell the sto - ry, be - cause I know it's true;
I love to tell the sto - ry, for some have nev - er heard
And when, in scenes of glo - ry, I sing the new, new song,
to ev - 'ry sin - ful crea- ture up - on this earth- ly place;

it sat - is - fies my long- ings as noth - ing else would do.
the mes - sage of sal - va - tion from God's own ho - ly word.
I'll sing the old, old sto - ry that I have loved so long.
how Christ, the gift from hea - ven, is God's great gift of grace.

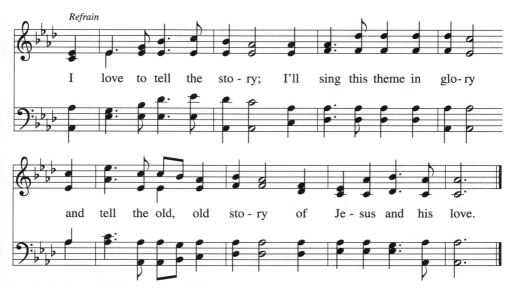

Refrain

I love to tell the sto-ry; I'll sing this theme in glo-ry

and tell the old, old sto-ry of Je-sus and his love.

Text: Katherine Hankey, 1834-1911, sts. 1-3, Jeffrey E. Burkart, st. 4
Music: HANKEY, William G. Fischer, 1835-1912
Text st. 4 © Jeffrey E. Burkart

Who Is to Condemn?   229

If Jesu, Lord, I come to thee,
And freely thou receivedst me,
    Who shall say, nay?
Who shall bring up the days of sin,
When earthly passions raged within?

If Jesu, Lord, I should profess
Thy name—Thy boundless love confess,
    Who shall deny?
That thou thyself hast made me bold
To claim the blessings long foretold?

If Jesu, in the throng I raise
My voice in notes of praise,
    Who say, be still?
Who chide me for the words I speak
And tell me I should be more meek?

Dear Jesu, 'tis thy precious Name
That doth alone my heart inflame—
    My heart inspire.
And makes me fearless of the world—
Thy children—of the arrows hurled.

Benjamin Tucker Tanner (1835-1923), "Who?" *Christian Recorder*, January 10, 1895

I, the Lord of Sea and Sky

Here I Am, Lord

1 "I, the Lord of sea and sky, I have heard my peo - ple cry.
2 "I, the Lord of snow and rain, I have borne my peo - ple's pain.
3 "I, the Lord of wind and flame, I will tend the poor and lame.

All who dwell in deep - est sin my hand will save.
I have wept for love of them. They turn a - way.
I will set a feast for them. My hand will save.

I, who made the stars of night, I will make their dark-ness bright.
I will break their hearts of stone, give them hearts for love a - lone.
Fin- est bread I will pro - vide till their hearts be sat - is - fied.

Who will bear my light to them? Whom shall I send?"
I will speak my word to them. Whom shall I send?"
I will give my life to them. Whom shall I send?"

Refrain

Here I am, Lord. Is it I, Lord? I have heard you calling in the night. I will go, Lord, if you lead me. I will hold your peo-ple in my heart.

Text: Daniel Schutte
Music: HERE I AM, LORD, Daniel Schutte; arr. Michael Pope, Daniel Schutte, and John Weissrock

Time Is Filled with Swift Transition

Hold to God's Unchanging Hand

231

1 Time is filled with swift tran - si - tion, naught of earth un-moved can stand;
2 Trust in him who will not leave you, what - so - ev - er years may bring;
3 Cov - et not this world's vain rich - es that so rap - id - ly de - cay;
4 When your jour-ney is com - plet - ed, God will keep the prom-ise true;

build your hopes on things e - ter - nal, hold to God's un-chang-ing hand.
if by earth - ly friends for-sak - en, still more close-ly to him cling.
seek to gain the heav'n-ly trea-sures: they will nev - er pass a - way.
fair and bright the home in glo - ry your en - rap-tured soul will view.

Refrain

Hold to God's un-chang-ing hand; hold to God's un-chang-ing hand;
Hold to his hand, hold to his hand.

build your hopes on things e - ter - nal; hold to God's un - chang-ing hand.

Text: Jennie Wilson
Music: GOD'S UNCHANGING HAND, F. L. Eliand

Let Us Talents and Tongues Employ

232

1 Let us tal - ents and tongues em-ploy, reach-ing out with a shout of joy:
2 Christ is a - ble to make us one, at the ta - ble he sets the tone,
3 Je - sus calls us in, sends us out bear - ing fruit in a world of doubt,

bread is bro - ken, the wine is poured, Christ is spo - ken and seen and heard.
teach-ing peo - ple to live to bless, love in word and in deed ex - press.
gives us love to tell, bread to share: God (Im-man - u - el) ev - 'ry - where!

Refrain

Je-sus lives a-gain, earth can breathe a-gain, pass the Word a-round: loaves a-bound!

Text: Fred Kaan, b. 1929
Music: LINSTEAD, Jamaican traditional; arr. Doreen Potter, 1925-1980
© 1975 Hope Publishing Co.

233   I'd Rather Have Jesus

1 I'd rath - er have Je - sus than sil - ver or gold,
2 I'd rath - er have Je - sus than your ap - plause,
3 He's fair - er than lil - ies of rar - est ... bloom,

I'd rath - er be his than have rich - es un - told;
I'd rath - er be faith - ful to his ... dear cause;
he's sweet - er than hon - ey from out ... the comb;

I'd rath - er have Je - sus than hous - es or lands,
I'd rath - er have Je - sus than world - wide .. fame,
he's all that my hun - ger - ing spir - it ... needs,

I'd rath - er be led by his nail - pierced hand—
I'd rath - er be true to his ho - ly name—
I'd rath - er have Je - sus and ... let him lead—

Refrain

Than to be the king of a vast do - main,

or be held in sin's dread sway;

I'd rath - er have Je - sus than an - y - thing

this world af - fords to - day.

Text: Rhea Miller
Music: George Beverly Shea
Text © 1922, 1950 and music © 1939, 1966 Chancel Music, admin. Word Music, Inc.

234 Lord, I Want to Be a Christian

1 Lord, I want to be a Chris-tian in my heart, in my heart;
2 Lord, I want to be more lov-ing in my heart, in my heart;
3 Lord, I want to be more ho-ly in my heart, in my heart;
4 Lord, I want to be like Je-sus in my heart, in my heart;

Lord, I want to be a Chris-tian in my heart,
Lord, I want to be more lov-ing in my heart,
Lord, I want to be more ho-ly in my heart,
Lord, I want to be like Je-sus in my heart,

in my heart, in my heart,
in my heart, in my heart,

Lord, I want to be a Chris-tian in my heart.
Lord, I want to be more lov-ing in my heart.
Lord, I want to be more ho-ly in my heart.
Lord, I want to be like Je-sus in my heart.

Text: African American spiritual
Music: African American spiritual

All to Jesus I Surrender

I Surrender All

1 All to Je-sus I sur-ren-der, all to him I free-ly give;
2 All to Je-sus I sur-ren-der, hum-bly at his feet I bow;
3 All to Je-sus I sur-ren-der, Lord, I give my-self to thee;

I will ev-er love and trust him, in his pres-ence dai-ly live.
world-ly pleas-ures all for-sak-en, take me, Jes-sus, take me now.
fill me with thy love and pow-er, let thy bless-ings fall on me.

Refrain

I sur-ren-der all, I sur-ren-der all,
I sur-ren-der all, I sur-ren-der all,

all to thee, my bless-ed Sav-ior, I sur-ren-der all.

Text: Judson W. Van DeVenter, 1855-1939
Music: SURRENDER, Winfield S. Weeden, 1847-1908

Some Folk Would Rather Have Houses

236

I've Decided to Make Jesus My Choice

1 Some folk would rath - er have hous - es and land.
2 These clothes may be rag - ged that I'm wear - ing.

Some folk choose sil - ver and gold.
Heav - y is the load that I'm bear - ing,

These things they trea - sure and for - get a - bout their souls;
these old . . . . . . bur - dens that I'm car - rying.

I've de - cid - ed to make Je - sus my choice.
I've de - cid - ed to make Je - sus my choice.

Refrain

The road is rough; the go-ing gets tough, and the hills are hard to climb.

I've start-ed out a long time a-go, there's no doubt in my mind;

I've de-cid - ed to make Je - sus my choice.

Text: Harris Johnson
Music: Harris Johnson

237   Must Jesus Bear the Cross Alone

1 Must Je-sus bear the cross a-lone and all the world go free?
2 The con-se-crat-ed cross I'll bear till death shall set me free;
3 Up-on the crys-tal pave-ment, down at Je-sus' pierc-ed feet,
4 Oh, pre-cious cross! Oh, glo-rious crown! Oh, res-ur-rec-tion day!

No, there's a cross for ev-'ry-one, and there's a cross for me.
and then go home my crown to wear, for there's a crown for me.
joy-ful, I'll cast my gold-en crown and his dear name re-peat.
Ye an-gels, from the stars come down and bear my soul a-way.

Text: Thomas Shepherd, 1665-1739
Music: MAITLAND, George N. Allen, 1812-1877

238   A Deacon's Prayer

Holy and righteous, everlasting unto everlasting, thou art God,
the giver of all good and perfect gifts, the author and finisher of our faith.

Again our Father, we, a few of your childrens, has assembled ourselves
at this appointed place, and at this particular time.

And as we come together, our Father,
we don't come for no shape, form, or fashion,
neither do we come for an outside show to a sin-cursed world.
But, our Father, we come as disobedient children
would come before a good parent,
asking if thou would forgive us for our many mistakes,
and own us as your children.

And as we come, our Father, we don't come beggin' thee
but we come thankin' thee, thankin' thee for thy lovingkindness
and tender mercy, realizing that you been a good God to us,

better to us than we have been to ourselves,
better to us, our Father, than we have been to one another,
because you told us to love one another as you have loved us.

Somewhere, someway, or somehow,
we've come shorter than thy glory;
but you being God, and such a good God,
you didn't stop us there, but you kept on blessing us.

We come just now, Master, to say thank you, thank you, thank you,
thank you, Jesus, for being so good to us.

You brought us from a mighty long ways; O Lord, have mercy.

We pray, our Father, for our childrens today;
not only our childrens, but our neighbors,
their childrens, and their children's childrens;
please, Sir, have mercy.

O Lord, we realize that they are living down here in a sin-torn world.
A world, our Father, that's no friend to grace,
a world, my Master, where man will say all manner of evil about you,
call you everything but a child of God.
A world, my Master, where murder, rape, dope, war and sex seem to be
the order of the day.

We pray, our Father, that you will let our lives be an example,
that we may go into a mean world,
tellin' men, women, girls and boys everywhere
that the wages of sin is death.

But there is a gift: the gift of God is eternal life.
There is a reality in serving a true and living God.
Hell is too hot, and eternity is too long; please, Sir, have mercy.

Now Lord, now Lord, one day when we like others
must quit the busy walks of life,
when this world can afford us a home no longer,
we pray that we will be able to look back and see a well-spent life.

As you receive us unto yourself, say to us,
"Well done, well done, thou good and faithful servant."
These blessings we ask in the name of him who gave himself to us,
Jesus Christ our Lord.
Amen

The prayers of the church or "deacon's prayer" prayed aloud in "free prayer" form by lay minister James Williams of St. John Lutheran Church,
Detroit, Michigan, 1995

239

What Shall I Render

1 What shall I ren-der un-to God for all his mer-cies?
2 All I can ren-der is my bod-y and my soul; . . . that's

What shall I ren-der, what shall I give?
all I can ren-der, that's all I can give.

Refrain

God has ev-'ry-thing; ev-'ry-thing be-longs to him.

God has ev-'ry-thing; ev-'ry-thing be-longs to him.

What shall I ren-der, what shall I give?

Text: Margaret J. Douroux, b. 1941; based on Psalm 116:12
Music: Margaret J. Douroux, b. 1941
© 1975 Margaret J. Douroux

It's Me, O Lord
Standing in the Need of Prayer

Refrain

It's me, *it's me,* it's me, O Lord, stand-in' in the need of prayer;

it's me, *it's me,* it's me, O Lord, stand-in' in the need of prayer.

1 Not my broth - er, not my sis - ter, but it's me, O Lord,
2 Not the preach - er, not the dea - con, but it's me, O Lord,
3 Not my fa - ther, not my moth - er, but it's me, O Lord,
4 Not the strang - er, not my neigh - bor, but it's me, O Lord,

stand-in' in the need of prayer; not my broth - er, not my sis - ter, but it's
stand-in' in the need of prayer; not the preach-er, not the dea - con, but it's
stand-in' in the need of prayer; not my fa - ther, not my moth - er, but it's
stand-in' in the need of prayer; not the strang - er, not my neigh-bor, but it's

Refrain

me, O Lord, stand- in' in the need of prayer.
me, O Lord, stand- in' in the need of prayer.
me, O Lord, stand- in' in the need of prayer.
me, O Lord, stand- in' in the need of prayer.

Text: African American spiritual
Music: African American spiritual

241

Every Time I Feel the Spirit

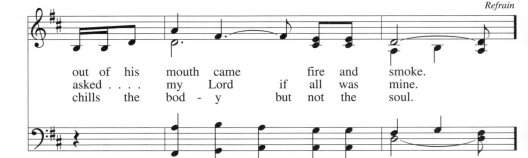

Refrain

Ev - 'ry time I feel the spir - it mov - ing in my heart, I will pray. Ev - 'ry time I feel the spir - it mov - ing in my heart, I will pray.

1 Up - on the moun - tain my Lord spoke,
2 All a - round me looked so fine,
3 Jor - dan riv - er, chilly and cold,

out of his mouth came fire and smoke.
asked . . . . my Lord if all was mine.
chills the bod - y but not the soul.

Refrain

Text: African American spiritual
Music: African American spiritual

Sweet Hour of Prayer

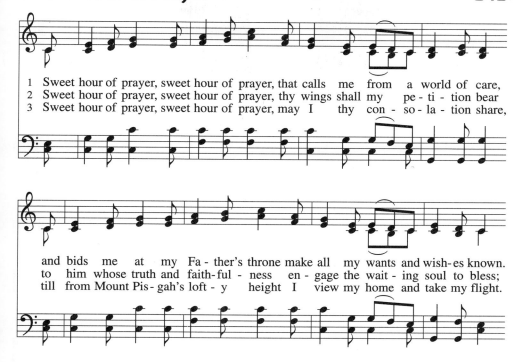

1 Sweet hour of prayer, sweet hour of prayer, that calls me from a world of care,
2 Sweet hour of prayer, sweet hour of prayer, thy wings shall my pe - ti - tion bear
3 Sweet hour of prayer, sweet hour of prayer, may I thy con - so - la - tion share,

and bids me at my Fa - ther's throne make all my wants and wish-es known.
to him whose truth and faith-ful - ness en - gage the wait - ing soul to bless;
till from Mount Pis-gah's loft - y height I view my home and take my flight.

In sea-sons of dis - tress and grief my soul has of - ten found re - lief.
and since he bids me seek his face, be - lieve his word and trust his grace,
With joy I'll has-ten to the place where God my Sav - ior shows his face,

and oft es-caped the tempt - er's snare by thy re - turn, sweet hour of prayer.
I'll cast on him my ev - 'ry care, and wait for thee, sweet hour of prayer.
and glad - ly take my sta - tion there, thy prom - ise gained, sweet hour of prayer.

Text: William Walford, 1772-1850, alt.
Music: SWEET HOUR, William B. Bradbury, 1816-1868

Your Will Be Done

Mayenziwe

Your will be done on earth, O Lord.
Ma - ye - nzi - we 'nta - ndo ya - kho.

Your will
Ma - ye -

Your will be done on earth, O Lord.
Ma - ye - nzi - we 'nta - ndo ya - kho.

Your will
Ma - ye -

Your will be done on earth, O Lord.
Ma - ye - nzi - we 'nta - ndo ya - kho.

Your will be done on earth, O Lord.
Ma - ye - nzi - we 'nta - ndo ya - kho.

Your will be done on earth, O Lord.
Ma - ye - nzi - we 'nta - ndo ya - kho.

Text: South African, from the Lord's Prayer
Music: South African traditional; taught by Gobingca Mxadana; transc. John L. Bell, b. 1949
Arr. © 1990 Iona Community, admin. GIA Publications, Inc.

Send Me, Jesus
Thuma mina

1 Send me, Lord. Send me, Je-sus, send me, Je-sus, send me,
Je-sus, lead me, Je-sus, lead me,
Je-sus, fill me, Je-sus, fill me,

1, 2
Lead me, Lord.
Fill me, Lord.

3

Je-sus, send me, Lord. 2 Lead me,
Je-sus, lead me, Lord. 3 Fill me,
Je-sus, fill me, Lord.

1 Thuma mina.
Thuma mina, thuma mina.
Thuma mina, somandla.

2 Roma nna.
Roma nna, roma nna.
Roma nna, modino.

Text: South African
Music: THUMA MINA, South African
Tr. and arr. © 1984 Ultryck, admin. Walton Music Corp.

Send Me, Jesus
Thuma mina

245

1 Send me, Je-sus; send me, Je-sus; send me, Je-sus; send me, Lord.
2 I am will-ing; I am will-ing; I am will-ing, will-ing, Lord.
1 Thu-ma mi-na, thu-ma mi-na, thu-ma mi-na, Nko-si yam.
2 Ndi-ya vu-ma, ndi-ya vu-ma, ndi-ya vu-ma, Nko-si yam.

Send me, Je-sus.

Text: South African
Music: South African

246   # Somebody Prayed for Me

1 Some-bod-y prayed for me,   had me on their mind,
2 My moth-er prayed for me,   had me on her mind,
3 My fa-ther prayed for me,   had me on his mind,
4 The peo-ple prayed for me,   had me on their mind,

took some time to pray for me.
took some time to pray for me.
took some time to pray for me.
took some time to pray for me.

I'm so glad they prayed,   I'm so glad they prayed,
I'm so glad she prayed,   I'm so glad she prayed,
I'm so glad he prayed,   I'm so glad he prayed,
I'm so glad they prayed,   I'm so glad they prayed,

I'm so glad they prayed for me.
I'm so glad she prayed for me.
I'm so glad he prayed for me.
I'm so glad they prayed for me.

Text: traditional
Music: James M. Capers, b. 1948
Arr. © 1999 Augsburg Fortress

Lord, Listen to Your Children Praying 247

Lord, lis-ten to your chil-dren pray-ing, Lord, send your Spir-it in this place;

Lord, lis-ten to your chil-dren pray-ing, send us love, send us pow'r, send us grace.

Text: Ken Medema, b. 1943
Music: CHILDREN PRAYING, Ken Medema, b. 1943
© 1973 Hope Publishing Co.

In My Life, Lord, Be Glorified 248

1 In my life, Lord, be glo-ri-fied, be glo-ri-fied;
2 In my song, Lord, be glo-ri-fied, be glo-ri-fied;
3 In your church, Lord, be glo-ri-fied, be glo-ri-fied;

in my life, Lord, be glo-ri-fied to-day.
in my song, Lord, be glo-ri-fied to-day.
in your church, Lord, be glo-ri-fied to-day.

Text: Bob Kilpatrick, b. 1952
Music: Bob Kilpatrick, b. 1952
© 1978 Bob Kilpatrick Music, admin. Lorenz Publishing Co.

249

Jesus Loves Me!

1 Je - sus loves me! this I know, for the Bi - ble tells me so;
2 Je - sus loves me! he who died heav - en's gates to o - pen wide;
3 Je - sus loves me! loves me still, though I'm ver - y weak and ill;
4 Je - sus loves me! he will stay close be - side me all the way;

lit - tle ones to him be - long, they are weak, but he is strong.
he will wash a - way my sin, let his lit - tle child come in.
from his shin - ing throne on high, comes to watch me where I lie.
when at last I come to die, he will take me home on high.

Refrain

Yes, Je - sus loves me, yes, Je - sus loves me,

yes, Je - sus loves me, the Bi - ble tells me so.

Text: Anna Warner, 1820-1915, alt.
Music: JESUS LOVES ME, William B. Bradbury, 1816-1868

There Is a Name I Love to Hear

Oh, How I Love Jesus

1 There is a name I love to hear, I love to sing its worth;
2 It tells me of a Sav-ior's love, who died to set me free;
3 It tells me what my mak-er hath in store for ev-'ry day;
4 It tells of one whose lov-ing heart can feel my deep-est woe,

it sounds like mu-sic in my ear, the sweet-est name on earth.
it tells me of his pre-cious blood, the sin-ner's per-fect plea.
and though I tread a dark-some path, yields sun-shine all the way.
who in each sor-row bears a part that none can bear be-low.

Refrain

Oh, how I love Je-sus, oh, how I love Je-sus,

oh, how I love Je-sus, be-cause he first loved me!

Text: Frederick Whitfield, 1829-1904
Music: traditional

Like a Ship That's Tossed and Driven

The Lord Will Make a Way Somehow

1 Like a ship that's toss'd and driv-en, bat-tered by an an-gry sea;
2 Try to do my best in ser-vice, try to live the best I can;
3 Of-ten there's mis-un - der-stand-ing out of all the good I do;

when the storms of life are rag - ing and their fu - ry falls on me,
when I choose to do the right thing, ev-il's pres-ent on ev - 'ry hand;
go to friends for con-so - la - tion and I find them com-plain-ing too.

I won-der what I have done that makes this race so hard to run;
I look up and won-der why..... that good for-tune pass me by.
So man-y nights I toss in pain, won - der-ing what the day will bring,

then I say to my soul, take cour-age; the Lord will make a way some-how.
Then I say to my soul, be pa - tient; the Lord will make a way some-how.
but I say to my heart, don't wor-ry; the Lord will make a way some-how.

Text: Thomas A. Dorsey, 1899-1993
Music: Thomas A. Dorsey, 1899-1993

Why Should I Feel Discouraged

His Eye Is on the Sparrow

1 Why should I feel dis-cour-aged, why should the shad-ows come,
2 "Let not your heart be trou-bled," his ten-der word I hear,
3 When-ev-er I am tempt-ed, when-ev-er clouds a-rise,

why should my heart be lone-ly and long for heav'n and home,
and rest-ing on his good-ness, I lose my doubts and fears;
when song gives place to sigh-ing, when hope with-in me dies,

when Je-sus is my por-tion? My con-stant friend is he:
though by the path he leads me but one step I may see:
I draw the clos-er to him, from care he sets me free:

his eye is on the spar-row, and I know he watch-es me;
his eye is on the spar-row, and I know he watch-es me;
his eye is on the spar-row, and I know he watch-es me;

his eye is on the spar-row, and I know he watch-es me.
his eye is on the spar-row, and I know he watch-es me.
his eye is on the spar-row, and I know he watch-es me.

Refrain

I sing be-cause I'm hap-py, I sing be-cause I'm free,
I'm hap-py, I'm free,

for his eye is on the spar-row, and I know he watch-es me.

Text: Civilla D. Martin, 1860-1948
Music: HIS EYE IS ON THE SPARROW, Charles H. Gabriel, 1856-1932

253

Just a Closer Walk with Thee

Refrain

Just a clos-er walk with thee, grant it, Je-sus, is my plea;

dai-ly walk-ing close to thee, let it be, dear Lord, let it be.

1 I am weak but thou art strong: Je-sus, keep me from all wrong;
2 Through this world of toil and snares, if I fal-ter, Lord, who cares?
3 When my fee-ble life is o'er, time for me will be no more;

Refrain

I'll be sat-is-fied as long as I walk, let me walk close to thee.
Who with me my bur-den shares? None but thee, dear . . Lord, none but thee.
guide me gent-ly, safe-ly o'er to thy king-dom . . shore, to thy shore.

Text: traditional
Music: CLOSER WALK, traditional

Savior, Like a Shepherd Lead Us

254

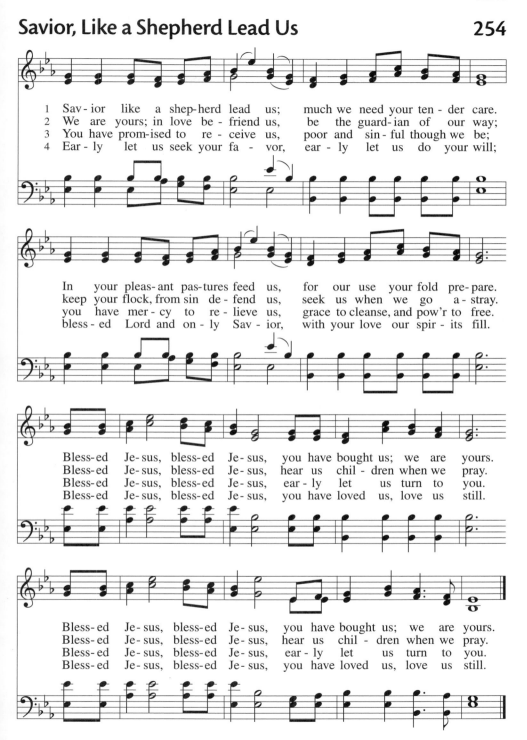

1 Sav-ior like a shep-herd lead us; much we need your ten-der care.
2 We are yours; in love be-friend us, be the guard-ian of our way;
3 You have prom-ised to re-ceive us, poor and sin-ful though we be;
4 Ear-ly let us seek your fa-vor, ear-ly let us do your will;

In your pleas-ant pas-tures feed us, for our use your fold pre-pare.
keep your flock, from sin de-fend us, seek us when we go a-stray.
you have mer-cy to re-lieve us, grace to cleanse, and pow'r to free.
bless-ed Lord and on-ly Sav-ior, with your love our spir-its fill.

Bless-ed Je-sus, bless-ed Je-sus, you have bought us; we are yours.
Bless-ed Je-sus, bless-ed Je-sus, hear us chil-dren when we pray.
Bless-ed Je-sus, bless-ed Je-sus, ear-ly let us turn to you.
Bless-ed Je-sus, bless-ed Je-sus, you have loved us, love us still.

Bless-ed Je-sus, bless-ed Je-sus, you have bought us; we are yours.
Bless-ed Je-sus, bless-ed Je-sus, hear us chil-dren when we pray.
Bless-ed Je-sus, bless-ed Je-sus, ear-ly let us turn to you.
Bless-ed Je-sus, bless-ed Je-sus, you have loved us, love us still.

Text: attr. Dorothy A. Thrupp, 1779-1847
Music: BRADBURY, William B. Bradbury, 1816-1868

255

Will Your Anchor Hold

1 Will your an - chor hold in the storms of life,
2 Will your an - chor hold in the straits of fear,
3 Will your an - chor hold in the floods of death,
4 Will your eyes be - hold through the morn - ing light

when the clouds un - fold their wings of strife;
when the break - ers roar and the reef is near;
when the wa - ters cold chill your fi - nal breath?
the . . . . . city of gold, and the har - bor bright?

when the strong tides lift and the ca - bles strain,
while the surg - es rave, and the wild winds blow,
On the ris - ing tide you can nev - er fail
Will you an - chor safe by the heav'n - ly shore,

will your an - chor drift, or firm re - main?
shall the an - gry waves then your bark o'er - flow?
while your an - chor holds with - in the veil.
when life's storms are past for - ev - er - more?

Refrain

We have an an - chor that keeps the soul

stead-fast and sure while the bil - lows roll, fas-ten'd to the Rock which

can - not move, ground-ed firm and deep in the Sa - vior's love!

Text: Priscilla J. Owens, 1829-1907
Music: William J. Kirkpatrick, 1838-1921

256

I Will Trust in the Lord

1 I will trust in the Lord, I will trust in the Lord,
2 Sis - ter, will you trust in the Lord, sis - ter, will you trust in the Lord,
3 Broth - er, will you trust in the Lord, broth - er, will you trust in the Lord,

I will trust in the Lord till I die.
sis - ter, will you trust in the Lord till you die?
broth - er, will you trust in the Lord till you die?

I will trust in the Lord, I will trust in the Lord,
Sis - ter, will you trust in the Lord, sis - ter, will you trust in the Lord,
Broth - er, will you trust in the Lord, broth - er, will you trust in the Lord,

I will trust in the Lord till I die.
sis - ter, will you trust in the Lord till you die?
broth - er, will you trust in the Lord till you die?

Additional stanzas ad lib:
Deacon, will you trust . . .
Preacher, will you trust . . .
People, will you trust . . .

Text: African American spiritual
Music: African American spiritual; arr. J. Jefferson Cleveland, 1937-1986
Arr. © 1981 Abingdon Press, admin. The Copyright Company

I've Got the Joy, Joy, Joy

257

1 I've got the joy, joy, joy, joy,
2 I've got the peace that pass - es un - der - stand - ing,
3 I've got the love of Je - sus, love of Je - sus,

down in my heart, down in my heart, down in my heart;
down in my heart, down in my heart, down in my heart;
down in my heart, down in my heart, down in my heart;

I've got the joy, joy, joy, joy,
I've got the peace that pass - es un - der - stand - ing,
I've got the love of Je - sus, love of Je - sus,

down in my heart, down in my heart to stay.
down in my heart, down in my heart to stay.
down in my heart, down in my heart to stay.

Text: George W. Cooke
Music: George W. Cooke

258

I've Got Peace Like a River

1 I've got peace like a riv-er, I've got peace like a riv-er,
2 I've got joy like a foun-tain, I've got joy like a foun-tain,
3 I've got love like an o-cean, I've got love like an o-cean,

I've got peace like a riv-er in my soul;
I've got joy like a foun-tain in my soul;
I've got love like an o-cean in my soul;

I've got peace like a riv-er, I've got peace like a riv-er,
I've got joy like a foun-tain, I've got joy like a foun-tain,
I've got love like an o-cean, I've got love like an o-cean,

I've got peace like a riv-er in my soul.
I've got joy like a foun-tain in my soul.
I've got love like an o-cean in my soul.

Text: traditional
Music: African American spiritual

All the Way My Savior Leads Me

1 All the way my Sav-ior leads me; what have I to ask be-side?
2 All the way my Sav-ior leads me, cheers each wind-ing path I tread,
3 All the way my Sav-ior leads me; oh, the full-ness of his love!

Can I doubt his ten-der mer-cy, who through life has been my guide?
gives me grace for ev-'ry tri-al, feeds me with the liv-ing bread.
Per-fect rest to me is prom-ised in my Fa-ther's house a-bove.

Heav'n-ly peace, di-vin-est com-fort, here by faith in him to dwell!
Though my wear-y steps may fal-ter, and my soul a-thirst may be,
When my spir-it, clothed im-mor-tal, wings its flight to realms of day,

For I know, what-e'er be-fall me, Je-sus do-eth all things well;
gush-ing from the rock be-fore me, lo, a spring of joy I see;
this my song through end-less a-ges—Je-sus led me all the way;

for I know, what-e'er be-fall me, Je-sus do-eth all things well.
gush-ing from the rock be-fore me, lo, a spring of joy I see.
this my song through end-less a-ges—Je-sus led me all the way!

Text: Fanny J. Crosby, 1820-1915
Music: ALL THE WAY, Robert Lowry, 1826-1899

A Wonderful Savior Is Jesus

He Hideth My Soul

260

1 A won - der - ful Sav - ior is Je - sus, my Lord, a
2 A won - der - ful Sav - ior is Je - sus, my Lord, he
3 With num - ber - less bless - ings each mo - ment he crowns, and,
4 When clothed in his bright-ness trans - port - ed I rise to

won - der - ful Sav - ior to me; he hid - eth my soul in the
tak - eth my bur - den a - way; he hold - eth me up, and I
filled with his good - ness di - vine, I sing in my rap - ture, oh,
meet him in clouds of the sky, his per - fect sal - va - tion, his

cleft of the rock, where riv - ers of plea - sure I see.
shall not be moved, he giv - eth me strength as my day.
glo - ry to God for such a re - deem - er as mine!
won - der - ful love I'll shout with the mil - lions on high.

Refrain

He hid - eth my soul in the cleft of the rock that shad - ows a dry, thirst - y

land;   he hid - eth my life   in the   depths of his   love,   and

cov - ers me there with his   hand,   and cov - ers me there with his   hand.

Text: Fanny J. Crosby, 1820-1915
Music: William J. Kirkpatrick, 1838-1921

Calling on You, O Lord   261

O God, you have prepared in peace
the path I must follow today.
Help me to walk straight on that path.
If I speak, remove lies from my lips.
If I am hungry, take away from me all complaint.
If I have plenty, destroy pride in me.
May I go through the day calling on you,
you, O Lord,
who know no other Lord.
Amen

Anonymous, from Ethiopia

262

This Is the Day

This is the day, this is the day that the Lord has made, that the
Lord has made; we will re-joice, we will re-joice and be
glad in it, and be glad in it. This is the day that the
Lord has made; we will re-joice and be glad in it.
This is the day, this is the day that the Lord has made.

Text: Psalm 118:24
Music: Les Garrett, b. 1944

I'm a-Goin'-a Eat at the Welcome Table

Welcome Table

1 I'm a-goin'-a eat at the wel-come ta - ble,
2 I'm a-goin'-a feast on milk . . . and hon - ey,
3 I'm a-goin'-a wade 'cross Jor - dan's riv - er,

I'm a-goin'-a eat at the wel-come ta-ble, some of these days.
I'm a-goin'-a feast on milk . . . and hon-ey, some of these days.
I'm a-goin'-a wade 'cross Jor - dan's riv-er, some of these days.

I'm a-goin'-a eat at the wel-come ta - ble,
I'm a-goin'-a feast on milk . . . and hon - ey,
I'm a-goin'-a wade 'cross Jor - dan's riv - er,

I'm goin'-a eat at the wel-come ta - ble, some of these days.
I'm goin'-a feast on . . . milk and hon-ey, some of these days.
I'm goin'-a wade 'cross . . Jor-dan's riv - er, some of these days.

Text: African American spiritual
Music: African American spiritual; arr. Carl Diton, 1886-1969
Arr. © 1930 G. Schirmer, Inc.

264 To God Be the Glory

1 To God be the glo - ry, great things he has done;
2 Oh, per - fect re - demp - tion, the pur - chase of blood,
3 Great things he has taught us, great things he has done,

so loved he the world that he gave us his Son,
to ev - 'ry be - liev - er the prom - ise of God;
and great our re - joic - ing through Je - sus the Son;

who yield - ed his life an a - tone - ment for sin,
the vil - est of - fend - er by grace may be - lieve,
but pur - er, and high - er, and great - er will be

and o - pened the life - gate that all may go in.
that mo - ment from Je - sus a par - don re - ceive.
our won - der, our vic - t'ry, when Je - sus we see.

Refrain

Praise the Lord, praise the Lord, let the earth hear his voice!

Praise the Lord, praise the Lord, let the peo - ple re - joice!

Oh, come to the Fa - ther, through Je - sus the Son,

and give him the glo - ry, great things he has done.

Text: Fanny J. Crosby, 1820-1915
Music: TO GOD BE THE GLORY, William H. Doane, 1832-1915

265

In the Name of Jesus

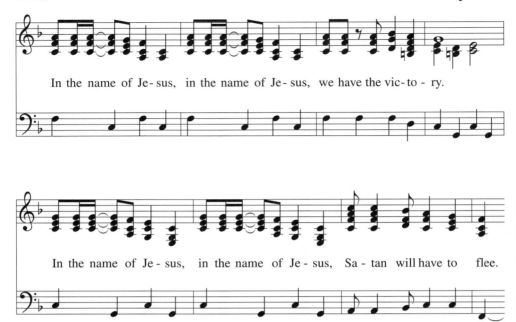

In the name of Je-sus, in the name of Je-sus, we have the vic-to-ry.

In the name of Je-sus, in the name of Je-sus, Sa-tan will have to flee.

Oh, tell me: who can stand a-gainst us when we call on that great name?

Je-sus, Je-sus, pre-cious Je-sus; we have the vic-to-ry.

Text: traditional
Music: traditional; arr. James M. Capers, b. 1948
Arr. © 1999 Augsburg Fortress

Victory Is Mine

1 Vic - to - ry   is mine;   vic - to - ry   is mine;
2 Joy . . . . .   is mine;   joy . . . .   is mine;
3 Peace . . .   is mine;   peace . . . .   is mine;

vic - to - ry   to - day   is   mine.
joy . . . . . .   to - day   is   mine.
peace . . . . .   to - day   is   mine.

I   told   Sa - tan,   "Get   thee   be - hind."
I   told   Sa - tan,   "Get   thee   be - hind."
I   told   Sa - tan,   "Get   thee   be - hind."

1, 2   *3*

Vic - to - ry   to - day   is   mine.
Joy . . . . .   to - day   is   mine.
Peace . . .   to - day   is   mine.

Text: traditional
Music: traditional; arr. James M. Capers, b. 1948
Arr. © 1999 Augsburg Fortress

267

All Hail the Power of Jesus' Name!

1 All hail the pow'r of Je - sus' name!
2 O seed of Is - rael's cho - sen race,
3 Let ev - 'ry kin - dred, ev - 'ry tribe,
4 Oh, that with yon - der sa - cred throng

Let an - gels pros-trate fall; let an - gels pros - trate fall;
now ran - somed from the fall, now ran - somed from the fall,
on this ter - res - trial ball, on this ter - res - trial ball,
we at his feet may fall, we at his feet may fall!

bring forth the roy - al di - a - dem,
hail him who saves you by his grace,
to him all maj - es - ty as - cribe,
We'll join the ev - er - last - ing song,

Refrain

and crown

and crown him, crown him, crown him,

and crown

and crown him, crown him, crown him,

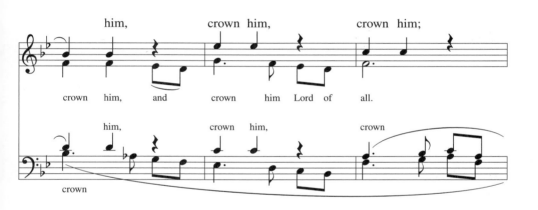

him, crown him, crown him;

crown him, and crown him Lord of all.

him, crown him, crown

crown

crown him;

crown him; and crown him Lord of all!

him; and crown him Lord of all!

Text: Edward Perronet, 1726-1792
Music: DIADEM, James Ellor, 1819-1899

268
Jesus, Name Above All Names

Je - sus, name a-bove all names, beau-ti-ful Sav - ior, glo-ri-ous Lord, Em-man-u-el, God is with us, bless-ed Re-deem - er, liv-ing Word. Word.

Optional repeat

Last time

Text: Naida Hearn
Music: Naida Hearn
© 1974 Scripture in Song, a division of Integrity Music, Inc.

When I Think of the Goodness of Jesus

269

When I think of the good-ness of Je - sus,

and what he has done for me,

my soul cries out, "Hal-le - lu - jah!"

Praise God for sav - ing me.

Text: traditional
Music: traditional; arr. James M. Capers, b. 1948
Arr. © 1999 Augsburg Fortress

270

Have You Thanked the Lord?

Have you thanked the Lord? Have you praised God's name? Don't you know that no to-mor-row is quite the same? Have you thanked the Lord?

Have you knelt in prayer, and re-joiced that, rain or sun-shine, our God is there?

Text: Bill LaMotta, 1919-1980
Music: Bill LaMotta, 1919-1980; arr. *This Far by Faith*

271

I Will Rejoice

I will re - joice, I will be glad.

I will praise God who holds my life

in his hands.

I will praise the Fa - ther, I will praise the Son,

I will praise the Spir - it for - ev - er - more.

I will re - joice,

I will be glad. I will praise

God, who holds my life in his hands.

Text: Grayson Warren Brown, b. 1948
Music: Grayson Warren Brown, b. 1948; arr. Larry Adams

To God Be the Glory
My Tribute

272

To God be the glo - ry, to God be the glo - ry,

to God be the glo - ry for the things he has done.

With his blood he has saved me; with his power he has raised me;

to God be the glo - ry for the things he has done.

Text: Andraé Crouch, b. 1942
Music: MY TRIBUTE, Andraé Crouch, b. 1942

Bless the Lord

Bless His Holy Name

Bless the Lord, O my soul: and all that is within me, bless his ho - ly name.
He has done great things, he has done great things,
he has done great things: bless his ho - ly name!

D.C. al fine

Text: Psalm 103:1, adapt.
Music: Andraé Crouch, b. 1942
Music © 1973 Bud John Songs, Inc., admin. EMI Christian Music Publishing

Oh, Sing to the Lord
Cantad al Señor

274

1 Oh, sing to the Lord, oh, sing God a new song.
2 For God is the Lord, and God has done won-ders.
3 So dance for our God and blow all the trum-pets.
4 Oh, shout to our God, who gave us the Spir-it.
5 For Je-sus is Lord! A - men! Al-le - lu - ia!

Oh, sing to the Lord, oh, sing God a new song.
For God is the Lord, and God has done won-ders.
So dance for our God and blow all the trum-pets.
Oh, shout to our God, who gave us the Spir-it.
For Je-sus is Lord! A - men! Al-le - lu - ia!

Oh, sing to the Lord, oh, sing God a new song.
For God is the Lord, and God has done won-ders.
So dance for our God and blow all the trum-pets,
Oh, shout to our God, who gave us the Spir-it.
For Je-sus is Lord! A - men! Al-le - lu - ia!

Oh, sing to our God, oh, sing to our God.
Oh, sing to our God, oh, sing to our God.
and sing to our God, and sing to our God.
Oh, sing to our God, oh, sing to our God.
Oh, sing to our God, oh, sing to our God.

1 Cantad al Señor un cántico nuevo.
Cantad al Señor un cántico nuevo.
Cantad al Señor un cántico nuevo.
¡Cantad al Señor, cantad al Señor!

2 Pues nuestro el Señor ha hecho prodigios.
Pues nuestro el Señor ha hecho prodigios.
Pues nuestro el Señor ha hecho prodigios.
¡Cantad al Señor, cantad al Señor!

3 Cantad al Señor, alabadle con arpa.
Cantad al Señor, alabadle con arpa.
Cantad al Señor, alabadle con arpa.
¡Cantad al Señor, cantad al Señor!

4 Es él que nos da el Espíritu Santo.
Es él que nos da el Espíritu Santo.
Es él que nos da el Espíritu Santo.
¡Cantad al Señor, cantad al Señor!

5 ¡Jesús es Señor! ¡Amén, aleluya!
¡Jesús es Señor! ¡Amén, aleluya!
¡Jesús es Señor! ¡Amén, aleluya!
¡Cantad al Señor, cantad al Señor!

Text: Brazilian folk song; tr. Gerhard Cartford, b. 1923
Music: CANTAD AL SEÑOR, Brazilian folk tune; arr. Gerhard Cartford, b. 1923
Tr. and arr. © Gerhard Cartford

God Is So Good 275

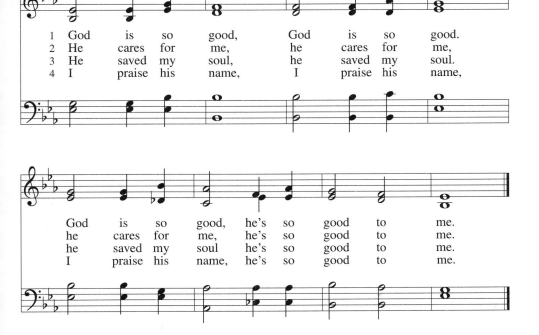

1 God is so good, God is so good.
2 He cares for me, he cares for me,
3 He saved my soul, he saved my soul.
4 I praise his name, I praise his name,

God is so good, he's so good to me.
he cares for me, he's so good to me.
he saved my soul, he's so good to me.
I praise his name, he's so good to me.

Text: traditional
Music: GOD IS SO GOOD, traditional

276 **Praise God, from Whom All Blessings Flow**

1 Praise God from whom all bless - ings flow,

praise him all crea - tures here be - low.

Praise him a - bove, ye heav - en - ly host,

praise Fa - ther, Son and Ho - ly Ghost.

2 Peo - ple and realms of ev - 'ry tongue
3 Sing to the Lord with cheer - ful voice,

dwell on his love with sweet - est song,
come ye be - fore him and re - joice,

to him shall end - less prayer be made,
all peo - ple that on earth do dwell,

and end - less prais - es crown his head.
serve him with mirth, his prais - es tell.

A - men, a - men.

Text: Thomas Ken, 1637-1711, st. 1; Isaac Watts, 1675-1748, st. 2; William Kethe, d. 1593, st. 3
Music: attr. John Hatton, d. 1793; adapt. George Coles; arr. Roberta Martin, 1912-1969

277

I Will Call Upon the Lord

Optional descant

I will call up-on the Lord

I will call up-on the Lord who is wor-thy to be

who is wor-thy to be praised. So shall I be

praised. So shall I be saved from my en-e-mies.

saved from my en-e-mies. I will call up-on the Lord. The

I will call up-on the Lord. The

Lord liv-eth, and bless-ed be the Rock, and let the God of my sal-va-tion be ex-alt - ed. The Lord liv-eth, and bless-ed be the Rock, and let the God of my sal-va-tion be ex-alt - ed.

278

Praise, Praise, Praise the Lord

Praise, praise, praise the Lord! Praise God's ho - ly name. Al - le - lu - ia!

Praise, praise, praise the Lord! Praise God's ho - ly name. Al - le - lu - ia!

Praise God's ho - ly name. Al - le - lu - ia! Praise God's ho - ly name. Al - le - lu - ia!

Praise God's ho - ly name. Al - le - lu - ia! Praise God's ho - ly name. Al - le - lu - ia!

This song may be repeated, adding a vocal part on each repetition:
melody (alto) alone; melody + tenor; melody + lower parts; all voices.

Text: traditional; collected by Elaine Hanson
Music: Cameroon processional; arr. Ralph M. Johnson
© 1994 earthsongs

Amen, We Praise Your Name

Amen, siakudumisa

Text: South African traditional
Music: AMEN SIAKUDUMISA, attr. S. C. Molefe, as taught by Gobingca Mxadana
Music © Gobingca Mxadana

280 Thank You, Jesus

Leader: Thank you, Je-sus. Thank you, Je-sus.

Congregation: Thank you, Je-sus, a-men. Thank you, Je-sus, a-men.

Thank you, Je-sus.

Thank you, Je-sus, a-men. Hal-le-lu-jah, a-men.

Text: Namibian traditional
Music: Namibian traditional; arr. James M. Capers, b. 1948
Arr. © 1999 Augsburg Fortress

281 We Will Glorify

1 We will glo-ri-fy the King of kings, we will glo-ri-fy the Lamb;
2 Lord Je-ho-vah reigns in maj-es-ty, we will bow be-fore his throne;
3 He is Lord of heav-en, Lord of earth, he is Lord of all who live;
4 Hal-le-lu-jah to the King of kings, hal-le-lu-jah to the Lamb;

we will glo-ri-fy the Lord of lords, who is the great I AM.
we will wor-ship him in righ-teous-ness, we will wor-ship him a - lone.
he is Lord a-bove the u - ni - verse, all praise to him we give.
hal-le - lu - jah to the Lord of lords, who is the great I AM.

Text: Twila Paris, b. 1958
Music: We Will Glorify, Twila Paris, b. 1958
© 1982 Singspiration Music/ASCAP, admin. Brentwood-Benson Music Publishing

Let All That Is within Me Cry, "Holy!" 282

1 Let all that is with - in me cry, "Ho - ly!"
2 Let all that is with - in me cry, "Bless - ed!"
3 Let all that is with - in me cry, "Wor - thy!"

Let all that is with - in me cry, "Ho - ly!"
Let all that is with - in me cry, "Bless - ed!"
Let all that is with - in me cry, "Wor - thy!"

Ho - ly! Ho - ly! Ho - ly is the Lamb that was slain.
Bless-ed! Bless-ed! Bless-ed is the Lamb that was slain.
Wor - thy! Wor - thy! Wor-thy is the Lamb that was slain.

Text: anonymous; transc. Melvin Harrel
Music: arr. Charles High

Text © 1963 Gospel Publishing House, admin. The Lorenz Corp.
Arr.© 1978 Word of God Music, admin. The Copyright Company

283

Great Is Thy Faithfulness

1 Great is thy faith-ful-ness, O God my Fa-ther; there is no
2 Sum-mer and win-ter and spring-time and har-vest, sun, moon, and
3 Par-don for sin and a peace that en-dur-eth, thine own dear

shad-ow of turn-ing with thee; thou chang-est not, thy com-
stars in their cours-es a - bove join with all na-ture in
pres-ence to cheer and to guide; strength for to - day and bright

pas-sions, they fail not; as thou hast been, thou for-ev-er wilt be.
man-i-fold wit-ness to thy great faith-ful-ness, mer-cy, and love.
hope for to-mor-row, bless-ings all mine, with ten thou-sand be-side!

Refrain

Great is thy faith-ful-ness! Great is thy faith-ful-ness! Morn-ing by

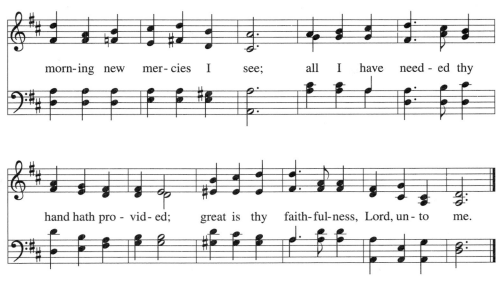

morn-ing new mer-cies I see; all I have need-ed thy

hand hath pro-vid-ed; great is thy faith-ful-ness, Lord, un-to me.

Text: Thomas O. Chisholm, 1866-1960
Music: FAITHFULNESS, William M. Runyan, 1870-1957

For He Alone Is Worthy 284

1 For he a-lone is wor-thy, for he a-lone is wor-thy,
2 We'll give him all the glo-ry, we'll give him all the glo-ry,
3 Oh, come, let us a-dore him, oh, come, let us a-dore him,

for he a-lone is wor-thy, Christ the Lord.
we'll give him all the glo-ry, Christ the Lord.
oh, come, let us a-dore him, Christ the Lord.

Text: traditional
Music: ADESTE FIDELES, John Francis Wade, 1711-1786

285   # Praise Him! Jesus, Blessed Savior

1 Praise him,   praise him,   praise him,   praise him!
2 Glo - ry!   Glo - ry!   In   all   things give him glo - ry.
3 Praise him,   praise him,   praise him,   praise him!
4 Praise him,   praise him,   praise him,   praise him!

Alternate accompaniment

Je - sus,   bless-ed   Sav - ior,   he's wor-thy to   be   praised.
Je - sus,   bless-ed   Sav - ior,   he's wor-thy to   be   praised.
Je - sus,   bless-ed   Sav - ior,   he's wor-thy to   be   praised.
Je - sus,   bless-ed   Sav - ior,   he's wor-thy to   be   praised.

1 From the ris - ing of the sun un - til the
2 For . . . . God . . . is our rock, hope of sal -
3 From the ris - ing of the sun un - til the

go - ing down of the same; he's wor - thy, Je - sus is
va - tion; a strong . . de - liv - er -
go - ing down of the same; he's wor - thy, Je - sus is

wor - thy, he's wor - thy to be praised.
er, ... in him I will al - ways trust.
wor - thy, he's wor - thy to be praised.

I Am Thanking Jesus
Tandi Tanga Yesus

286

English   I am thank-ing Je-sus,   I am thank-ing Je-sus,   I am thank-ing
Swahili   A-san-te   sa-na Ye-su,   a-san-te   sa-na Ye-su,   a-san-te   sa-na
Otji-vambo Tan-di   tan-ga Ye-sus,   tan-di   tan-ga Ye-sus,   tan-di   tan-ga

Je-sus from my   heart.   I   am thank-ing Je-sus,
Ye-su mo-yo-ni.   A-san-te   sa-na Ye-su,   a-
Ye-sus mo-mu-ti-ma.   Tan-di   tan-ga Ye-sus,

I   am thank-ing Je-sus,   I   am thank-ing Je-sus from my   heart.
san-te   sa-na Ye-su,   a-san-te   sa-na Ye-su mo-yo-ni.
tan-di   tan-ga Ye-sus,   tan-di   tan-ga Ye-sus mo-mu-ti-ma.

Text: Namibian and Tanzanian traditional
Music: African traditional, arr. *This Far by Faith*
Tr. © 1986, arr © 1999 Augsburg Fortress

287

I Just Came to Praise the Lord

C   G/B   Am   F   C/E   Dm⁷   G⁷

1 I just came to praise the   Lord,   I just came to praise the   Lord,
2 I just came to thank the   Lord,   I just came to thank the   Lord,
3 I just came to love the   Lord,   I just came to love the   Lord,

I just came to praise his ho-ly name, I just came to praise the Lord.
I just came to thank his ho-ly name, I just came to thank the Lord.
I just came to love his ho-ly name, I just came to love the Lord.

Text: Wayne Romero
Music: Wayne Romero

© 1975 Paragon Music Corp./ASCAP, admin. Brentwood-Benson Music Publishing

I Love You, Lord

288

I love you, Lord, and I lift my voice to wor-ship

you. Oh, my soul, re - joice! Take joy, my king, in what you hear:

may it be a sweet, sweet sound in your ear.

Text: Laurie Klein
Music: Laurie Klein

© 1978 House of Mercy Music, admin. Maranatha! Music c/o The Copyright Company

289

Holy, Holy

1 Ho - ly, ho - ly, ho - ly, ho - ly,
2 Gra - cious Fa - ther, gra - cious Fa - ther,
3 Pre - cious Je - sus, pre - cious Je - sus,
4 Ho - ly Spir - it, Ho - ly Spir - it,
5 Hal - le - lu - jah, hal - le - lu - jah,

ho - ly, ho - ly, Lord God Al - might - y!
we're so blest to be your chil - dren, gra - cious Fa - ther;
we're so glad that you've re - deemed us, pre - cious Je - sus;
come and fill our hearts a - new, . . . Ho - ly Spir - it;
hal - le - lu - jah, ... hal - le - lu - jah;

and we lift our hearts be - fore you as a to - ken of our love,
and we lift our heads be - fore you as a to - ken of our love,
and we lift our hands be - fore you as a to - ken of our love,
and we lift our voice be - fore you as a to - ken of our love,
and we lift our hearts be - fore you as a to - ken of our love,

ho - ly, ho - ly, ho - ly, ho - ly.
gra - cious Fa - ther, gra - cious Fa - ther.
pre - cious Je - sus, pre - cious Je - sus.
Ho - ly Spir - it, Ho - ly Spir - it.
hal - le - lu - jah, hal - le - lu - jah.

Text: Jimmy Owens, b. 1930
Music: HOLY, HOLY, Jimmy Owens, b. 1930

Praised Be the Rock

290

1 Praised be the Rock of our sal - va - tion,
2 God grants the needs of ev - 'ry na - tion,
3 To spare us all from con - dem - na - tion,
4 In Je - sus Christ our con - so - la - tion,
5 We now a - wait the con - sum - ma - tion,

a bul - wark stead - y and a sure place:
and charts the course that e - ven birds trace:
God's Son was sent our sins to ef - face:
made one with him for - ev - er by grace:
to see God's glo - ry then in Christ's face:

Refrain

God's good - ness shown through - out cre - a - tion

for our whole race.

Text: Aaron Lwehabura; tr. Howard S. Olson, b. 1922
Music: AHIMIDWE MWAMBA WANO, Haya tune; arr. A. Louise Anderson Olson
Tr. and arr. © Lutheran Theological College, Makumira, Tanzania

I Will Enter His Gates

He Has Made Me Glad

I will en-ter his gates with thanks-giv-ing in my heart,

I will en-ter his courts with praise.

I will say this is the day that the Lord has made;

I will re-joice for he has made me glad.

He has made me glad, he has made me glad,

I will re-joice for he has made me glad.

He has made me glad, he has made me glad,

I will re-joice for he has made me glad.

Text: Psalm 100:4 and 118:24, adapt.
Music: Leona von Brethorst

292

Give Thanks

Give thanks with a grate-ful heart, give thanks to the Ho-ly One,

give thanks be-cause he's giv-en Je-sus Christ, his Son.

And now let the weak say, "I am strong," let the poor say, "I am

rich," be-cause of what the Lord has done for us. And

now let the weak say, "I am strong," let the poor say, "I am rich," be-cause of

what the Lord has done for us. Give thanks!

Text: Henry Smith
Music: Henry Smith
© 1978 Integrity's Hosanna! Music

Thank You, Lord 293

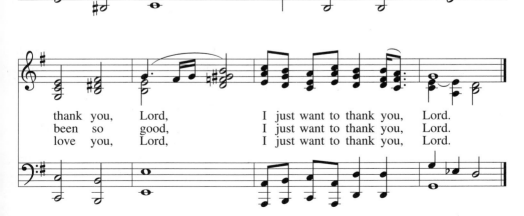

1 Thank you, Lord, thank you, Lord,
2 Been so good, been so good,
3 Love you, Lord, love you, Lord,

thank you, Lord, I just want to thank you, Lord.
been so good, I just want to thank you, Lord.
love you, Lord, I just want to thank you, Lord.

Text: traditional
Music: traditional; arr. J. Jefferson Cleveland, 1937-1986; and Verolga Nix, b. 1933
Arr. © 1981 Abingdon Press, admin. The Copyright Company

294

O Christ the King, Anointed

1 O Christ the king, a-noint-ed, by God him-self ap-point-ed
2 In Christ the king, Lord Je-sus, from sin and death God frees us;
3 In Christ the king, oh, hear it! A new life in the Spir-it!
4 In Christ the king, our Sav-ior, we learn a new be-hav-ior,
5 Now Christ the king is reign-ing, our peace and joy re-gain-ing.

to save by grace the hu-man race: we praise thy name.
and we are free e-ter-nal-ly: we praise thy name.
We learned it, Lord, from thine own word: we praise thy name.
to be as he, since we are free: we praise thy name.
Our sins are gone through Christ a-lone: we praise thy name.

We praise thy name, we praise thy name, we praise thy name!

To save by grace the hu-man race: we praise thy name!
And we are free e-ter-nal-ly: we praise thy name!
We learned it, Lord, from thine own word: we praise thy name!
To be as he, since we are free: we praise thy name!
Our sins are gone through Christ a-lone: we praise thy name!

Text: Richard C. Dickinson
Music: Richard C. Dickinson
Text and music © Richard C. Dickinson

What a Mighty God We Serve!

What a might - y God we serve!

What a might - y God we serve!

An-gels bow be - fore him, heav-en and earth a - dore him;

what a might - y God we serve.

Text: traditional
Music: traditional

296

Lift Every Voice and Sing

1 Lift ev - 'ry voice and sing till earth and heav - en ring,
2 Ston - y the road we trod, bit - ter the chas - t'ning rod,
3 God of our wea - ry years, God of our si - lent tears,

ring with the har - mo - nies of lib - er - ty.
felt in the days when hope un - born had died;
thou who hast brought us thus far on the way;

Let our re - joic - ing rise high as the lis - t'ning skies,
yet with a stead - y beat, have not our wea - ry feet
thou who hast by thy might led us in - to the light,

let it re - sound loud as the roll - ing sea.
come to the place for which our par - ents sighed?
keep us for - ev - er in the path, we pray.

Text: James Weldon Johnson, 1871-1938
Music: LIFT EVERY VOICE, J. Rosamund Johnson, 1873-1954

NATIONAL AND CULTURAL RESOURCES

Mine Eyes Have Seen the Glory

Battle Hymn of the Republic

297

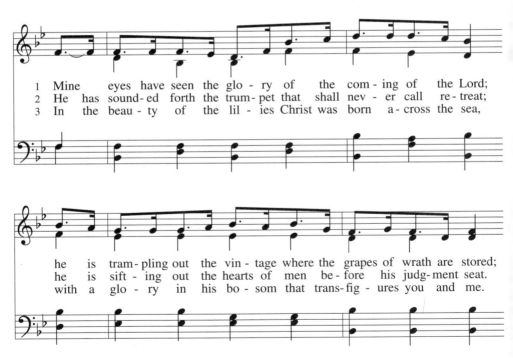

1 Mine eyes have seen the glo - ry of the com - ing of the Lord;
2 He has sound - ed forth the trum - pet that shall nev - er call re - treat;
3 In the beau - ty of the lil - ies Christ was born a - cross the sea,

he is tram - pling out the vin - tage where the grapes of wrath are stored;
he is sift - ing out the hearts of men be - fore his judg - ment seat.
with a glo - ry in his bo - som that trans - fig - ures you and me.

he has loosed the fate-ful light-ning of his ter-ri-ble swift sword:
Oh, be swift, my soul, to an-swer him; be ju-bi-lant, my feet!
As he died to make men ho-ly, let us live to make men free,

his truth is march-ing on.
Our God is march-ing on.
while God is march-ing on.

Refrain

Glo-ry, glo-ry! Hal-le-lu-jah! Glo-ry, glo-ry! Hal-le-lu-jah!

Glo-ry, glo-ry! Hal-le-lu-jah! His truth is march-ing on.

Text: Julia Ward Howe, 1819-1910
Music: BATTLE HYMN, North American, 19th cent.

298 — O Beautiful for Spacious Skies

1 O beau-ti-ful for spa-cious skies, for am-ber waves of grain,
2 O beau-ti-ful for pil-grim feet, whose stern, im-pas-sioned stress
3 O beau-ti-ful for he-roes proved in lib-er-at-ing strife,
4 O beau-ti-ful for pa-triot dream that sees be-yond the years

for pur-ple moun-tain maj-es-ties a-bove the fruit-ed plain:
a thor-ough-fare for free-dom beat a-cross the wil-der-ness:
who more than self their coun-try loved, and mer-cy more than life:
thine al-a-bas-ter cit-ies gleam, un-dimmed by hu-man tears:

A-mer-i-ca! A-mer-i-ca! God shed his grace on thee,
A-mer-i-ca! A-mer-i-ca! God mend thine ev-'ry flaw,
A-mer-i-ca! A-mer-i-ca! May God thy gold re-fine,
A-mer-i-ca! A-mer-i-ca! God shed his grace on thee,

and crown thy good with broth-er-hood from sea to shin-ing sea.
con-firm thy soul in self-con-trol, thy lib-er-ty in law.
till all suc-cess be no-ble-ness, and ev-'ry gain di-vine.
and crown thy good with broth-er-hood from sea to shin-ing sea.

Text: Katherine L. Bates, 1859-1929
Music: MATERNA, Samuel A. Ward, 1848-1903

Holy God, You Raise up Prophets

299

1 Ho - ly God, you raise up proph-ets; praise and hon-or do we sing
2 Mor - al con-science of his na - tion, re - con-cil-ing black and white,
3 Teach - er of Christ-like non - vio-lence to the out-cast, poor and meek;
4 Preach-er of Christ's love for neigh-bor, he won No-bel's prize for peace;

for your faith-ful, hum - ble ser - vant, Doc-tor Mar-tin Luth-er King.
dreamed he of a just so - cie - ty; we must car-ry on his fight.
great - er weap-on 'gainst op-pres - sion is to turn the oth-er cheek.
peo - ples, beat your swords to plough-shares, wars 'twixt na-tions all shall cease.

Refrain

Bless-ed Mar-tin, pas - tor, proph-et, who the moun-tain-top did see!

Bless-ed Mar-tin, ho - ly mar-tyr! Oh, that we may all be free.

5 Champion of oppressed humanity
suff'ring throughout all the world;
he offered pride and dignity,
let Christ's banner be unfurled!
Refrain

6 So, when felled by sniper's bullet,
under heavens overcast,
he could cry, "Thank God Almighty,
I am free, I'm free at last."
Refrain

Text: Harold T. Lewis, b. 1947, alt.
Music: MARTIN'S SONG, Carl Haywood, b. 1949

300

The Right Hand of God

1 The right hand of God is writ-ing in our land,
2 The right hand of God is point-ing in our land,
3 The right hand of God is strik-ing in our land,
4 The right hand of God is heal-ing in our land,

writ - ing with pow-er and with love,
point - ing the way . . . we must go,
strik-ing out at en - vy, hate, and greed.
heal-ing bro - ken bod-ies, minds, and souls,

our con - flicts and our fears, our tri - umphs and our tears
so cloud-ed is the way, so eas - i - ly we stray,
Our self - ish - ness and lust, our pride and deeds un - just
so won-drous is its touch with love that means so much,

are re - cord-ed by the right hand of God.
but we're guid-ed by the right hand of God.
are de - stroyed by the right hand of God.
when we're healed by the right hand of God.

Optional stanza
5 The right hand of God is planting in our land,
   planting seeds of freedom, hope, and love.
   In these Caribbean lands,
   let people all join hands,
   and be one by the right hand of God.

Text: Patrick Prescod
Music: Noel Dexter

Bless, O Lord, Our Country

Prayer for Africa

301

English Bless, O Lord, our coun- try, Af - ri - ca,   so that she may wak - en
Swahili Bwa - na, i - ba - ri - ki Af - ri - ka,   i - li - i - pa - te . . .
Zulu   Nko - si si - kel -el' i Af - ri - ka,   mal -u - pa -kam' u - pon -

from her sleep. Fill her horn with plen - ty, guide her feet.
ku - am - ka. Ma - om - bi ye ta ya - si - ki lel.
do - lway - o; yi - va im - i - tan - da - zo ye - tu.

Hear us, Faith - ful One. Hear us, Faith - ful One.
U - tu - ba - ri - ki. U - tu - ba - ri - ki.
U - si - si -kel -el - e. U - si - si -kel -el - e.

Spir - it, de -scend, Spir - it, Spir - it; Spir - it, de -scend, Spir - it, Spir - it;
U - je Ro - ho, U - je, U - je; U - je Ro - ho, U - je, U - je;
Yih -la Moy - a, Yih - la Mo - ya; Yih - la Moy - a; Yih - la Mo - ya;

Spir - it, de - scend. Spir - it, de -scend, Spir - it di - vine.
U - je Ro - ho. U - je Ro - ho. U - tu - ja - ze.
Yih -la Moy - a. Oy - ing cwel - e.

Text: Enoch Sontonga, Zulu; tr. Katherine F. Rohrbough.
Music: PRAYER FOR AFRICA, Enoch Sontonga

302   Commemoration of Martin Luther King Jr.

As an example of ways that the church may remember witnesses to the faith, the following resources are offered as suggestions for congregations that observe the commemoration of Martin Luther King Jr.

Prayer of the Day
Martyrs, Renewers of Society (p. 118)

Psalms
5; 31:1-20; 46; 56; 72; 94:1-14

Readings
Amos 5:24; Deut. 34:1-12; Isa. 43:1-7; Ezek. 20:40-42; Hos. 2:18-23
Rom. 12:9-21; Eph. 6:10-20; Phil. 4:4-9; Rev. 6:9-11
Matt. 10: 16-31; Mark 8:34-38; Luke 6:20-36; John 15:12-21

Hymns
296 Lift Every Voice and Sing   213 We Shall Overcome
197 We've Come This Far by Faith   70 Lead Me, Guide Me
299 Holy God, You Raise Up Prophets   46 Freedom Is Coming

Intercessions
Silence for prayer may follow each of the spoken petitions.

We remember the conviction of Martin Luther King Jr. that
"freedom is never voluntarily given by the oppressor; it must be demanded by the oppressed."
Therefore, let us pray
for courage and determination by those who are oppressed.

We remember Martin's warning that
"a negative peace which is the absence of tension" is less than "a positive peace which is the presence of justice."
Therefore, let us pray
that those who work for peace in our world may cry out first for justice.

We remember Martin's insight that
"injustice anywhere is a threat to justice everywhere. We are caught in an inescapable network of mutuality tied in a single garment of destiny. Whatever affects one directly affects all indirectly."
Therefore, let us pray
that we may see nothing in isolation, but may know ourselves bound to one another and to all people under heaven.

We remember Martin's lament that
"the contemporary church is often a weak, ineffectual voice with an uncertain sound. It is so often the arch-supporter of the status quo. Far from being disturbed by the presence of the church, the power structure of the average community is consoled by the church's silent and often vocal sanction of things as they are."

Therefore, let us pray
    that neither this congregation nor any congregation of Christ's people may be silent in the face of wrong, but that we may be disturbers of the status quo when that is God's call to us.

We remember Martin's hope that
    "dark clouds of racial prejudice will soon pass away and the deep fog of misunderstanding will be lifted from our fear-drenched communities, and in some not so distant tomorrow the radiant stars of love and brotherhood will shine over our great nation with all their scintillating beauty."
Therefore, in faith, let us commend
    ourselves and our work for justice to the goodness of almighty God.

Quotations from *Letter from the Birmingham City Jail*, Martin Luther King Jr., 1929-1968
© 1963 Martin Luther King Jr., ren. 1991 Coretta Scott King, admin. Joan Daves Agency
Litany by W. B. McClain and L. H. Stookey
© 1986 Abingdon Press

Charge to the People
When we let freedom ring,
when we let it ring from every village and every hamlet,
from every city and every state,
we will be able to speed up that day
when all God's children, Black men and White men,
Jews and Gentiles, Protestants and Catholics
will be able to join hands and sing that old Negro spiritual,
"Free at last! Free at last!
Thank God almighty, we are free at last!"

Martin Luther King Jr., 1929-1968

Black History Month   303

Background
Black History Month is an annual observance of the history and accomplishments of African Americans. The month designated for the observance is February, which was chosen to coincide with the birthdays of Abraham Lincoln (February 12) and Frederick Douglass (February 14). Lincoln is significant for signing the Emancipation Proclamation, which ended slavery in the United States, and Douglass for his prominence as an African American leader in the nineteenth century.

The concept for the observance originated with African American historian, Carter G. Woodson, who in 1926 called for the establishment of Negro History Week. Woodson observed that both the struggles and accomplishments of African Americans were not widely studied or recognized, and that this deficit of knowledge was unhealthy for American society in general and the African American community in particular. Woodson believed that studying and remembering the past was a prerequisite to living successfully in the present and being prepared for the future.

The observance has been sponsored by the Association for the Study of Afro-American Life and History (ASALH), an organization founded by Woodson in 1915. Each year ASALH has chosen a theme to focus the observance, which became known as Black History Week in the early 1970s. In 1976 the observance was lengthened to a month.

Observance in the congregation

Although not a religious observance, Black History Month is appropriately marked and celebrated by congregations as a secondary focus during the seasons of Epiphany and Lent. Possibilities for observance include the following:

▶ Sponsor adult and youth forums on African American history. These forums may be sponsored jointly by several area congregations.

▶ Sponsor plays or dramas recalling important events or figures in African American history. Consider having parish youth write, organize, and act in the performances.

▶ Publish articles, poetry, and prose on African American history or by African American writers in the parish newsletter.

▶ Sponsor a congregational banquet and invite members to wear African-inspired clothing. Consider including a special speaker and serving traditional foods.

▶ Hold soup suppers with storytelling times. Invite elders (older members) to share their recollections of African American history, drawing from the experiences of their own lives.

▶ Include teaching moments about African American history during worship times.

▶ Use various African and African American musical styles in worship. Decorate the worship spaces with African cloth that coordinates with the seasonal liturgical color.

304   Juneteenth

Juneteenth is a holiday that commemorates the end of slavery in the United States. It recalls how the states of Louisiana and Texas heard the news that President Abraham Lincoln had signed the Emancipation Proclamation on January 1, 1863. Slavery continued in those two states for more than two years after the proclamation was signed because the word had yet to travel there. Texas and Louisiana finally got the good news on June 19, 1865. Former slaves broke out in spontaneous celebration.

Legend has it that the good word was spread by a black man who rode a mule from the east all the way to Texas. Historians credit Union General Gordon Granger, who arrived in Galveston, Texas, on June 19, 1865, with making the announcement. In any case, the announcement marked the end of slavery for the nation.

More recently, the United States House and Senate have passed a resolution calling for Juneteenth to be recognized as Independence Day for African Americans and celebrated by all. At the time of this printing some were working to see that Juneteenth becomes an official American holiday.

The Hurricane Season 305

The hurricane season often has a profound impact on those who live in tropical and coastal regions. The following prayers, from a Danish Lutheran missionary manual, have been used for decades in parts of the Caribbean.

Prayer for the Beginning of the Hurricane Season

O Lord God, heavenly Father, in this perilous season of the year our island/region *name* is often visited with tempests and gales, calamities and distresses by land and sea. From such evil spare us, we pray.

But if you loosen the wings of the gale and the earth trembles at your bidding—your will, O Lord, be done. Almighty Creator and heavenly Father, keep us in your mercy through your beloved Son, Jesus Christ our Lord, who lives and rules with you, in the unity of the Holy Spirit, one true God, forever and ever. Amen

Prayers for the End of the Hurricane Season

O merciful God and heavenly Father, you asked us to call upon you in all our need and distress, and moreover, you promised to hear our prayers and to help us, thereby causing us to give thanks. During this past perilous season, we have felt nature weigh heavily upon us. Keep us from anger, that we might turn our hearts to you, as the ruinous gale passes over us and the earth trembles.

We give ourselves to you with humble hearts, and pray that you will graciously grant by your Holy Spirit, that we are found thankful, not only in word, but also in deed and in truth, that our lives may give glory and praise to you, through your beloved Son, Jesus Christ our Lord, who lives and reigns with you, In the unity of the Holy Spirit, one true God, forever and ever. Amen

OR

O merciful God and heavenly Father, you asked us to call upon you in all need and distress, and moreover promised to hear our prayers and to help us, thereby causing us to give thanks. During this past perilous season, we have felt your help and assistance, as you have preserved our lives and homes, and kept the ruinous gale from afflicting us and the earth from trembling.

Therefore we give thanks to you from humble hearts, and we pray that you will graciously grant by your Holy Spirit, that we are found thankful, not only in word, but also in deed and in truth, that our lives may give glory and praise to you, through your beloved Son, Jesus Christ our Lord, who lives and reigns with you, in the unity of the Holy Spirit, one true God, forever and ever. Amen

Adapt. from *The Lutheran Manual of Hymns, Liturgy and Prayers*, 2nd edition, Copenhagen: Bianco Luno, 1880.

Kwanzaa

In recent years, many African Americans have begun to celebrate the festival of Kwanzaa. Kwanzaa is a cultural rather than a religious festival. It is not affiliated with any particular religious faith or tradition. Kwanzaa affirms ethical principles that emanate from traditional African societies and that resonate with the ethical traditions of the major religious traditions of Christianity, Judaism, and Islam.

Civil rights activist Maulana Karenga formulated and introduced Kwanzaa in 1966 to encourage African American families to build upon the spiritual strengths of their cultural heritage. On each of the seven days of Kwanzaa—December 26 to January 1—candles are lighted to signify seven foundational principles (*Nguzo Saba*, listed on the following page). Various combinations of red, green, and black candles may be used.

Many African Americans relate Kwanzaa to their Christian faith and traditions. The rituals associated with Kwanzaa are familial and take place primarily in the home, but on occasion they are adapted for use in congregational settings. Some who celebrate Kwanzaa in this way call its observance "Christkwanzaa," while others simply observe it as a cultural festival.

The following are activities and practices that may be observed on the days of Kwanzaa.

▶ Families may place a straw mat, *mkeka*, on the table as a sign of the tradition that is foundation for the celebration.

▶ On the first day of Kwanzaa, the *mtume* (leader) calls the family together. When everyone is present, the *mtume* greets them with the words *"Habari gani"* ("What's the news?") and the family responds *"Umoja"* (unity). On each succeeding day, the principle associated with that day is named.

▶ A member of the family offers prayer while all are standing.

▶ The group then says *"Harambee"* ("Let's pull together"), a call for unity and the collective work and struggle of the family. Each member raises up the right arm with open hand and, while pulling the arm down, closes the hand into a fist.

▶ *"Harambee"* is repeated in sets of seven in honor and reinforcement of the *Nguzo Saba*, Kwanzaa's seven spiritual and communal principles.

▶ The group sings a Kwanzaa song.

▶ The leader talks about the concept of Kwanzaa and the principle of the day.

▶ An elder performs the *tambiko* (libation), pouring juice or water in honor of the ancestors.

▶ A family member, preferably a youth, lights the candle appropriate to the day.

▶ After the lighting ceremony is complete, a story, song, or object reflective of the principle of the day is shared, and a scripture passage related to the principle may be read.

▶ The family distributes *zawandi*, handmade gifts.

▶ The leader conducts a closing prayer.

▶ On December 31, a *karamu*, an African-style feast, may be eaten, often without Western utensils, and accompanied by indigenous music.

NGUZO SABA (THE SEVEN PRINCIPLES)
with related biblical passages

Umoja (unity)
To strive for and maintain unity in the family, community, nation, and race.

> There is one body and one Spirit . . . one Lord, one faith, one baptism, one God and Father
> of all. *Ephesians 4:4-6; see also Acts 10:1-37*

Kujichagulia (self-determination)
To define ourselves, name ourselves, create for ourselves, and speak for ourselves instead
of being defined, named, created for, and spoken for by others.

> But you are a chosen race, a royal priesthood, a holy nation, God's own people.
> *1 Peter 2:9; see also Numbers 13:31—14:9*

Ujima (collective work and responsibility)
To build and maintain our community together and make our sisters' and brothers'
problems our problems and to solve them together.

> Bear one another's burdens, and in this way you will fulfill the law of Christ.
> *Galatians 6:2; see also Nehemiah 3:1-31*

Ujamaa (cooperative economics)
To build and maintain our own stores, shops, and other businesses and to profit from them
together.

> Whoever does not provide for relatives, and especially for family members, has denied the faith
> and is worse than an unbeliever. *1 Timothy 5:8; see also Acts 2:42-47*

Nia (purpose)
To make our collective vocation the building and developing of our community in order to
restore our people to their traditional greatness.

> Therefore, since we are surrounded by so great a cloud of witnesses . . . let us run with perse-
> verance the race that is set before us. *Hebrews 12:1; see also Esther 4:1-17*

Kuumba (creativity)
To do always as much as we can, in the way we can, in order to leave our community more
beautiful and beneficial than we inherited it.

> Whatever your hand finds to do, do with your might.
> *Ecclesiastes 9:10; see also 2 Kings 12:1-16*

Imani (faith)
To believe with all our heart in our people, our parents, our teachers, and the righteousness
and victory of our struggle.

> This is the victory that conquers the world, our faith.
> *1 John 5:4; see also 2 Kings 16:8-17*

Acknowledgments

The material on pages 1–118 and at #302–306 is covered by the copyright of this book except where noted.

Material used with permission from the following sources is acknowledged:

Lutheran Book of Worship, © 1978 Lutheran Church in America, The American Lutheran Church, The Evangelical Lutheran Church of Canada, and The Lutheran Church—Missouri Synod.

Lutheran Worship, © 1982 Concordia Publishing House.

Service Book and Hymnal, © 1958, admin. Augsburg Fortress.

With One Voice, © 1995 Augsburg Fortress.

All-Africa eucharistic prayer, adapted (East Africa).

Book of Common Prayer (1979) of The Episcopal Church (psalm texts, offertory sentences).

Book of Common Worship, © 1993 Westminster John Knox Press (charges to the people).

The Book of Occasional Services 1994, © 1995 Church Pension Fund (Way of the Cross, adapted).

International Consultation on English Texts: the Apostles' Creed, the Nicene Creed, the Lord's Prayer; the canticle texts "Glory to God in the highest," "Holy, holy, holy Lord," "Lamb of God," "Lord, now you let your servant go in peace."

New Revised Standard Version of the Bible, © 1989, Division of Christian Education of the National Council of Churches of Christ in the United States of America (scripture quotations).

Sundays and Seasons, Cycle B, © 1996 Augsburg Fortress (offertory prayers).

Authors/translators of liturgical texts are acknowledged: Donald Anthony, John W. Arthur, Joseph A. Donnella II, Emmanuel F. Y. Grantson, John Nunes, Martin A. Seltz, Frank Stoldt, Karen M. Ward, Maxine Washington, Gregory Wismar.

Composers of liturgical music are acknowledged: Tillis Butler (setting I), James Capers (setting II), Joseph Chouinard (setting I, arrangement), Dennis Friesen-Carper (setting II, arrangement).

Writers of introductory material are acknowledged: Joseph A. Donnella II, John Nunes, Karen M. Ward (Worship and Culture); Mellonee Burnim (Leading African American Song); Melva Wilson Costen (A Musical Timeline).

Publishing house editorial staff and associates: Becky Brantner-Christiansen, Suzanne Burke, Ryan French, M. Alexandra George, Aaron Koelman, Kristine Oberg, Linda Parriott, Martin A. Seltz, Frank Stoldt, Mark Weiler, Lani Willis.

Art and design: Lynn Joyce Hunter, Ellen Maly, Barbara Zuber.

Music engraving and composition: Jürgen Selk, Music Graphics International.

Copyright and Permissions

Copyright acknowledgment: The publisher gratefully acknowledges all copyright holders who have granted permission to reproduce copyrighted materials in this book. Every effort has been made to determine the owner and/or administrator of each copyright and to secure needed permission. The publisher will, upon written notice, make necessary corrections in subsequent printings.

Permission information: Permission to reproduce Holy Communion (Shape of the Rite), pp. 22–23 and the service outlines of Holy Communion, setting III (Pattern for the Service), pp. 60–63, Service of the Word, p. 69, and Service of Prayer and Preaching (Revival), p. 70–71, for one-time congregational use in weekly worship folders is hereby granted to any purchaser of this volume provided that no part of such reproduction is sold and the following credit line is used: Reprinted from *This Far by Faith*, copyright © 1999 Augsburg Fortress. Used by permission.

Permission to reproduce any other copyrighted words or music contained in this book must be obtained from the copyright holder(s) of that material. For contact information of copyright holders not listed on the following page or for further copyright information, please contact Augsburg Fortress.

COPYRIGHT HOLDERS AND ADMINISTRATORS

AUGSBURG FORTRESS
426 S. Fifth St., PO Box 1209
Minneapolis, MN 55440
(800) 421-0239
(612) 330-3252 FAX

BRENTWOOD-BENSON MUSIC PUBLISHING, INC.
365 Great Circle Road
Nashville, TN 37228
(800) 688-2606

COPYRIGHT COMPANY
40 Music Square East
Nashville, TN 37203
(615) 244-5588
(615) 244-5591 FAX

EARTHSONGS
220 NW 29th St.
Corvallis, OR 97330
(541) 758-5760

EMI CHRISTIAN MUSIC
PO Box 5085
101 Winners Circle
Brentwood, TN 37024-5085
(615) 371-4400
(615) 371-6897 FAX

G. SCHIRMER
257 Park Ave. S.
New York, NY 10010
(212) 254-2100
(212) 254-2013 FAX

GAITHER COPYRIGHT MANAGEMENT
Box 737
Alexandria, IN 46001
(765) 724-8233
(765) 724-8290 FAX

GIA PUBLICATIONS
7404 S. Mason Ave.
Chicago, IL 60188
(708) 496-3800
(708) 496-3828 FAX

HAL LEONARD CORPORATION
7777 West Bluemound Rd.
PO Box 13819
Milwaukee, WI 53213-0819
(414) 774-3630
(414) 774-3259 FAX

HOPE PUBLISHING COMPANY
380 S. Main Place
Carol Stream, IL 60188
(800) 323-1049
(630) 665-2552 FAX

INTEGRATED COPYRIGHT GROUP
Box 24149
Nashville, TN 37202
(615) 329-3999
(615) 329-4070 FAX

INTEGRITY INCORPORATED
1000 Cody Road
Mobile, AL 36695
(334) 633-9000
(334) 633-5202 FAX

LILLY MACK MUSIC (BMI)
417 East Regent Street
Inglewood, CA 90301

LORENZ PUBLISHING CORPORATION
501 E. Third St.
Box 802
Dayton, OH 45401
(513) 228-6118
(513) 223-2042 FAX

LUTHERAN THEOLOGICAL COLLEGE AT MAKUMIRA
(Contact Augsburg Fortress for permission, or)
Box 55
Usa River (near Arusha)
Tanzania, East Africa
011-255-57-3858 FAX

LUTHERAN WORLD FEDERATION
Box 2100
150 route de Ferney
CH1211 Geneva 2 Switzerland
011-41-22-791-6360
011-41-22-798-8616 FAX

MANNA MUSIC INC.
Box 218
Pacific City, OR 97135
(503) 965-6112
(503) 965-6880 FAX

MORNINGSTAR MUSIC PUBLISHERS
2117 59th St.
St. Louis, MO 63110-2807
(800) 647-2117
(314) 647-2777 FAX

MUSIC SERVICES
209 Chapelwood Dr.
Franklin, TN 37064
(615) 244-5588

OCP PUBLICATIONS/ NEW DAWN MUSIC
5536 NE Hassalo PO Box 18030
Portland, OR 97218-0030
(800) 548-8749
(503) 282-3486 FAX

PILGRIM PRESS/ UNITED CHURCH PRESS
700 Prospect Ave.
Cleveland, OH 44115-1100
(216) 736-3700
(216) 736-3703 FAX

PRINCE OF PEACE PUBLISHERS/ CHANGING CHURCH INC.
200 East Nicollet Blvd.
Burnsville, MN 55337
(612) 435-8102

WALTON MUSIC CORPORATION
c/o Plymouth Music Corporation
170 NE 33rd St. Box 24330
Fort Lauderdale, FL 33307
(305) 563-1844
(305) 563-9006 FAX

WESTMINSTER JOHN KNOX PRESS
100 Witherspoon St.
Louisville, KY 40202
(502) 569-5060
(502) 569-8090 FAX

WORD MUSIC, INC.
3319 West End Ave., Suite 200
Nashville, TN 37203
(615) 385-9673
(615) 269-3190 FAX

WORLD COUNCIL OF CHURCHES
150 route de Ferney
PO Box 2100
CH1211 Geneva 2 Switzerland
011-41-22-791-6111
011-41-22-798-1346 FAX

Topics and Themes

Scripture References

Micah

6:8	253	Just a Closer Walk with Thee

Habakkuk

2:20	143	The Lord Is in His Holy Temple

Zechariah

13:1	72	Down at the Cross
13:1	78	There Is a Fountain

Matthew

1:18-25	47	All Earth Is Hopeful
1:23	45	Emmanuel
2:1-2	58	There's a Star in the East
2:10-11	182	Ride On, King Jesus
4:18-22	154	You Have Come Down to the Lakeshore
5:16	65	This Little Light of Mine
6:6	175	Steal Away
6:9-13	33	Our Father, Who Art in Heaven
6:9-13	34	Let the Words of My Mouth
6:19-23	231	Time Is Filled with Swift Transition
6:25-39	252	Why Should I Feel Discouraged
6:33	149	Seek Ye First
7:7	149	Seek Ye First
8:5-13	42	Come by Here
8:5-13	43	Come by Here
9:27	20	Kyrie
9:27	21	Lord, Have Mercy
9:27	22	Lord, Have Mercy
9:27	23	Lord, Have Mercy
10:8	187	God Forgave My Sin in Jesus' Name
11:28-30	62	I Heard the Voice of Jesus Say
11:28-30	183	I Must Tell Jesus
13:8-23	131	Lord, Let My Heart Be Good Soil
15:21-28	120	Lord, I Hear of Showers of Blessings
17:1-9	64	Shine, Jesus, Shine
17:8	98	Open Our Eyes, Lord
18:20	145	Jesus, We Want to Meet
19:13-15	161	Go, My Children, with My Blessing
19:16-30	233	I'd Rather Have Jesus
21:22	244	Send Me, Jesus
21:22	245	Send Me, Jesus
24:29	40	My Lord, What a Morning
24:36	38	Soon and Very Soon
25:31	172	If When You Give the Best of Your Service
28:5-7	96	Christ Has Arisen, Alleluia
28:16-20	130	Listen, God Is Calling
28:18-20	187	God Forgave My Sin in Jesus' Name
28:19	142	In the Name of the Father

Mark

3:24-37	40	My Lord, What a Morning
4:8	226	You Are the Seed
10:13-16	161	Go, My Children, with My Blessing
10:35-45	83	Jesu, Jesu, Fill Us with Your Love
11:15-32	134	O Lord, Open My Eyes
14:36	243	Your Will Be Done
16:16	113	Have You Got Good Religion?

Luke

1:46-55	168	My Soul Does Magnify the Lord
2:1-21	50	I Wonder As I Wander
2:7	54	That Boy-Child of Mary
2:7	60	Sister Mary
2:8-20	52	Go Tell It on the Mountain
2:11-22	55	Mary Had a Baby
2:13-14	51	Jesus, What a Wonderful Child

2:21	54	That Boy-Child of Mary
2:33, 38	47	All Earth Is Hopeful
5:1-11	154	You Have Come Down to the Lakeshore
5:3	199	'Tis the Old Ship of Zion
9:23	237	Must Jesus Bear the Cross Alone
9:28-36	64	Shine, Jesus, Shine
10:33	150	Pass Me Not, O Gentle Savior
14:27	237	Must Jesus Bear the Cross Alone
17:15	269	When I Think of the Goodness of Jesus
18:15-17	161	Go, My Children, with My Blessing
18:38-39	20	Kyrie
18:38-39	21	Lord, Have Mercy
18:38-39	22	Lord, Have Mercy
18:38-39	23	Lord, Have Mercy
22:19	121	This Is My Body
22:33	86	King of My Life
23:32-34	74	Days Are Filled with Sorrow and Care
23:40-43	178	Do, Lord, Remember Me
24:1-8	86	King of My Life
24:6	94	Low in the Grave He Lay
24:13-28	91	Alleluia! Jesus Is Risen!

John

1:4-9	37	He Came Down
1:16	127	Fill My Cup, Let It Overflow
1:29	35	Lamb of God
1:29	36	O Lamb of God
1:29	128	Now Behold the Lamb
2:1-11	133	A Mighty Fortress Is Our God
4:5-15	124	Fill My Cup, Lord
4:7-15	62	I Heard the Voice of Jesus Say
4:23	102	There's a Sweet, Sweet Spirit in This Place
5:24	174	Deep River
6	125	Eat This Bread
6	158	Hallelujah! We Sing Your Praises
6:1-13	232	Let Us Talents and Tongues Employ
6:33-37	156	Come to Jesus
6:35	124	Fill My Cup, Lord
8:12	62	I Heard the Voice of Jesus Say
8:36	114	Wade in the Water
8:36	116	Free at Last
14:1	256	I Will Trust in the Lord
14:3	181	To Go to Heaven
15:13	249	Jesus Loves Me!
15:26	107	Holy Spirit, Descend
16:13	193	Precious Lord, Take My Hand
17:18	159	Take the Name of Jesus with You
20:11-18	88	O Mary, Don't You Weep

Acts

1:8	106	Come, O Holy Spirit, Come
2	105	Oh, Let the Son of God Enfold You
2:14	41	I Want to Be Ready
2:42	220	What a Fellowship, What a Joy Divine
2:42	123	Let Us Break Bread Together
3:1	242	Sweet Hour of Prayer
4:20	228	I Love to Tell the Story
4:20	225	I Believe I'll Testify
8:12	112	Wash, O God, Our Sons and Daughters
8:18-19	246	Somebody Prayed for Me
8:36	117	Take Me to the Water
10:12	253	Just a Closer Walk with Thee
18:20	140	Jesus, We Are Gathered
20:17	145	Jesus, We Want to Meet
20:24	225	I Believe I'll Testify

Tunes—Alphabetical

Authors, Composers, and Sources

First Lines and Common Titles

Resources from the Tradition

Graphic Art

Artist Barbara Zuber based *This Far by Faith*'s cover cross design on a carved motif from a Yoruba wooden door in Nigeria. She adapted and stylized the Yoruba design by varying the line weights and adding an African American geometric pattern found in the Mississippi quilting tradition. This quilt pattern, called a "log cabin," also has its origin in a design from West Africa. The Yoruba people of Nigeria were among those most profoundly affected by the American slave trade; thus their traditions are particularly relevant to African Americans.

The woven cross represents the weaving of traditions and faith that African Americans celebrate today. Tied together by the knot of faith and the log cabin respite of home, the African American journey is symbolized in the woven lines of the cross, through which the people have come *This Far by Faith*.

The art featured within this book is typical of Barbara Zuber's style. Influenced by artists of the African American "Harlem Renaissance," the artist prefers to represent a two dimensional flat plane, creating figures that are elongated to enhance movement and complement the composition. The geometric designs incorporated into the art are stylizations of African textile patterns, including kente cloth.

Barbara Zuber was born in Philadelphia, raised in New York City, and educated at Yale University, New York University and the Art Students League of New York. She has exhibited with Georgia O'Keeffe and Fernando Garassi, and been featured in the traveling exhibit *Forever Free, Art by African American Women*. Zuber has taught the arts of the African and African American traditions to students of all ages. Her Christian faith has been shaped by both Southern Baptist and Episcopal traditions. She resides in Troy, New York, with her family.

AN INDEX TO THE ART

Christian Burial, the Saints	113	Music	13	Times and Seasons	72
Holy Baptism	64	Prayers and Blessings (1)	104	Way of the Cross	96
Holy Communion	26, 43, 60	Prayers and Blessings (2)	110, 112	Witnesses to the Faith	114
Journey of Faith	103	Preaching, Revival	70		
Marriage	107	The Word	19, 69		

ISBN 0806633335-2

3–520
Augsburg Fortress